Officially Gay

*The Political Construction
of Sexuality by the U.S. Military*

In the series

Queer Politics, Queer Theories

Officially Gay

The Political Construction of Sexuality by the U.S. Military

Gary L. Lehring

 Temple University Press
Philadelphia

Temple University Press, Philadelphia 19122
Copyright © 2003 by Temple University
Published 2003
Printed in the United States of America

∞ The paper used in this publication meets the requirements of
the American National Standard for Information Sciences—Permanence
of Paper for Printed Library Materials, ANSI Z39.48-1984

Library of Congress Cataloging-in-Publication Data
Lehring, Gary L., 1966–
    Officially gay : the political construction of sexuality by the U.S.
military / Gary L. Lehring.
        p.   cm. — (Queer politics, queer theories)
    Includes bibliographical references and index.
    ISBN 1-59213-034-8 (cloth : alk. paper) — ISBN 1-59213-035-6 (pbk. :
alk. paper)
        1. United States—Armed Forces—Gays—Government policy.
I. Title. II. Series.
    UB418.G38 L44 2003
    355'.0086'640973—dc21
                                                                    2002043554

2 4 6 8 9 7 5 3 1

For Mary Geske
and
for my parents

Contents

Acknowledgments

I AM INDEBTED to many people for their assistance with this book. John Brigham and Nicholas Xenos provided helpful critiques and guidance on early versions of the manuscript. Cynthia Enloe and Craig Rimmerman freely shared their insights and suggestions on various sections. Peter Wissoker at Temple University Press provided consistent encouragement and direction. Jane Mercier helped prepare the manuscript with her trademark humor and efficiency. And my research assistants at Smith College, Tatiana Bertsch, Elizabeth Donoghue, and Kate Stineback, were invaluable as they tirelessly and cheerfully helped the project come to fruition by pursuing references, gathering information, scrutinizing footnotes, and providing useful feedback.

I am grateful to the Committee on Faculty Compensation and Development at Smith College for its generous financial support as I revised the manuscript. An earlier version of Chapter 7 appeared as "Essentialism and the Political Articulation of Identity" in Shane Phelan's *Queer Politics, Queer Theories*, and portions of Chapter 6 appeared as "Constructing the 'Other' Soldier" in Craig Rimmerman's *Gay Rights, Military Wrongs: Perspectives on Gays and Lesbians in the Military*. I am also grateful to Billy Bragg and BMG music for allowing me to reprint part of Billy's song "Tender Comrade" at the beginning of Chapter 4 and to David LaChappelle for allowing me to use his incredible photograph for the paperback book cover.

I must also acknowledge the significant and prominent roles that Martha Ackelsberg, Cynthia Enloe, Mary Hawkesworth, and Nancy Whittier have played in my life and my career. Each has contributed greatly to my professional growth and development, serving as a role model for all academics. Excelling as administrators, scholars, teachers, colleagues, and friends, they are possessed of a contagious enthusiasm for and love of "the life of the mind." I am truly fortunate to be so completely in their debt. More than anyone else, Nancy Whittier helped me fine-tune my arguments and my prose. She also pushed me to finish when I thought I could not; this project could not have been completed without her.

I am especially grateful to my colleagues at Smith College for their advice, humor, and unflagging support. Martha Ackelsberg, Don Baumer, Donna Divine, Velma Garcia, Alice Hearst, and Greg White never failed to check on my progress, providing collegial support during the many months of revisions. Howard Gold and Nancy Whittier provided useful insights into the publication process, answering my endless questions with great patience and grace. I will always be obliged to Howard and his wife, Jennifer Innes, who had me to dinner more times during the revision process than I will ever be able to repay. Marilyn Schuster and Susan Van Dyne have also assisted me in countless ways since I came to Smith College. Their enthusiasm for gay and lesbian and queer studies has put Smith on the map with one of the most forward-thinking women's studies programs in the country. Collectively, these individuals have made my affiliation with Smith College a rich, rewarding, productive experience.

I have received support of a more personal nature from a number of friends and family members. Martha Ackelsberg, Marc Benda, Elizabeth (Betsy) Brooks-Bartlett, Fiona Cooke, Julie Drucker-Donnelly, Leyla Ezdinli, Velma Garcia, Howard Gold, Gail Lehring-Elliott, Dorian Leslie, Kathleen Moore, Seng Quah, Janice Savitz, Paul Shepard, Cristina Suarez, Kate Weigand, and Nancy Whittier make up an extended family that has provided me with an embarrassment of friendship riches. Velma Garcia, Cristina Suarez, and Nancy Whittier, above all, helped keep me alive and sane throughout the book production process. Constituting the core of "the lesbian commune," they have offered emotional support in each of my many misguided adventures, supporting me even in my darkest days of fear and self-doubt. Cristina, my "lesbian wife," and I have shared more of ourselves with each other than most people ever do. It is a testament to her patience and saintly nature that we remain the best of friends. During the final revisions of this manuscript, I lost my dear personal friend and colleague Mary Geske. Her kindness, intelligence, courage, and deliciously wicked wit are missed every single day.

Finally, and most significantly, I thank my parents, Melvin Charles Lehring and Burnetta Catherine Gardner-Lehring, without whose constant love and support this book would not have been possible. I cannot express how much they mean to me, although I trust that they know. To my parents, Burnetta and Melvin, and to the memory of Mary Geske I dedicate this book.

Officially Gay

The Political Construction
of Sexuality by the U.S. Military

Introduction

ON SEPTEMBER 11, 2001, the world changed. In the months following this late summer day when commercial jetliners flew purposely into both the World Trade Center and the Pentagon and the United States perceived itself as vulnerable to international terrorism at home for the first time, these words have been written or spoken thousands of times. This excess of rhetoric regarding a changed world can be forgiven a naïve people accustomed to conflating their nation with the world; still, it is true that for many citizens of the United States their nation would never be the same. But just how the world or the nation has changed or will change as a result of the terrorist attacks of September 2001 is as yet unclear. In the weeks following the attacks, CNN gave its network over to what it called "America's New War," and attempts to understand anew international political struggles and the intricacies of foreign policy, diplomacy, and military hardware eclipsed much of what would otherwise be considered newsworthy.

One such example came less than a week after the terrorist attacks: The Pentagon issued a "stop loss order" to all branches of the military, an order that suspended discharges—including those of service members who disclose their homosexuality. On the face of it, this might have seemed an amazing victory for gay rights. After all, less than a decade earlier, the nation's Democratic president, Bill Clinton, had met with months of angry protestation for

1

suggesting that gay men and lesbians should be allowed to serve in the military. As finally implemented, Clinton's Don't Ask, Don't Tell policy permitted gay men and lesbians to serve but also continued to leave them subject to discharge for disclosing their gay or lesbian identity. In effect, gay men and lesbians could serve as long as no one knew they were gay or lesbian. Under this policy, predictably, discharges of gay and lesbian service members skyrocketed. But in 2001, in the aftermath of the terrorist attacks and under the more socially conservative Republican administration of George W. Bush, gays would be allowed to serve regardless of any declarations of their sexual identity.

That this seemingly momentous change in military policy was adopted by a Republican president is not the most amazing part of this story (indeed, during the Gulf War, the administration of the first George Bush had similarly suspended all discharges, including those for violations of the military's gay ban). More dramatic was the deafening cultural and societal silence surrounding this change in policy. In 1993, the mere idea that lesbians and gay men should be permitted to serve openly in the military had inspired right-wing extremist groups and powerful social conservatives to launch a firestorm of protest that threatened to derail the entire agenda of a newly elected president. How can it be explained, then, that eight short years later the Pentagon's suspension of discharges went largely overlooked and unremarked by political pundits, news organizations, military experts, religious leaders, and gay activists? Was it the sheer gravity of President Bush's declared war against terrorism that made all other news pale by comparison? Was it the newly discovered unity of the U.S. people, content finally to join the armed forces of the world in permitting gay men and lesbians to serve openly in uniform? Or had the perceived threat to morale, order, and discipline—presented with such certainty a decade before—vanished in the presence of a new enemy, one simultaneously outside and inside the United States?

No doubt these explanations help account for some of the lack of fanfare by gay people and straight people alike, but for many the explanation was somewhat simpler: ignorance. And the importance of this pervasive lack of awareness of changes in military policy lies not in what it tells us about 2001 but rather in what it can teach us about Clinton's failed attempt to lift the ban in 1993 and the general progress of gay rights in the United States.

In 2001, permitting gay men and lesbians to serve openly in the U.S. military was not perceived as an important issue precisely because the military did not want it to be perceived as an important issue. The nation was at war; nations at war take extraordinary measures, and their militaries take even more extraordinary measures. Thousands of reserves were called into active duty as the Pentagon contemplated military strikes, and the National Guard was deployed in all major airports around the country as the nation entered a new era of domestic militarization. Huge budget increases for the U.S. Border Patrol passed Congress with few waves, allowing increased militarization of both the U.S.-Mexican and U.S.-Canadian borders. In this climate of national uncertainty and fear, with dissenting voices in the nation's capital few and far between, it is not surprising that many people found it inappropriate to question the military; in fact, it would not have been surprising even if the change in policy regarding the suspension of gay discharges had been widely known.[1]

Still, as many who had been involved in the 1993 debate knew only too well, the military has always curtailed discharges—including those of gay and lesbian service personnel—during times of war. In World War II, in Korea, in Vietnam, and in the Gulf War, U.S. armed forces discharges of gay men and lesbians dropped dramatically or (in the case of the Gulf War) were suspended altogether. Sadly, however, as soon as the nation's conflicts come to an end, so too does the fleeting tolerance of the U.S. military toward its gay and lesbian service members.

The history of selective objections to gay and lesbian military participation is interesting from a number of different perspectives. First, it has made a lie of the military's long-standing contention that the presence of homosexuals negatively affects the ability of the armed services to accomplish their mission. If this were true, then why in times of war, when the stakes of mission failure are so much higher, would gay men and lesbians be allowed to serve? And why would the presence of gay and lesbian soldiers among the ranks be more threatening to "morale, good order, and discipline" in times of peace than in times of war?

Second, on the surface, the military's suspension of discharges during times of conflict appears punitive: When bodies are needed to put in harm's way, what more culturally disposable bodies are there than gay and lesbian bodies (a huge number of which are also bodies of color and working-class bodies, as these groups are overrepresented among the nation's fighting forces)? While this is no doubt a publicly unacknowledged part of the military justification, there is another reason for the suspension of discharges during wartime. Having created a policy that excludes homosexuals, the military *must* suspend discharges when the need for person power is at its peak. Again never admitted publicly, the military's own policy that prohibits "out" gay and lesbian personnel from serving in the military functions as a kind of reverse recruitment process in times of war. If discharges were not suspended, some soldiers might be tempted to declare themselves openly gay, regardless of their sexual orientation, to avoid having to go to war. The Pentagon's fear is familiar to anyone who has ever seen Corporal Klinger in a dress. Not as obvious, however, is the way the Pentagon itself has increased the effectiveness of this strategy for anyone who wishes to deploy it.

During the 1980s and 1990s, simple declarations of gay identity became grounds for removal from the U.S. military, regardless of the existence of sexual contact. Simultaneously, the type of discharge granted to servicepersons who declared they were gay or lesbian was upgraded to "honorable," which meant that separation from the military for homosexuality would carry neither social stigma nor individual punishment. As a result, the very Pentagon ban that prohibits participation of "out" gay men and lesbians in the military makes wartime suspension of the policy to rid the military of gay men and lesbians absolutely necessary.

Third, and perhaps most interesting of all, is the role that military policy has played in the creation of a "homosexual" identity. In the policies adopted to exclude homosexuals, in the medical justifications for the exclusion of homosexuals, and in both the military and civil court cases given the task of adjudicating disputes that arise from the policies and medical findings, a new kind of person emerges: the gay and lesbian subject. I am not suggesting that military policy is responsible for making people queer (although perhaps); I am simply suggesting that, in the struggle for gay equality in the twentieth and twenty-first centuries, the military has played a central role.

As medical scientists joined forces with the military, and as military courts scrambled to make new rulings that would support the Pentagon's position, much of the nineteenth-century science of sexology became the basis of twentieth- and twenty-first-century military policy. What emerged from this fusion was a new way of making truth of human sex acts and sexual behaviors long practiced but seldom acknowledged. The new truth to be discerned from these acts was not focused on discovering new techniques for sexual pleasure; its target was more interior. If, as Michel Foucault suggested, in the nineteenth century sex had become the way to tell the truth about oneself, then in the twentieth and twenty-first centuries, new techniques and strategies of power would be invented to extract that truth from others less willing to "give it up" freely. In the hands of overzealous medical scientists armed with the power of the State, unapproved sexual acts would be indications of something far more sinister about a person: a degenerative condition, a character flaw, a criminal mind.

Often, changes in the strategies of gay and lesbian activists were in response to these changes in military policy—sometimes directly, sometimes indirectly. Centrally, the military is a place where arguments about what gay men and lesbians *are* could be witnessed often at a decibel level reserved only for those accustomed to making war. These debates about identity frequently mirrored debates that would later occur in society, but it was in the military that the question of gay and lesbian identity and the presence of gay and lesbian persons first made an appearance in the official records of the U.S. government.

How did the creation of sexuality as a new category of person bring the "homosexual" into being, not only as a new form of person but also as a new category of social and legal *subject*? It is this process that I explore in the pages that follow. As I have suggested, the U.S. military has played a central role in defining the "homosexual" juridically, presenting authoritatively and *officially* who and what lesbians and gay men *are*, creating a category of identity that would serve both as a new site of regulation and a new form of resistance to regulation. The military forms a constant frame of reference for this exploration, but the arguments here are applicable to all areas of public policy where lesbians and gay men are "put into the law."

Whenever the law is invoked, whenever debates erupt about rights and equality, differing conceptions of *identity* circulate just below the surface. Are homosexuals people, or is homosexuality a series of sexual *acts* that people engage in? Do they have control over *what* they do and *who* they are, or is sexuality a question simply beyond our control? Finally, are "gay" and "lesbian" nouns, or are they adjectives? The debate about *who* and *what* gay men and lesbians *are* is the subject of Chapter 1.

Before turning to the examination of policy debates, legislation, and adjudication in which gay men and lesbians come to be identified and addressed by the State, I examine the discourses and the institutions from which these discourses emanate, creating understandings that circulate still in our modern perception of the gay and lesbian subject. I look at the religious, medical, and psychiatric/psychological models of homosexuality, first from within the respective epistemological institutions that gave birth to them and then by tracing the influences that these institutions of "truth creation" have had on the formal State bureaucracies and policymakers. The *official* representative of the State adopted, reflected, and codified this sexual "truth" constructed by religious, medical, and psychiatric discoveries and consolidated the Foucaultian triad of "power-knowledge-pleasure that sustains the discourse on human sexuality in our part of the world."[2] As official public policy, these epistemological "truths" about sexuality were granted new life, and with this new life heightened levels and increased forms of scrutiny affected/infected the personal and private lives of all human beings, gay and straight alike. Tracing the historical evolution of these epistemological discourses, their originating institutions, and the institutional lobbying for access to the corridors of State power is the subject of Chapter 2.

Chapters 3 through 6 examine the way that the State came to reflect these epistemological models of homosexuality in a single policy area—military policy—and investigate the consequences of these policies for gay men and lesbians. Military service, as one of the primary means for distinguishing between a nation's citizens and noncitizens, provides an interesting example of the way in which arguments about *who* and *what* lesbians and gay men *are* are deployed to legitimize and legalize discrimination against them. Military service is a natural place to begin to search for the concretization of sexual identities by the State. The massive military mobilization of human resources during both world wars proved to be one of the greatest expansions of governmental bureaucratization of everyday life ever experienced in the history of this country. Clearly seen in military policy are the religious, medical, and psychiatric/psychological models of homosexuality, as the "expertise" of physicians and psychiatrists becomes institutionalized as one of the regulatory arms of the government in this intensifying process of screening, examining, and determining the military fitness of soldiers during wartime.

Chapter 7 expands on this discussion, drawing from various policy areas to illustrate the extent to which these epistemological models of homosexuality have shaped the social and political quests for "liberation" pursued by contemporary gay and lesbian activists. Even more, the question of definition of self—the philosophic, academic, and personal musings about "identity"— although present prior to these modern policy debates, is elevated to a new plateau, as gay men and lesbians attempt to control the way in which the government comes to regulate aspects of their lives and their *being*. And finally, the Conclusion, returning to the theme of identity, offers some culminating (though not final) observations about the consequences and possibilities that lesbian and gay identity has created for State regulation and individual liberation.

1

What Is an Official Gay Identity?

---

official: adj. 1. of or relating to an office, position, or trust. 2. holding an office. 3. authoritative, authorized; prescribed or recognized as authorized.

gay: adj. 1. happily excited: merry; keenly alive and exuberant. 2. bright, lively. 3. given to social pleasures; licentious. 4. homosexual, being a socially integrated group oriented toward and concerned with the welfare of the homosexual.

—*The Random House Dictionary of the English Language,* 1987

WHAT DOES it mean to suggest that there is an *official* construction of sexuality? Sexuality, for many people, connotes sexual practices, and we think of sexual practices as a private concern; hidden away and out of view, they are tolerated in a liberal society *because* they are private. Sexuality in the more contemporary sense connotes sexual *identity* and does not, at least on the surface, invite public scrutiny and discourse, for many people live their entire lives without giving a thought to their own sexual identity. Just what does it mean, then, to suggest that there is an official construction of sexuality, and how can it be said to emerge from an analysis of public policy texts?

Before we can begin to answer these questions and simplify the discussion, however, we must first complicate it further. It is clear to virtually everyone that gay and lesbian people exist. Since the 1970s, the struggle for lesbian and gay equality in the United States has achieved ever-increasing levels of recognition, attention, and understanding. In most major cities today, gay men and lesbians can choose to live freely and openly among other men and women who share their sense of identity. Bars, bookstores, health clubs, and crisis lines that cater specifically to their needs have become commonplace. Hotels, bed-and-breakfasts,[1] libraries, doctors, insurance agents, realtors, even car salespersons frequently advertise in gay and lesbian newspapers, periodicals, and telephone directories.[2] Gay youth organizations have been created to help adolescents who are struggling with their sexual identity, and even mainstream comic books aimed at a children's market have expanded their universe to include gay superheroes.[3]

These changes include increasing levels of political activity. Nonprofit organizations such as the National Gay and Lesbian Task Force and the Human Rights Campaign Fund lobby Congress, while Lambda Legal Defense and Education Fund and the National Gay Rights Advocates press for reform in the nation's courts. Openly gay and lesbian candidates have won election to local city councils, state legislatures, and the U.S. Congress. In the latter part of the twentieth century, gay men and lesbians created a culture, a politics, and a sense of community based on a shared sense of self. A number of scholars see the strategies and techniques that are employed by the gay and lesbian community to realize increased levels of societal recognition and political mobilization as patterned after the politics of racial and ethnic minorities.[4]

To complicate matters, however, unlike racial and ethnic minorities, the gay and lesbian communities lack many of the common secondary characteristics that demographers employ to describe group similarities. Gay men and lesbians come from every religious, ethnic, and racial background. They come from widely divergent classes, reflect diverse levels of educational and occupational achievement, and have no primary nation of origin. They are Republicans and Democrats, conservatives and liberals. They assume no predictable "gay" or "lesbian" position with regard to most policy issues, and many have lived decades of their lives without defining themselves as gay or lesbian.

For all the material evidence that gay men and lesbians do indeed exist, there has been great disagreement over the true meaning of sexual identity. There is little agreement over *why* a person is gay, and debates have erupted over what the categories "gay" and "lesbian" actually describe. Are these terms descriptive of something natural, something fixed, something immutable? Or are sexual identities more fluid, malleable, and hence open to social influences? Are they historical categories that come into existence at a certain time and place? Are there anthropological similarities between the sexual identities and practices of gay and lesbian people today and the sexual identities and practices of people from different cultures both ancient and modern, or do these terms really signal a late Western identity that appeared only in the past 125 years? If newly emergent, then are modern sexual identities tied to certain levels of economic development? Finally, are gay and lesbian identities fixed and unchangeable, or do they include some element of personal choice?

These questions are not simply academic. How we answer them will help determine what kind of public policies nations may wish to pursue. For example, polling data for the years between 1993 and 2001 have been remarkably consistent on the issue of the believed fluidity of gay sexual identity. In 1993, 44 percent of those who responded to a *New York Times*/CBS News poll believed that gay men and lesbians choose to be gay, whereas 43 percent believed that being gay or lesbian is something that individuals cannot change.[5] Almost a decade later, the results of a second poll were nearly identical, with 42 percent of respondents believing that gay men and lesbians can change their sexual orientation and 45 percent believing that sexual identity cannot be changed.[6]

Although equally divided on this issue, polls further reveal that this question of identity is central to how people feel about whether gay men and lesbians are deserving of social and political equality. For example, as Table 1 indicates, although 78 percent of respondents support equal job opportunities for gay men and lesbians, how we perceive sexual orientation clearly influences

TABLE 1   Jobs and Rights

Total % of Respondents	Response	Perception of Homosexuality	
		It Is a Choice (%)	It Cannot Be Changed (%)
78	Homosexuals should have equal rights in terms of job opportunities.	69	90
42	It is necessary to pass laws to ensure that homosexuals have equal rights.	30	58
49	It is objectionable to have a doctor who is homosexual.	64	34
55	It is objectionable to have a homosexual as an elementary school teacher.	71	39
46	Homosexual relations between consenting adults should be legal.	32	62
55	Homosexual relations between adults are morally wrong.	78	30
43	Homosexuals should be permitted to serve in the military.	32	54

Source: Data from the *New York Times*/CBS News poll, Febrary 9–11, 1993.

this support. To illustrate, 90 percent of those who believed that sexual identity is unchangeable also believed that homosexuals should have equal employment opportunities, whereas only 69 percent of those who believed that gay men and lesbians can choose their sexual orientation supported equal job opportunity for gay men and lesbians. This gap widens to nearly 50 percent when respondents are asked whether, in their personal judgment, homosexual relations between adults are morally wrong.

Right or wrong, the question of identity clearly affects public opinion about gay rights. Unfortunately, students of public policy have dismissed these very questions of beliefs and values as unscientific or inapplicable to the "science" of policy studies. Failing to recognize the interrelationship of facts and values has led to both a theoretical bankruptcy on the part of most policy analysts and a gulf between policy studies and political theory. Most policy analysts "take the view that values must be accepted as an arbitrary decision posited by the will or by passion, while 'factual' premises are grounded in reality. There is therefore a gulf between goals and value judgments, on the one hand, and the universe of facts which can be arranged and ordered in an objective, scientific, rational and coherent fashion on the other."[7] Most studies of public policy look toward purely technical considerations, as "on all sides theoretical requirements are abandoned, by considering inputs or outputs alone."[8]

But what is public policy if not a snapshot of the values, beliefs, and preferences of a culture at a given point in history? Today one would hardly advocate the segregation of African Americans or the forced sterilization of the poor and the mentally challenged, although both represented official government policy at particular times in this country's history and both were widely accepted and supported among large segments of the general population. This is not to suggest that all public policy decisions are doomed to be judged as unenlightened mistakes by the generations that follow. However, it is clear that federal policy texts are interesting "stuff" for theoretical investigation, as the privileges, convictions, predispositions, and prejudices of a culture are all too present in the "rational" outcomes of the policy process. Rather than reprehend these values and beliefs as "soft," as many policy analysts do, I suggest that, *because* of their softness, these decisions reveal much about the political climate and the culture that produce them. Policy decisions do not function unidirectionally; in other words, they do not flow simply from the institutions of government to the people. Indeed, much of what government representatives do is carefully crafted to meet with the approval of the people, to embody their desires and opinions. In this sense, the policy-making process is interactive, permeable, and subject to change—not at all the reasoned and studied decision-making process that some policy analysts describe.

Initiating as well as reflecting beliefs and values, the decisions of public policy help shape the values of a culture and are in turn shaped by them, creating *official* meanings and accepted under-

standing while granting legitimacy and recognition. When striking the perfect balance between representing cultural values and
helping to authorize and legitimate new ones, the policy process
can often appear objective, rational, and scientific, so completely
have we been implicated in the framing of the questions during
the policy-making process. Kathy Ferguson's description of framing is relevant here, as public policy questions are often framed
in such a way that the answers become obvious the moment the
question is asked. Ferguson writes, "The questions we can ask
about the world are enabled, and other questions disabled, by the
frame that orders the questioning. When we are busy arguing
about the questions that appear within a certain frame, the frame
itself becomes invisible; we become *enframed* within it."[9]

The power of undertaking a theoretical analysis of policy texts
comes in its ability to (re)move the frame or to decenter the object
of study and to reveal the epistemological systems and cultural
values cross-dressing as a kind of "rational objectivity" known as
positivism. An examination of the public construction of sexuality seeks to explain how homosexuality has been imagined and
defined in such a way as to make possible various forms of scrutiny and invasion, regulation and prohibition. Using military policy texts as a constant *frame* for investigation, I aim to reveal the
epistemological systems at work that authorize and legitimate the
policies that exclude lesbians and gay men from participation in
the U.S. armed forces.

At the philosophic level, this understanding of an official sexuality has implications beyond its effect on the study of military
policy or of policy making in general. The implications of revealing the way that sexuality is politically constructed extend even
beyond the scholarly research into homosexuality. The question of
sexual identity is central to thousands, if not millions, of men and
women, who seek to justify, legitimate, and promote understanding of their existence and to explain and defend their struggles for
equal protection and fundamental civil rights guaranteed to citizens by the Constitution of the United States. Identity, then, is
being. It is who we *are* and how we wish others to see, perceive,

and respond to us. But where does it come from? People do not choose to remake their identities totally, although the Western emphasis on individualism and freedom of choice attempts to convince us that they do. To do so would be to create an identity that would be unintelligible to anyone else. As Erik Erikson—the man who helped popularize the word "identity" in the 1950s through his psychological term "identity crisis"—suggests, identity concerns "a process 'located' *in the core of the individual* and yet also *in the core of his communal culture,* a process which establishes, in fact, the identity of these two identities."[10] Erikson's psychological approach can be contrasted with the sociological tradition in which role theory and reference group theory understand identification as the "process by which a person comes to realize what groups are significant for him, what attitudes concerning them he should form, and what kind of behavior is appropriate."[11] In both of these early understandings of identity, cultural structures play a role in the making of identity, though in very different ways. In both examples, individuals play a role in producing their own identity, but Erikson's process is a negotiation between an individual and the larger culture to determine an identity in which the individual plays a more active role, reconciling his or her individuality with a knowledge of communal practices and preexisting identities.

One actor central to this process of identification is the State. In this battle over "naming names" the State's actions will determine who receives rights and benefits, what activities are legal, and which identities constitute citizenship. The State will depend on other instruments of truth production to justify and legitimate its decisions, making an analysis of the way that gay men and lesbians are treated by the State dependent on a knowledge of other, sometimes older, discourses of truth production. In other words, in its interrogation of gay and lesbian subjects, the State will often turn to other arenas—tradition, religion, medicine, science—to help it decide what gay and lesbian identity *is*.

In this context, this philosophic discussion takes on a political hue. If sexual expression is medicalized, criminalized, or anathematized, then individuals and groups that attempt to secure rights of citizenship by positing a social and political identity based on this problematized sexual expression will encounter deeply ingrained prejudice and stiff resistance at best and moral outrage, hatred, and violence at worst. Answers to the questions "What are we?" "Why are we?" and "Why do we do what we do?" become the ideological battleground, the disputed epistemological territory, as individuals and institutions, authors and authorities struggle for control over the most basic political power: the power to name, to classify, to tell the "truth"; the taxonomic power to determine self and other. Louis Althusser's famous description of interpellation, found in his essay "Ideology and Ideological State Apparatuses," is a helpful lens through which to frame this discussion of an *official* sexuality:

> Ideology "acts" or "functions" in such a way that it recruits subjects among the individuals . . . or "transforms" the individuals into subjects . . . by the very precise operation which I have called interpellation or hailing, and which can be imagined along the lines of the most commonplace everyday police (or other) hailing: "Hey, you there."
>
> Assuming that the theoretical scene I have imagined takes place in the street, that hailed individual will turn around. By the mere hundred and eighty degree physical conversion, he becomes a *subject*. Why? Because he recognized that the hail was "really addressed to him and that 'it was really him who was hailed'" (and not someone else).[12]

Althusser's description of interpellation, which describes the making of a subject, one who knows and understands that it is he (or she) who is addressed, is a helpful way to think about the process embedded in the making an *official* construction of identity.

But there is another somewhat different definition that is equally interesting and important to the analysis that I undertake. The 1987 *Random House Dictionary of the English Language* (second edition) defines "interpellation" as "a process in some legislative bodies of asking a government official to explain an act or policy, sometimes leading, in parliamentary government, to a vote of confidence of the dissolution of government." "Interpellation" in this definition is not simply the calling into being or the making of a subject but also the interrogation of that subject, the calling of the subject to account before the official administrators of the State. For gay men and lesbians, this State accounting asks *who* they are, *what* they are, and even *why* they are. The State asks in order to know *how* they can be put into the law and how the law will account for them. These two different definitions of "interpellation"—the conversion of undifferentiated individuals into subjects as these individuals come to understand that it is they who are summoned and the interrogation or calling to account of these individuals by officials of the State—are the two processes that contribute to the constitution of an *official* gay identity.

Most, although not all, of the policy texts that I have examined depend on deployments of discursive productions of homosexual identity that treat gay men and lesbians as evil, unnatural, physiologically deviant, medically ill, mentally disturbed, or immoral. Yet many of these policymakers, as well as many in the general population, know gay and lesbian individuals and find little resemblance between these people and the culturally constructed gay and lesbian Other. Indeed, the remarkable thing is how many of those who express homophobic views about the evil and immorality of homosexuality have perfectly civil, perhaps even warm, relationships with lesbian and gay family members and friends. Perhaps the explanation for the inconsistency found among many social critics of homosexuality is that the lesbians and gay men they know personally are exempted from vituperation because they are perceived to be just like everyone else and simply want to be treated equally by law and society. This view that gay men and lesbians are just like everyone else can also be dangerous, as it builds acceptance of lesbians and gay men through an erasure of some very real differences. The danger for gay men and lesbians occurs as it adversely affects our desire to combine "what we regard as the better parts of the alternative; we want equality without its compelling us to accept identity; but also difference without its degenerating into superiority/ inferiority."[13]

What, then, do gay men and lesbians share? What are the elements that bring otherwise disassociated individuals together to form a community? To answer sexuality, or sexual difference, might at first seem to be stating the obvious, but beyond this simplistic rejoinder there is little agreement. Indeed, even this answer refracts into more questions. Is this sexual difference a deviance, a form of perverse sexuality? Is it an illness, a sexuality gone awry? Is "homosexual" a noun or a verb? Is being gay an orientation, a preference, a lifestyle? Do gay men and lesbians *choose* to be the way they are, or does sexuality reside outside the realm of choice, a matter of "genetic predetermination"? Are there any theoretical possibilities between these two extremes? In sum, upon what does lesbian and gay "identity" depend?

Over the past decade, those interested in the study of sexuality have been embroiled in a debate aimed at addressing just this overall question. According to some, the debate has "outlived its usefulness,"[14] creating an "impasse predicated on the difficulty of theorizing the social in relation to the natural,"[15] thereby paralyzing the study of homosexuality in the disciplines of history and the social sciences.[16] Nevertheless, even critics agree that this debate has reoriented our thinking about sexuality, calling into question some of the general assumptions of the twentieth century regarding homosexuality.[17] At the center of this debate stand political actors, scientists, and public policymakers, who have helped shape the way that we think about sex and sexual identity in the contemporary United States.

This debate, first coming into its modern expression in the study of feminist theory, was adopted quickly by scholars and activists interested in creating an academic field committed to the study of gay men and lesbians. Known as the essentialist/constructivist controversy, this debate has fueled the fire of speculation about the causes of homosexuality and its recognition as a lesbian or gay identity. The word "identity" as used in the expressions "homosexual identity," "gay identity," or "lesbian identity" is of relatively recent origin. Vivienne Cass has noted that "a perusal of the pages and indices of early bibliographies clearly shows the lack of reference to, and interest in, the construct [identity] prior to [the 1970s]."[18] But the roots of this debate have a genealogy that is traceable both to the twentieth-century development of the academic fields of psychology and sociology and to the search for self-definition and self-understanding pursued by early gay and lesbian political organizations.

Eriksonian psychology and U.S. sociology illustrated an academic interest in the concept of personal identity—what makes a person who he or she is—that would resurface again in the form of academic debates regarding essentialism and social constructivism during the 1970s and 1980s. But psychologists and sociologists were not the only people interested in issues of identity in the 1950s.

In fact, it would be a mistake to conclude that because *identity* has only recently become the focus of medical or scientific understandings of homosexuality or that because the *word* "identity" does not appear in the academic literature on homosexuality before the 1970s, the *concept* of identity, as a way of understanding who and what one is, was not an issue for gay men and lesbians in their lives before then. For decades before "homosexual identity" came into common usage in the academic communities, homosexuals had been battling the stigmatizing effects of this medical classification, just as, before them, sodomites had fought their legal/moral classification attributed by church and State. It was these struggles that led to the birth of organizations that aimed to foster understanding and acceptance of homosexuals. It was in the arguments put forward by these organizations that the idea of identity first approached the meaning that Erikson assigned to it: a deeply internal structure located within an individual's psyche.

In the United States, one of the first of these organizations, the Mattachine Society, originated in Los Angeles in the early 1950s. Making use of the name of a secret medieval society of unmarried French men who conducted rituals and dances during festivals, members of the modern Mattachine Society organized themselves into secret cells reminiscent of those of the communist party, in which the founders had been active.[19] In its mission statement, the Mattachine Society proposed to foster an "ethical homosexual culture" comparable to "the merging cultures of our fellow-minorities—the Negro, Mexican and Jewish Peoples." Stressing the importance of education, unification, and consciousness-raising, the society also called for its members to engage in "political action to erase from our law books the discriminatory and oppressive legislation presently directed at the homosexual minority."[20]

The members of this early gay rights organization claimed that a hidden homosexual minority existed and, by implication, had always existed. It was only the oppression of the heterosexual majority's culture, language, and legal strictures that had prevented gay men and lesbians from discovering their common heritage and their shared essentialism. As Jeffrey Escoffier writes, "This analysis seemed consistent with the experience of many gay women and men at the time as well as with subsequent history." This minority, they argued, could be discovered, united, and led to emancipation through education, political activity, and the creation of an "ethical homosexual culture."[21] This group clearly had an understanding of gay and lesbian identity that mirrored Erikson's presentation of identity as an "internal" part of an individual, although academicians would not apply this conceptualization of identity to gay men and lesbians for two decades. Still, not everyone in the Mattachine Society agreed with this assessment of gay and lesbian identity. Others in the Mattachine Society, called "middle class" and "status quo types" by founder Henry Hay, believed that the "the cultural and social characteristics of gay life" were "the result of ostracism and oppression"[22] rather than a reflection of essential differences realized and then projected outward into the creation of a specialized culture.

Arguing from a sociological/interactionist perspective and relying on the pioneering works of Alfred Kinsey (*Sexual Behavior in the Human Male* in 1948 and *Sexual Behavior in the Human Female* in 1953) and the position developed by writers such as Donald Webster Corey in his 1951 publication *The Homosexual in America: A Subjective Approach*, these activists claimed that the only "real" difference between heterosexuals and homosexuals was their sexual preference.[23] In all other respects, homosexuals and heterosexuals were alike. They agreed with the supporters of the "ethical homosexual culture" thesis that having a different sexual preference often led to oppression of homosexuals. They also agreed that shared oppression led to the development of some kind of homosexual subculture, but they disagreed that this subculture was the result of some unchangeable essential difference inherent in gay men and lesbians, and they clearly did not find this subculture something to celebrate. Believing that the homosexual subculture was premised on self-hatred and isolation, the "assimilationists," as they were dubbed by their opponents in the Mattachine Society, saw a distinct, disparate homosexual culture more as a byproduct of oppression than as a solution to it. Arguing against creating a different culture, the proponents of the assimilationist position advocated working within the system, "adopting a pattern of behavior that is acceptable to society" and compatible with the political and social institutions of "home, church and state."[24] Their position became the pattern for the developing gay and lesbian rights movement in the fifties and sixties.[25]

This quick examination of the history of the U.S. gay rights movement illustrates a number of interesting points. The concept of a politicized homosexual identity first emerged among gay men who attempted to explain and justify their existence and to achieve some form of political equality. Although they had yet to apply the term "identity" to their efforts to organize and record their history and opinions about *who, what,* and *why* they were, gay men and lesbians saw themselves as engaged in the process of truth telling, the process of explaining, justifying, and at times inventing who they were and thereby hoping to alter the medicalized and criminalized representation of "homosexual."

The actions and the controversies of the early Mattachine Society mirror the academic debate surrounding "personal identity formation" espoused by Erikson and the sociologists of the time. Although the term "identity" was yet to enter everyday, or even common, academic usage, the concept and its importance in the battle over representations of self were being debated in the gay and lesbian community long before it became a hot academic topic or a colloquial mainstay. These early debates over identity also accurately foreshadow the theoretical split that was to develop within the research on homosexuality in the late 1970s.

More important than the historical genealogy of *identity*, this historical digression illustrates that the debate over *being* (known in its current manifestation as the essentialist/constructivist debate) has been present, at some level, since the beginning of the gay rights movement in the United States. In other words, this debate about identity has been political since its origin. Politics helps shape and motivate the theories (scientific and philosophic) behind the search for causes of gay identity, and theory in turn contributes to the political debate about who lesbians and gay men are and what civil and social rights they are to be afforded. That academicians, pursuing the study of sexuality, would come to reflect the debate over the meaning of lesbian and gay being in their deliberations, albeit in a more detailed, analytic, and sometimes tedious manner, is both predictable and understandable. But these debates are not merely interesting philosophically; they also have far-reaching consequences for many of the political battles being fought today. From the policies that have excluded gays from serving in the U.S. armed forces to the political debates over lesbian and gay marriage, essentialist and constructivist understandings of sexuality emerge as central. We cannot understand public policy without considering these theoretical debates; thus, the study of public policy is a theoretical undertaking.

The Essentialist/Constructivist Debate

Although many scholars believe that the essentialist/constructivist debate is in essence a debate between constructivists and their socially constructed "straw man" of essentialism,[26] the philosophic roots of essentialism can be traced to the work of Aristotle, whose Book Z of the *Metaphysics* conducts a systematic examination of the distinction between essence and accident.[27] In this form, the debate between the essentialists and the social constructivists reflects the ancient polemic between nature and nurture that has reverberated for millennia in the works of philosophers who have conceptualized and justified the roles that women have occupied in society.

Fueled by the Enlightenment fascination with *reason* and *science*, this debate, as it was applied to women, reached a fevered pitch in the writings of Jean Jacques Rousseau. His explanations for the differences in the treatment of women, which sound like weak and sometimes comical rationalizations to many modern listeners, reflect an understanding of the roles of nature and socialization that circulate still in the modern understanding of sex and gender differences. Of course, few today would argue, as did Rousseau, that "however lightly we may regard the disadvantages peculiar to women, yet, as they necessarily occasion intervals of inaction, this is a sufficient reason for excluding them from . . . supreme authority."[28] However, the rapidity with which the concept of premenstrual syndrome (PMS) exploded into common usage as a medically scientific explanation of the "unpredictable mood swings" that women experience as a result of biological differences indicates the ancient roots of our modern understanding of nature and biology.

Essentialism, as it applies to the study of sexuality, has historically dominated this debate that marshals nature and biology against social and cultural explanations of the causes and origins of sexual difference. Essentialists believe that a true, unchanging, irreducible essence constitutes sexual identity. Sexuality, in this understanding, carries the weight of a biological force, and sexual identity represents the cognitive realization of genuine underlying differences. To be gay, then, constitutes a core of one's being that exists independent of, prior to, and outside of the influence of culture. It is a fixed and unchanging property, like height, eye color, or body type, and it is objectively verifiable. It is a real, existing, determinative difference that, whatever the cause, already has been or will be in the future empirically verified.

As much of the recent constructivist criticism indicates, essentialism contains within it a variety of causal explanations. Not unlike constructivism, essentialism is compatible with a variety of understandings of sexuality.[29] Whether they view sexuality as a biological force, a product of hormonal or genetic differences, or a consequence of psychological elements of early adult/child relationships, essentialists agree that there is something central, some core part of individuals that *makes* them the "way they are."

Social constructivists, on the other hand, are concerned with the philosophic refutation of essentialism. Believing that sexuality and sexual identity are social constructs, belonging to the nexus between society, culture, and the production of meaning, they reject biological and deterministic accounts of sexual difference. The constructivist objective is to examine, interrogate, and explain the complicated and interlocking processes that work together to create the appearance of "natural" or given "sexualities."

Included in this agenda is the defamiliarization of the signifier "natural" and a critique of science, as constructivists argue that nature and science are both products of social interaction and are rooted in culturally specific meanings. Nature, it is argued, has meanings that differ among people at various periods in history, and much of what was considered scientifically sound and irrefutable in the past is seen today as remarkably naïve, simplistic, and shaped by a cultural/political context. According to the constructivists, sexuality and sexual identity, like history, are culturally dependent and rooted in practices unique to a specific culture at a specific period in time. Constructivists assume that sexual relations, identities, and differences inhere in the practices created by a culture's language. And whereas they admit that sexual acts between members of the same gender occur in almost every society and at almost every period in history, they argue that those who have created a sexual identity based on these sexual acts or on deeply personal sexual feelings and emotions have only recently come into being.

The genealogy of the social constructivists does not stretch back nearly as far as the Aristotelian musings about essence, but its relatively recent origin belies the speed with which it has become "received wisdom" among many leftist academics. Although there are some disagreements about the more obscure tenets of the social constructivist position as it is applied to questions of sexuality,[30] there is general agreement over the central figures: Mary McIntosh and Michel Foucault.

In 1968, Mary McIntosh wrote an article that sought to "take on" the medical understanding of the "homosexual" as a transhistorical, natural category of person. Central to the current constructivist critique, McIntosh's discussion of a "homosexual role" as a modern development provides the crux of the constructivist argument that, although homosexual acts can be found in every society, homosexual persons have arisen only recently. McIntosh describes the role the medical community played in the spread of our cultural understanding of the homosexual:

> Many scientists and ordinary people assume that there are two kinds of people in the world: homosexuals and heterosexuals. Some of them recognize that homosexual feelings and behavior are not so confined to the persons they would like to call "homosexuals" and that some of these people do not actually engage in homosexual behavior. This should pose a crucial problem, but they evade the crux by retaining their assumption and puzzling over the question of how to tell whether someone is "really" homosexual or not. Lay people too will discuss whether a certain person is "queer" in much the same way as they might question whether a pain indicated cancer. And in much the same way will often turn to scientists or to medical men for a surer diagnosis.[31]

In place of a primarily essentialist medical discourse that treats homosexuality as an internal property, McIntosh argues that in modern societies the homosexual has come to occupy a unique social role. This role developed because homosexual practices are widespread yet threatening, and a stigmatized category of "being" was required to help distinguish between good and evil and to help keep the rest of society "pure." This category serves, McIntosh argues, as a threshold that distinguishes between permissible and impermissible behavior. As an individual's behavior approaches that threshold, he or she immediately risks being labeled a full-fledged deviant. Finally, McIntosh adds that a homosexual *identity* is created not through engaging in a certain sexual activity (what labeling theorists would call primary deviance) but through the reactions of the deviant individual to being described as a homosexual and then internalizing that description and its imposed categorization (secondary deviance). McIntosh's work created room for doubt in the prevailing essentialist understandings of a medicalized homosexuality in 1968, and it opened the door to even greater investigation as to the causes of homosexuality and the origins of gay and lesbian people.

More important than McIntosh's "The Homosexual Role" was the 1978 appearance of Michel Foucault's *History of Sexuality.* Foucault argues that sexuality has been the site of an explosion of discourses of power and knowledge. Sexual meanings, sexual strictures, and sexual beings have come to be produced endlessly by societies and cultures that have become obsessed with the significance of the sexual, elevating it to dimensions never before witnessed in the history of the world. In Foucault's words, we have come to look toward sex and sexuality to tell the "truth of our being."[32]

Bringing a historical approach to the constructivist debate, Foucault employs this perspective to explain the origin of "the homosexual." Tracing the shift from sexual acts to sexual persons, from verb to noun, Foucault argues that the shift occurred as the result of an increase in (1) the fascination with sexuality in general, (2) the intensity and transformation in the structures of social control, by making these mechanisms for social control ever more individualized and disciplinary, and (3) the authority of, respect toward, and institutional power of the medical professionals to enforce social norms and punish aberrations and deviances.

Sounding a bit like Thomas Kuhn, whose book *The Structure of Scientific Revolution*[33] describes paradigm shifts that dramatically change the way in which we understand a given field of inquiry, Foucault argues that there is a definite point in history when the homosexual was brought to life:

> As defined by the ancient civil or canonical codes, sodomy was a category of forbidden acts; their perpetrator was nothing more

than the juridical subject of them, the nineteenth-century homosexual became a personage, a past, a case history, and a childhood,
in addition to being a type of life, a life form, and a morphology,
with an indiscreet anatomy and possibly a mysterious physiology.
Nothing that went into his total composition was unaffected by
his sexuality. It was everywhere present in him: at the root of all
his actions. . . . Homosexuality appeared as one of the forms of
sexuality when it was transposed from the practice of sodomy
onto a kind of interior androgyny, a hermaphroditism of the soul.
The sodomite had been a temporary aberration; the homosexual
was now a species.[34]

From these double roots, the social constructivists have developed a sophisticated new analysis of sexuality that affects our understanding of history, politics, anthropology, classical literature,
women's studies, and philosophy. Currently, there are quite im-
pressive numbers of people who call themselves social constructivists. Steven Epstein, Jeffrey Escoffier, Arnold Davidson, Robert
Padgug, Ian Hacking, Lenore Tiefler, Diane Richardson, Diana
Fuss, Jeffrey Weeks, and Kenneth Plummer are some of the more
notable scholars, although, among even this sample of individuals, there are differences in the approach to the social construction of sexuality.

Morality and Politics

A large part of the present debate over sexuality and sexual identity involves the moral and political implications that each of the
various positions creates. Unfortunately, the political and moral
implications are not always immediately obvious to those who articulate "proofs" and "theories" regarding the roots and causes of
sexuality, and many scholars make claims about "truth" without
acknowledging cultural or ideological influences on that truth
production.

Edward Stein has noted that many scholars and activists are not
honest about their reasons for articulating a theory of sexuality.
Stein describes their logic as rooted in the notion that "essentialism, *if true,* would be good for gay rights and/or writing social

criticism, literary criticism, or history; therefore essentialism *is true*."[35] This concern over creating a theory of sexual identity that is "safe" or one that creates space with which to fight bigotry and moral condemnation regardless of how tenuous the theory is not limited to essentialists. However, this conflation of "ought" with "is" does appear to be most prevalent among gay political activists who want essentialist claims about the origins of sexuality to be true.[36]

The logic behind activists making essentialist arguments is as follows: If homosexuality is biologically or genetically determined, then it rests outside the sphere of individual control and therefore should rest outside the realm of condemnation and discrimination. For many gay men and lesbians who have had their sexual identity declared immature or have been asked or sometimes pressured to become heterosexual, an essentialist claim to having always been gay provides more protection against bigotry and oppression than do constructivist claims that "gay" and "lesbian" are only textual, historical, or discursive productions.

To the extent that persecution, harassment, and discrimination do exist, then, essentialists argue that deterministic explanations for sexual orientation allow gay men and lesbians to seek and perhaps receive preferential treatment as members of a "protected class." From a religious point of view, essentialist explanations for homosexuality allow gay men and lesbians to challenge orthodox condemnations of homosexual feelings, acts, and identity. If sexual orientation does not depend on human choice, then homosexuals can claim to be the creation of God as much as can heterosexuals; thus, their form of sexual activity becomes less problematic.

The disagreement about what constitutes the "best" or most defensible position for gay men and lesbians to adopt with respect to the understanding of their sexual orientation and sexual identity is most bitter in academic circles where battle lines have been drawn. In leftist academic circles constructivism has become accepted wisdom, often manifested in a new "queer" critique, and essentialism has been rejected as a return to an unsophisticated biological determinism of the past; the constructivists' critics who often make essentialist arguments about sexuality and sexual identity argue that essentialist explanations are much more widely accepted among the gay and lesbian community. Epstein notes that "curiously, the historical ascendancy of the new constructivist orthodoxy [in academia] has paralleled a growing inclination in the gay movement in the United States to understand itself and project an image of itself in ever more 'essentialist' terms."[37] Many gay men and lesbians believe that an essentialist understanding of their sexuality is a truer expression of their understanding of self and identity and is likely to provide a more defensible political position with regard to civil rights protection. For example, if gays are born and not made, then a gay elementary school teacher who serves as a role model for, or in a position of authority over, children need present neither a threat to the children nor a legitimate concern for the children's parents, as the teacher's sexual identity cannot influence the sexual development of his or her students.

Dynes has written that "abandonment of the idea that homosexuals constitute a discrete social entity or minority will make it difficult to persuade already skeptical lawmakers that we deserve civil rights protection."[38] That this battle rages with the intensity of ecclesiastical differences over "revealed truth" and apostasy reveals both the great stakes involved for, and the very real oppression experienced by, gay men and lesbians. But what often is missing from both social constructivist and essentialist analyses of sexual identity is a distinctively political understanding of the way that political institutions, public policies, and the power of the State come to affect our choices and our understanding of sex and sexual identity.

The Philosophic and Political Dimensions of Sexual Identity and Its Use in Public Policy

Diana Fuss, perhaps more than anyone else, has offered a way to move the study of sexuality beyond its current philosophic and academic morass. In *Essentially Speaking: Feminism, Nature and Dif-*

ference, Fuss, who defines herself an "anti-essentialist," begins her investigation with the question "Has essentialism received a bad rap?" Impressed by the "sheer rhetorical power of essentialism," Fuss's objective is not to contribute to the current constructivist/essentialist debate; she believes that "essentialism itself is neither good or bad, progressive or reactionary, beneficial or dangerous." Instead, Fuss hopes to reorient the direction and emphasis of this debate, believing that "the question we should be asking is not, 'is this text essentialist (and therefore bad)?' but rather, 'if this text is essentialist, *what motivates its deployment?*' How does the sign 'essence' circulate in various contemporary critical debates? Where, how and why is it invoked? What are the political and textual effects?"[39] Of course, the same questions can and should be asked of texts that make constructivist claims about sexuality.

Fuss's focus on *how* and *by whom* essentialist arguments in texts are deployed reveals her indebtedness to Foucault, who similarly believed that *how* and *where* we talk about sex was as important as what we had to say. Foucault writes, "The central issue, then . . . is not to determine whether one says yes or no to sex, whether one formulates prohibitions or permissions, whether one asserts the importance or denies its effects, or whether one defines the words one uses to designate it, but to account for the fact that it is spoken about, to discover who does the speaking, the positions and viewpoints from which they speak, the institutions which prompt people to speak about it and which store and distribute the things that are said. What is at issue, briefly, is the overall 'discursive fact,' the way in which sex is 'put into the discourse.'"[40]

Foucault and Fuss's concern over the way that texts deploy ideas, beliefs, and values and their sensitivity to the social and political *effects* of these deployments is central to the examination that I undertake here. Narrating what I call an *official* sexuality, I explore the intersection between the body of laws and the identities of lesbians and gay men as they come to inhabit newly drawn and often illegal bodies that emerge through public/political discourse. Foucault understood the importance of these institutions for the creation and deployment of our sex and sexualities, writing that "sexuality owes its very definition to the action of the law: not only will you submit your sexuality to the law, but you will have no sexuality except by subjecting yourself to the law."[41] Examining the effects of these policy texts on the strategy, understanding, and even the very ontological debates over identity will involve an understanding of how both essentialist and constructivist arguments about sexuality are deployed and what effect they come to have on our political strategies and our personal lives.

Unlike Fuss, I believe that essentialist arguments about sexuality are indeed *bad*. As explanatory theories, they fail to account for much of the culturally variable and highly stylized sexual acts and presentations of self that are a part of what we mean today by "sexuality" or "sexual identity." Politically, these arguments open up possibilities for greater State regulation of sex than has heretofore been known. Still, the constructivist reply to an essentialist understanding of sexuality often seems even more dangerous and less accurate as a reflection of the way many lesbians and gay men feel about themselves. In fact, as most of the public understands it, the opposite of essentialism is not social constructivism per se but *choice*. And although choice may well be the rhetorical weapon with which to fight the battle to keep abortion legal (though even this is a contentious claim), it is decidedly not the preferred argument for those who seek State protection of the civil liberties of gay men and lesbians in the United States. Through an examination of the political effects of both positions, I articulate an argument that allows us to see constructivism—even in its most easily reducible manifestation as *choice*—as a defensible and, I believe, preferable alternative to the political essentialism that has become so predominant in our official construction of sexuality today.

Identity, then, is *being*. It is who we *are* and how we wish others to see, perceive, and respond to us. But this debate is also about *identification*, about how we are addressed, handled, and administered to by others. In the United States, gay men and lesbians do not enjoy social approval; they are judged evil and inferior by many in the dominant culture. To the extent that there is any recognition by those in the general population of a desire by gay men and lesbians for civil rights and legal protection, then, it is assumed that gay men and lesbians desire the same rights as heterosexuals. Although this is often the case, it carries the assumption that gay men and lesbians have the same desires and values as do heterosexuals. It denies the opportunity for difference, the opportunity for social and cultural transformation, by limiting rights and protection to only those rights and protections that are as defined by and granted to members of the dominant heterosexual culture.

Projecting these anticipated beliefs and desires for rights on the gay Other identifies this Other with the dominant heterosexual "self," predetermining the direction that civil rights debates and struggles will take. To the extent that gay men and lesbians accept this predetermined political agenda unreflectively, they do so without realizing that their demands did not originate in acts of political, social, or cultural creation of self and community by other gay men and lesbians and without realizing that the path to "liberation" is always already awaiting them. The concept of equal rights becomes a flight into similitude, as *equal* rights for gay men and lesbians comes to mean granting gay men and lesbians the *same* rights as "straights."

The notion of a social and political movement that would remake society, one that would liberate, change, or even question the existing social structures and the fundamental institutional arrangements of power, is relegated to the past—to a different, "less sophisticated" era of the movement's history—replaced by an agenda that seeks not to change society but to become one with it. This sinister, almost unconscious co-optation of the movement's agenda is but one of the associated costs to be borne as a result of this process of "identification" that takes place between the State and gay men and lesbians.

This process of identification and value integration is not unilateral; it does not flow only from the State, as the representative of the dominant culture, to gay men and lesbians, as members of a subculture. Often, lack of knowledge about gay men and lesbians and their subculture creates openings in the dominant culture's social fabric, points of resistance in a seemingly impregnable web of hegemonic cultural productions of sexualized and gendered selves, allowing elements of gay and lesbian identity to be mainstreamed. This "queering" of mainstream values can be seen in the widespread acceptance of earrings among "straight" men, pants and short hair among women, and alternative fashion styles and colors of clothing. Each of these is related to a gay sensibility that has become accepted, albeit unwittingly, by mainstream culture.[42]

Chapter 2 explores this nexus of collective identity formation and State identification from the discursive level, to ascertain how and where sex is put into the discourse of U.S. public policy.

2

The Emergence of Identity

Epistemological Tenets of the Modern Gay and Lesbian Subject

THE DEBATE over sexual identity, as we have seen, has spilled over into every facet of gay and lesbian existence, with important consequences for both State policy and the lives of lesbians and gay men. But how did sexuality come to be a State concern? Which epistemological systems were first concerned with articulating an understanding of "the homosexual," and how did these epistemologies represent who and what lesbians and gay men are? How were these epistemic conceptions—once developed—deployed in a way that increased the power of the State to recognize, define, and identify lesbians and gay men, summoning them into existence in ways that made their exclusion necessary and legitimate?

First, this chapter explores how the epistemological systems that produced the "truth" of the homosexual and his or her antecedents—be it the truth as revealed by religion or by medicine—came together to call the homosexual into existence. Through this process, individuals are turned into homosexual subjects, as they recognize that the noun "homosexual" refers to them. This process marks a reproblematization of sex, a shifting of the focus of regulation from anathematized sexual acts to medicalized sexual identities.

Second, this chapter begins the task that is undertaken through the remainder of the book: demonstrating how this new sexual identity—the homosexual—becomes the subject of the law, creating new forms of regulation and greater levels of official scrutiny than had previously been possible.

Elements of three different epistemological systems have contributed to this creation of the "homosexual subject." As systems of "truth" production, these three discursive systems have helped delineate and define gay identity as it emerged from prohibited sexual practices, medical case studies, and the therapist's couch and was transformed into an official and legal form of identity and identification. The three systems are (1) the Christian prohibitions of sodomy as an act contrary to "nature"; (2) the late-nineteenth-century medical "discovery" of "homosexuality" (a term invented by the medical establishment that would prescribe its treatment and cure); and (3) the psychiatric, psychological, and developmental models of homosexuality that emerged in the twentieth century.

These epistemologies, these ways of understanding sex, were produced by practitioners in institutions that had great authority in the society within which they operated. Although the medieval theologian, the nineteenth-century medical doctor, and the twentieth-century psychiatrist all differ, they came together in the position they shared in relationship to society and the State. The role of expert or authority is a powerful one, often carrying with it a great capacity to influence State policymakers, be they kings, legislators, or judges. Historically, each of these epistemological systems came to have some authoritative claim to knowing the "truth" about sexuality and sexual difference, and each was more than willing to share it with the rest of society. These practitioners, mouthpieces of various epistemologies, sought, and were often granted, the opportunity to "speak 'Truth' to power,"[1] with the consequence that their "truths" spilled over into the public policies of the modern State.

It is important to keep in mind that the intersections between epistemology, the institutions of its production, and the State shift over time, but as each shift occurs, the new discourse of authority and the new epistemology do not succeed completely in replacing earlier ones. As new epistemologies, social institutions, and discourses replace older ones as the bearers of "truth," older explanations are sifted and repackaged within the new framework rather than being abandoned, and their influence continues. As Jeffrey Weeks has noted, "All the major elements of the medieval taboos are present in the modern hostility toward homosexuality, but the contents of the kaleidoscope have been shaken and the pattern is different."[2]

For many centuries, for example, the Catholic Church controlled the production and dissemination of knowledge and "truth" about the purpose and intention of sexual acts. Procreation was the aim and goal of all sexual acts in this epistemological system. In the nineteenth and twentieth centuries, when medical science (including psychiatry and psychology) supplanted the church's monopoly on the creation of "truth" about sexual acts, the moral authority of the church's pronouncements did not completely cease. Although procreation is never explicitly posited as a standard of "normal sexuality" in the nineteenth-century medical epistemology, nonproductivity infiltrates the Darwinian, evolutionary model of homosexuality as biologically inferior, thus shaking the kaleidoscopic pattern of the cultural representation of sexual difference while retaining all its former elements. At different times, each has claimed the authority to define sexual difference, homosexuality, and gay and lesbian identity. Each shaped the public policy of the era in which it held sway. Understanding the processes of authority and influence lays the groundwork for a consideration of how each of the three epistemologies affects gay men and lesbians in terms of twentieth- and twenty-first-century military policy in the United States.

The Natural Law of Sexuality

The first epistemological discourse that helped summon forth the lesbian and gay subject is centuries old and rests on the dialectic natural/unnatural. The ideological and coercive power of the discourse of "nature" and "the natural" as it applies to sexual difference occurs around the medieval religious problematization of sodomy. The problematization of sodomy, in turn, is dependent on the moral equation of nature with a divine plan or an expressed will of God. Since the thirteenth century, most of the religious intolerance of sodomy depended on a definition of this act as unnatural, as contrary to both God and nature.

Invocations of the signifiers "nature," "the natural," and "natural law" are some of the most powerful that can be made. Plato was among the first to make this appeal, arguing in the *Laws* that homosexual acts were against nature and therefore warranted State regulation.[3] This has become a familiar rhetorical strategy, as the authority of nature is used alternately to create a realm of privacy independent of State regulation and to justify State incursions into this natural realm of privacy when nature is defi(l)ed.

Nature, as deployed within religious texts and arguments about sexual ethics, seems to be both fixed and malleable. On one hand, claims about nature attempt to affix us in a world of immutable truths; nature is called upon to illustrate God's intention, to illustrate the way things essentially *are*. Conversely, nature is offered as a moral standard, an ethical exemplar that helps human actors resist the corruptive influence of the unnatural.

This apparent contradiction rests on how the early and medieval Christians understood sexual difference. Their emphasis in this epistemology was on acts, not identities. The sodomite was merely someone who had committed the heinous *act* of sodomy. The act was essentially evil, although the person was not. Nature in this Christian epistemology represents what John Boswell has called an "idealized" conception of nature.[4] Contrasting this with "realistic" conceptions of nature, Boswell writes:

> Concepts of "ideal nature" are strongly conditioned by observation of the real world, but they are ultimately determined by cultural values. This is particularly notable in the case of "unnatural" which becomes in such a system a vehement circumlocution for "bad" or "unacceptable." Behavior which is ideologically so alien

or personally so disgusting to those affected by "ideal nature" that it appears to have no redeeming qualities whatever will be labeled "unnatural," regardless of whether it occurs in ("real") nature never or often, or among humans or lower animals, because it will be assumed that a "good" nature could not under any circumstances have produced it.[5]

Idealized notions of nature—whether understood to include all physical things or merely the nonhuman—are always believed to operate for the good. This is clear in the deployment of natural law, which is often conceptualized as representing a divine plan or the will of God. The church's observations of real nature serve to bolster its institutional and cultural values and its ideological agenda. As Boswell notes, "Adherents of 'ideal' concepts of nature frequently characterize as 'unnatural' sexual behavior to which they object on religious or personal grounds."[6]

This point is illustrated in the medieval church's claim that as homosexuality does not occur among animals in the wild, it must be unnatural. This argument, first introduced by Plato,[7] is still being made by those who wish to provide evidence of the unnaturalness of homosexual acts. But homosexual activity does occur among animals in nature. It "has been observed among many animal species in the wild as well as in captivity. This has been recognized since the time of Aristotle and . . . has been accepted by people who still objected to homosexual behavior as unknown to other animals."[8]

Boswell believes that this claim that the animal world represents the final word on what is natural is beside the point. He argues that even if human beings were the only species to engage in homosexual acts, this would not make these acts unnatural:

Many animals in fact engage in behavior which is unique to their species, but no one imagines that such behavior is "unnatural"; on the contrary, it is regarded as part of the "nature" of the species in question and is useful to taxonomists in distinguishing the species from other types of organisms. If man were the only species to demonstrate homosexual desires and behavior, this would hardly be grounds for categorizing them as "unnatural." Most of the behavior which human societies most admire is unique to humans:

this is indeed the main reason it is respected. No one imagines that human society "naturally" resists literacy because it is unknown among other animals.[9]

Idealized, coercive concepts of nature first become common in the centuries following the rise of Christianity among the philosophic schools of Rome. This idealized view of nature has profoundly affected Western philosophy and ethics and helped to popularize the belief that all nonprocreative sexuality is unnatural.[10] Although this argument fell into disfavor among early Christians, it was revived in the thirteenth century by Scholastics and became the definitive and controlling concept.[11]

It is Thomas Aquinas who makes idealized conceptions of nature and natural law a central part of the medieval church's epistemology. His thirteenth-century writings argue that there is an "eternal law" that governs all things in the universe. It is up to human beings to abide by these eternal laws to the extent that they can control their own lives and destinies. "This participation in the Eternal law by rational creatures is called the Natural law."[12] Aquinas believes Natural law can be discovered through examining what God intended in all things. With regard to sex, Aquinas argues that God intended procreation, and it is toward the creation of children that all sexual acts should intend. In Aquinas's epistemology, homosexual acts are grouped together with all acts that do not lead to procreation and are therefore in violation of right reason and natural law. This focus on opportunities for procreation as the only legitimate sexual activity led the late medieval church to a position that would be judged today as morally repugnant: the acceptance of rape, incest, and adultery as less problematic than either masturbation or sodomy.[13]

According to Aquinas, all lust is immoral, but some lustful acts are worse than others because they "are in conflict with the natural pattern of sexuality for the benefit of the species."[14] Called "unnatural vices" (*vitiae contra naturum*), homosexual acts are, according to Aquinas, among the worst kind of lustful sins. Aquinas's *Summa Theologiae* became the standard of Catholic orthodoxy and established the natural as the guide for Roman Catholic sexual ethics from the thirteenth century. The *essential* unnatural-ness and immorality of sodomy remains the official Catholic po-sition today.[15]

This emphasis on the *essential* goodness of nature and the *essential* evil of sodomy led to greater attention to these acts and those who performed them. In the view of Christian theologians concerned with the ethics and morality of individual acts of free will, those who practiced unnatural sexual acts deserved ever greater penance and punishment. Still, until the Inquisition, and arguably even after, the sodomite was persecuted not for who he was—sodomite was less an identity than a status—but because of what he did or, more to the point, what he failed to do. In the co-ercive legacy left by Aquinas, procreation was the only sexual goal, and sodomy was a temporary aberration that could and should be corrected. Sodomy was problematized as deserving of punish-ment, penance, and blame because it thwarts God's command-ment to "be fruitful and multiply." Sodomy is not a state of being, but a chosen path to perversion.

To the medieval church, sodomy represented the corruptive temptation, the moral morass into which people fell because of uncontrolled desire or were seduced by the corrupting influence of others. The flip side of this coin is that, although seen as an unnatural aberration, sodomy can also be resisted. It represents a sinful choice, but nonetheless a choice. And bad choices can be avoided or, when not avoided, forgiven. The sinner has the option of confession and penance, purification and reunification with God and God's natural procreative design. The problematization of sodomy, at least before the late Middle Ages, was aimed at the act of sodomy and not at the sodomite himself.[16]

An example of the way that the *essentially* unnatural sexual acts of sodomites are treated as constitutive acts of a free will gone awry is this deployment of "unnatural" as a synonym for "failure to procreate." Again, this religious problematization of sexuality is traceable to ideas expressed by Plato and amplified in the works of philosophers who followed. Plato argued that, for the health of society, all sexual acts outside of marriage should be encoded within a social taboo that would ensure citizens' compliance in a way that laws could not. Equating the taboo that he would create around *all* extramarital sexual acts with the incest taboo that receives unquestioned obedience, he proposed the following rhetorical strategy:

> In regard to this law I had an art that would promote the natural use of sexual intercourse for the production of children—by abstaining on the one hand from intercourse with males, the deliberate killing of the human race, as well as the wasting of sperm on rocks or stones where it will never take root and generate a *natural* offspring, and on the other hand by abstaining from any female field in which you wouldn't wish your sperm to grow.[17]

In one breath, Plato joined nature with procreation in a union that would last for millennia. His explanations, his taboos, circulate still in the Christian problematization of all sexual acts outside of marriage. Although Christian religious epistemology owes a debt to Plato's problematization of sexual acts, this epistemology is less than rigorously consistent when it insists that homosexual acts are unnatural because they violate God's desire or nature's design for procreation. As Boswell points out, "Non-productivity can in any case hardly be imagined to have induced intolerance of gay people in ancient societies which idealized celibacy or in modern ones which consider masturbation perfectly natural, since both of these practices have reproductive consequences identical with those of homosexual activity."[18]

Today, however, many of the claims that homosexuality is unnatural still rest on its nonreproductivity. But this judgment also exposes the moral and cultural contradictions that arise when an epistemology that was invented to explain the essential wickedness of *acts* is used to explain the essential wickedness of the *actors*. Behind this modern use of "unnatural," gay and lesbian persons are constructed as "barren," both physiologically and ethically, both essentially and constitutively: Either they do not procreate because they cannot, and hence are biologically inferior and unnatural, or because they will not, choosing to sin against God's desire that we procreate. This, of course, runs the risk of conflating the "unnaturalness" and "immorality" of gays with all the heterosexuals who cannot or choose not to have children.

This strange admixture of the medieval problematization of sodomitical acts and the modern hostility toward gay men and lesbians has influenced the way in which biblical texts have come to be translated and interpreted. For example, prior to the Inquisition, the Catholic Church's attitude toward homosexual acts and feelings was often one of tolerance. After this time, fueled by the work of Aquinas and the Scholastics, biblical scripture was reinterpreted, first problematizing homosexual acts and then retroactively attributing homosexual meanings and interpretations to texts where previously there were none.[19]

This process of reinterpreting and expanding biblical scripture to include condemnations that were not germane to those living at the time that the Bible was written continues today. For example, newer editions of the Christian Bibles use the word "homosexual" in Leviticus, despite the fact that there was no comparable word or concept at the time that Leviticus was written. This process of political redaction is especially true of New Testament sources that are deployed in contemporary debates as evidence of the Bible's hostility to homosexuality. Boswell argues that two of the three New Testament passages have nothing to do with homosexuality at all.[20]

The Old Testament citations are another story altogether. They are often marshaled as evidence of God's belief that homosexuality is unnatural and contrary to the "ideal nature" that God has created. References in Genesis and Leviticus are often used to justify attacks on gay men and lesbians. However, investigations such as Boswell's *Christianity, Social Tolerance and Homosexuality* (1980) and Derrick Bailey's *Homosexuality and the Western Christian Tradition* (1955)[21] have cast some doubt on whether homosexual acts are central to the moral message of even Genesis and Leviticus. Academic debates aside, there is no real debate about the enormous influence that religion and the religious tradition of an "ideal nature" played when the power of the nation-state was joined with the authority of the medieval church.

As late as the eighth century, there were few ecclesiastic injunctions against homosexual acts. Boswell argues that this was because the "church was largely unconcerned about exclusively homosexual behavior. Homosexuality was given no greater attention than other sins and, viewed comparatively, appears to have been thought less grave than such common activities as hunting."[22] But following the development of theories of natural law by Aquinas and the other Scholastics of the thirteenth century and the subsequent reinterpretation of scripture to problematize homosexual acts, sodomy became an area of increasing church regulation.

According to Michael Goodich, in *The Unmentionable Vice,* it was not until the end of the twelfth century that sodomy became a truly infamous crime in canonical law. Shortly thereafter, it also became a subject of greater civil legislation. Goodich points out that by the thirteenth century the church's epistemological construction of sodomy was reflected in civil edicts. The report of a Sienese city council meeting held in 1324 provides one example: "The council of nine provided for the appointment of men to pursue sodomites "in order to honor the Lord, ensure true peace, maintain the good morals and praiseworthy life of the people of Sienna.' . . . The councilor voiced the fear that those whose crime was repellant to both God and the Devil, and abhorrent to all peoples, unless prosecuted, would bring down the Lord's ire on the city."[23] The most interesting part of this quotation is the excerpted passage from the legislation of the council of nine. Clearly, for these civil authorities, the power of the church to interpret God's truth was unquestioned. If sodomy warranted church regulation, then it also warranted State regulation. The city officials were afraid that God might choose to castigate the city's residents if sodomy were sanctioned or even merely left unpunished. The criminal prosecution of those poor souls who were discovered by the State authorities and chastened was imbued with notions of sodomy as a sin against God.

Reflecting the problematization initiated by the Catholic Church centuries before, civil regulation of sexual sin spread and endured long after the church's preeminence in civil and social matters had ended. For example, in the 1787 English trial of the Earl of Castlehaven, accused of sodomizing his wife, the attorney general's arguments mirror those made by the Council of Sienna in the fourteenth century. Sodomy, he argued, was of such a "pestiferous and pestilential nature that if they not be punished [those who engage in it] will draw from Heaven heavy judgments upon the Kingdom."[24] By the nineteenth century, civil prohibitions against sodomy were widespread among European countries and many U.S. states. In Indiana, the church's tone of execration toward all forms of nonreproductive sexuality reverberated in the state's 1881 sodomy statute: "Whoever commits the abominable and detestable crime against nature by having carnal knowledge with mankind or beast; or who being a male, carnally knows any man or woman through the anus; and whoever entices, allures, instigates, or aids any person under the age of twenty-one to commit masturbation or self-pollution is guilty of sodomy, and upon conviction thereof, shall be imprisoned in the State prison not more than fourteen, nor less than two years."[25]

In many places, including the Earl of Castlehaven's England, sodomy was a capital crime, and it was in this climate of prosecution and persecution of sodomy that medical science first turned its attention to issues of sexuality. The attention of ecclesiastic and then juridical authorities to problematized sexual acts had begun the process of greater scrutiny of individuals in their exercise of desire and pleasure. But it would be left to the unique medical gaze of the nineteenth-century sexologists to issue the hail "Hey, you," thereby transforming those who engaged in certain sexual acts from undifferentiated individuals into subjects deserving of greater political attention by the State.

The Medical Model of Homosexuality

The increase in the attention directed toward sex during the nineteenth century, particularly by the medical "experts," came about for a variety of reasons. Michel Foucault catalogs a number of factors that contributed to medical science's greater interest in sex.

The rise of urbanization and industrialization created conditions of overcrowding as production became more and more labor intensive and more concentrated in the cities. This, in turn, created concerns about sanitation, disease, and crime that required new medical and scientific explanations.[26]

George Chauncey claims that the desire to preserve male superiority over women at a time when women's social and political roles were expanding motivated much of the early research into sexuality. Sexology thus played a policing function, inscribing new, scientific explanations onto old forms of social hierarchy. Seemingly progressive in its acknowledgment that women did indeed experience sexual desire, the true intention of this new openness was to tie women to men, making sexual desire "the basis for their involvement in heterosexual institutions."[27] Sexual relations outside of marriage were seen as a direct threat to civilized society.

Physicians were in a position to offer new theories and explanations to help prevent this decline of civilization. In Europe and the United States, they were already involved in writing and lobbying for legislation that dealt with other sex-related activities, including prostitution, abortion, and contraception.[28] In many European countries, physicians had organized and had run for public office with some success.[29] In the United States, where the medical profession had yet to attain the same stature it had in Europe, many doctors realized that an "expanded jurisdiction for physicians was very much in the interests of the entire profession; it meant not only potential sources of income but also greater prestige."[30] Physicians were eager to play a role in discovering and treating new ailments and diseases and to provide information on how to create new, improved societies and new, improved human beings.[31] At the same time, the rapid spread of Darwinian evolutionary theory was undermining traditional religious authority and establishing the power of science as the new interpreter of "truth."

The late nineteenth and early twentieth centuries were also years of great anxiety over the increasing numbers of people who immigrated to the United States. As more people began to crowd into smaller and smaller areas, the science of population studies spearheaded the drive toward "normalization" and the subsequent attention to "deviance" and "degeneration." In this atmosphere, experiments in eugenics, sterilization of the mentally ill, and public debates about forced birth control for immigrants flourished, affording physicians and medical "scientists" a role and an authority that they had not previously enjoyed. As Foucault writes, "It was in the name of medicine both that people came to inspect the layout of houses and, equally, that they classified individuals as insane, criminal or sick."[32]

Many modern scholars have pointed out, however, that the intent of the first physicians who addressed homosexuality was to offer a new theory that would break with the former religious problematization of sodomy as "sin" and thereby help to end its criminalization by the State. Philosopher Michael Ruse has argued that "undoubtedly the sickness model . . . has helped to remove some of the most oppressive laws against homosexuals and their orientations."[33] And John DeCecco contends that the shift from the term "sodomy" (an act) to "homosexual" (a person) "was the result of the social and political efforts of those who preferred their own sex to resist the ecclesiastical, secular and later, medical encroachments on their sexual activities. They transformed their sodomitical status . . . into a human species as a way of identifying fellow victims and fighting homophobia."[34] On the other hand, as Shane Phelan argues, although "the political consequence of this shift in paradigm was a trend toward medicalization of what had been a legal problem . . . this movement has never been completed, as the legal establishment has fought to retain control over an issue that has been within its purview throughout Judeo-Christian history."[35] Although there is evidence that medical explanations saved some from prison, many nations and thirty-two U.S. states today have laws that criminalize sodomy. And in at least one of these nations, sodomy has only recently been criminalized.[36]

Although many of the early researchers were sympathetic to the plight of "homosexuals," there were those who showed no such sympathy. Their cures and regulatory strategies can hardly be said to have brought the kind of liberation that the early sexologists desired. Together, however, both groups of medical researchers succeeded in shifting the focus of scrutiny from sexual acts and behaviors to "homosexual persons," persons with an innate, congenital basis for the desires and behaviors that they manifest.[37] It is in the pages of these physicians' theorizations that the Althusserian hail "Hey, you there" is first extended to the "homosexual." This shift also marked the beginning of the modern debate about identity that reverberates still in the study of lesbians and gay men.

The Birth of Homosexuality

The "scientific" investigations of sexual behavior and desires in the late nineteenth century led to an explosion of theories that addressed all forms of nonprocreative sexuality and to an expansion of the terminology used to discuss sexual phenomena. Richard von Krafft-Ebing compiled hundreds of cases of unusual sexual behaviors and desires and introduced a number of new terms to this expanding vocabulary of sexual "perversions," including "sadism," "masochism," and "antipathic sexual instinct" (his term for homosexuality).[38]

The English word "homosexuality," a painful philological combination of Greek and Latin elements, was first coined by a Hungarian pamphleteer named Karoly Maria Benkert. In 1869, writing under the pseudonym Kertbeny, Benkert published a pamphlet on homosexuality that was quickly forgotten but then republished by Magnus Hirschfield in 1905.[39] According to Jeffrey Weeks, the term "homosexuality" first entered the English language in the works of British physician Havelock Ellis published at the end of the nineteenth and the beginning of the twentieth centuries and came into common use nearly contemporaneously with the use of the term "inversion" to describe intragender sexual difference.[40]

But before the word "homosexuality" was coined, the debate about the status of "inverts" and "sodomites" was already well under way in increasingly "scientific" terms employed by early sexologists such as Benkert, Ellis, Hirschfield, and Krafft-Ebing. From these early debates, two competing yet related approaches emerged to explain homosexual acts and desires in the nineteenth century. The first of these might loosely be called "congenital biologism," as it sought to prove that homosexuality was innate. Related but with very different implications was "physiomoral degeneracy," the idea that homosexuality was either a symptom or a result of moral or physical degeneracy. It was speculated that this degeneracy might even be transmitted to an individual's children. The former approach would lead to the latter, as medical researchers sought to explain not merely the existence of a "third" or "intermediate" sex but also how this existence had come to be.

In 1862, Karl Heinrich Ulrichs, a German lawyer and writer and a homosexual himself, argued that sexual preference was as innate as were the sex organs themselves. Ulrichs contended that homosexuality was the result of an anomalous development of the human embryo. An accidental differentiation of the male fetus while still in utero was associated with a preference for sexual partners with a male body. The same was thought to occur with lesbians, who developed the genitals of a woman but the sex drive of a man. Ulrichs was the first to develop systematically the idea that homosexuality was caused by cross-sex identification. This would provide the basis for the later development of theories of an "intermediate sex" and sexual "inversion," in which the mind of one gender was believed to be trapped in the body of the other. The male members of this third sex were called Urnings (or in English, Uranians), after Aphrodite Uranus in Plato's *Symposium;* the female members were called Dionings. Believing this new third sex was a congenital condition, but not an inherited one, Ulrichs claimed that its members should be treated neither as criminals nor as victims of mental illness.[41]

Benkert, the linguistic father of "homosexuality," agreed with Ulrichs that homosexuality was a congenital condition and argued that homosexuals constituted a different sexual species—a third sex. Benkert, who believed that homosexuals were distinguished by their feelings, desires, or urges, apparently never felt Ulrichs's need to justify homosexual desire by explaining it as the product of biological cross-wiring. For Benkert, homosexual desire was "natural" to this third sex.

Hirschfeld, a member of one the early German homosexual liberation movements—the Scientific Humanitarian Committee —accepted this third-sex theory, again hoping to end the criminalization of same-gender sexual acts.[42] Hirschfeld spent a great deal of time lobbying legislators and appearing as an "expert" medical witness in criminal proceedings.[43]

Ellis, whose wife was a lesbian, wrote in *Sexual Inversion* that the presence of homosexual drives appeared at an early age in many of the subjects he had studied. He believed that this disproved many of the contemporary theories that posited environmental causes of homosexuality. He also claimed that the large number of successful and accomplished people who were homosexuals could not be reconciled with a theory of homosexuality as degeneration.[44] He argued that the families of homosexuals "do not usually possess such profound signs of nervous degeneration as we were once led to suppose." Ellis's conclusion: The causes of homosexuality were clearly congenital but not harmful.[45] Writing in a U.S. medical journal, Ellis sympathetically presented the claims of a lesbian who argued that "homosexual love is morally right when it is really part of a person's nature and provided that the nature of homosexual love is always made plain to the object of such affection."[46]

Englishman Edward Carpenter further extended the debate in *The Intermediate Sex,* exploring the presence and treatment of homosexuals among more "primitive" and therefore more "natural" cultures. Moving beyond his friend Ellis's claim that homosexuals were not dangerous or harmful, Carpenter argued that, in the "natural" environment of many of these primitive cultures, homosexuals tended to have special powers. As a result, they became shamans or medicine men, representing a higher stage of human evolution.[47]

The works of Carpenter, Ellis, Hirschfeld, and Ulrichs represent the theories of the early sexologists whose interest in bringing greater compassion and tolerance to those incarcerated for homosexual acts led them to theorize that homosexuality was an inherent characteristic. But not all of the theorists who posited a congenital basis for homosexuality did so with greater tolerance in mind. It is in their works that the full effect of the policeman's hail "Hey, you there" is understood. For example, in 1869, Karl Westphal argued that those who suffered from "perverted sexual instinct" were subject to a "contrary sexual feeling," a "congenital perversion of the sexual instinct." These individuals, he wrote, were "conscious of the morbid character of their condition."[48]

In the United States at the end of the nineteenth century, similarly negative conceptualizations of homosexuals were being added to the Althusserian hail of identity. One physician described homosexuals as being of a "morbid congenital type," and another pronounced the homosexual the result of "genital malformation caused by the fact that sensory nerves normally originating in the penis are displaced to the rectum and the erogenous zone is shifted correspondingly."[49] Robert W. Shufeldt, a major in the U.S. Army Medical Corps who published photographs of a "twenty-three year old 'fairy' from the slums of Brooklyn," concluded that the young man was a "typical example of contrary sexual instinct."[50] Medical science was becoming more confident in its identification of homosexual subjects and its explanations for why they were the way they were.

As theories of congenital homosexuality became common, the search for the causes of this inherent "morbidity" became more common as well. In 1887, Paul Moreau argued that homosexuals are a "mixed class constituting a real link between reason and madness, the nature of which are most frequently to be explained by one word: Heredity."[51] Earlier he had not only argued that it was "above all, important for the public morality and safety, that these individuals of defective organization, . . . these mental and moral mongrels . . . be eliminated from social consort" but also simultaneously identified homosexuals as a social problem and positioned physicians as the only reliable solution to the problem.[52]

Moreau's approach and tone is typical of much of the "scientific" work conducted on issues of homosexuality during the last half of the nineteenth century. Increasingly, medical researchers turned to evolution and heredity to explain the causes of homosexual "degeneracy." So did those who called for the institutionalization or imprisonment of those "afflicted." Moreau's emphasis on degeneration verging on madness was another theme that, although present all along in the works of the early medical researchers, would reach a fever pitch in the fin de siècle United States and Europe. Having located the "reform" for sodomitical activities within the corporeal constitution of the homosexual subject, this understanding of homosexuality gained quick and widespread acceptance.

Physical (De)Signs of Degeneration

In the last half of the nineteenth century, "scientists" and medical practitioners added volumes to the "knowledge" of sexual inversion. They were so insistent in their policeman's hail of "Hey, you there" that the scrutinized individuals who engaged in practices and pleasures considered unproductive were identified and constituted as new subjects, new kinds of beings. As is often the case in police work, however, identifying the subject/suspect is not enough. To the policeman's hail that first ushered in sexuality as a form of identity was added a list of identifying characteristics of likely suspects, which functioned as a kind of cultural "Most Wanted" poster, inviting citizens to assist in community policing of sexual identity. This effort at community policing would again rely on a taxonomy developed by medical science: physical qualities and descriptions that would enable other medical professionals and laypeople alike to recognize and identify homosexuals. If "homosexuals" were different and subject to a medical epistemology that constructed them as diseased, ill, or congenitally weak, then medical science must also "discover" a way to distinguish "them" from everyone else. This emphasis on detection, signs, and differentiation was important not only because homosexuality might be spread intergenerationally or by an environmental trigger but also because "normal" people must have a way to ensure that they were not "infected" or "afflicted" with homosexuality. In this search for signs, doctors were to become the modern-day prophets and oracles.

Many of these early sex researchers argued that homosexuals had physical and corporeal differences that were detectable. The prevalence and wide acceptance of third-sex and intermediate-sex theories made this a logical next area of exploration. These theories postulated that homosexuals represented a congenitally anomalous cross between the anatomy of one gender and the emotional psyche and sexual drives of the other. In this unnatural mixing of anatomy and gender functions, it followed that some of these "inverts" might manifest constitutional and secondary personality characteristics as well, characteristics normally associated with the opposite sex.

In 1889, one physician claimed that a large number of these "sexual perverts [were] physically abnormal rather than morally leprous." He concluded that "their physique is apt to be inferior —a defective physical makeup being general among them."[53] Another physician wrote that "inverts" retained "a youthful appearance through life" because of their mentally and physically arrested development.[54]

Some physicians believed that the psychic inversion that made male homosexuals possess a feminine psyche would lead to the degeneration of their bodies, again making them detectable. A feminine psyche, it was theorized, caused male homosexuals to think that "muscular exercise is repugnant. . . . Hence at about forty years of age we find them with fat, flabby bodies."[55] Alfred Adler was reminded of reptiles when he examined homosexuals; he professed that they exhibited "snake-like," "serpentine" qualities.[56]

Lesbians were not immune to this medical attention, although in general more attention was given to the male invert than to his female counterpart. Still, many doctors reported that female inverts were likely to possess an enlarged clitoris. One physician who claimed that he frequently found this characteristic among the female inverts he examined reported that he once discovered "an enlarged clitoris two and one-half inches when erect."[57] Incidentally, this focus on "erections" and "size" is typical of the almost exclusively male nineteenth-century medical profession, whose members found it impossible to imagine sexual pleasure without a penis or a penis substitute.

In a 1934 study of 250 adult patients, G. W. Henry found that homosexuals had "considerably greater constitutional deviations on a general average than the heterosexually adjusted." Henry continued that female homosexuals were "characterized by a firm adipose tissue, deficiencies of fat at the shoulders and at the girdle, firm muscles, excess hair on the chest, back and lower extremities, a tendency to masculine distribution of the pubic hairs and a small uterus and an over or underdevelopment of the labia or clitoris. There is also a tendency toward a shorter trunk, a contracted pelvis, underdevelopment of the breast, excessive hair on the face and a low-pitched voice."[58] This description appears again, almost verbatim, when the military turns its public policy-making function to the question of homosexual identity (see Chapters 3 and 4).

These same doctors claimed that homosexuals often manifested secondary personality characteristics—characteristics that went beyond bodily descriptions. Again offering a shortcut for homosexual identification that the military would later employ, one physician wrote that male homosexuals were often characterized by "effeminacy of voice, dress, and manner."[59] Other characteristics of male homosexuals to watch for included "extreme modesty toward males" and "intense liking for female occupations and dress,"[60] a "mimicking gait . . . and hips [that] are broad like those of women."[61] Secondary sexual characteristics were also attributed to female homosexuals. Lesbians were identifiable by their masculine dress, often "wearing stiff collars and plain fedora hats."[62]

The taxonomy of descriptive indicators for identifying homosexuals included such powerful insights as the observations that all homosexuals were "liars"[63] and that male homosexuals were unable "to lead in dancing, female homosexuals unable to follow."[64] In 1920, in a prominent medical journal, W. C. Rivers published the discovery of perhaps the definitive telltale indicator of male homosexuality: "cat loving."[65]

The power to control how this new medical discovery—homosexuality and those afflicted with it—would be described fell to the group that had first discovered it: physicians. The acceptance of congenital theories as an explanation for homosexuality also meant that the physical, sexual, social, psychological, and emotional characteristics of one sex would be employed to describe the appearance and behavior of homosexuals of the opposite sex. Lesbians would be described as mannish, masculine, hairy, assertive, and strong, since that was what was socially expected from men. Gay men would be described using the adjectives usually reserved for women: effeminate, artistic, emotional, sensitive, big-hipped, and flabby.

Often the line between description and inscription became blurred as homosexuals, expected by their doctors to behave in a certain way and facing the wrath of physicians armed with "cures," gladly conformed to their doctors' expectations. Another aspect of the community policing of identity, preventive policing, had many physicians turning their efforts toward penning books for parents to advise them about what signs to look for in children who could be potential homosexuals.

Jeffrey Weeks has argued that a "new recognition of the separateness of childhood by the eighteenth century went hand in hand with a socially felt need to preserve children's purity and innocence."[66] David Greenberg concludes that "as children were being redefined as asexual (and manifestations of childhood sexuality, such as masturbation, labeled pathological or pathogenic), the law was stepping in to place them 'off limits' to adults."[67] Prohibiting all childhood sexual acts was high on the list of ways of ensuring "purity," as physicians claimed that "the eradication of homosexuality is a question of the bringing up of the child."[68] It was believed that "congenital perversion" often began as early as age eight or nine in males, making closer scrutiny imperative.[69]

One advice book aimed at parents of young boys cautioned that it was unhealthful for young boys to sleep together as it "prevented [their] skin from breathing fresh air," making it "possible to absorb the poisons from another's skin." The author, a physician, advised that sleeping with other boys "sends blood to the sex organs" and "causes a feeling of attraction towards these delicate organs." Many boys "will be tempted to talk and play with each other," ending in "self abuse."[70] Parents were held responsible for regulating their sons' behavior. Such characteristics as a love of pretty things, a love of dressing well, and a love of art were listed as signs of a boy's perversion.[71]

Another physician similarly counseled parents to watch their daughters: "No thoughtful parent will . . . permit a [female child] of school age to go and sleep with another child. It is bad for their minds, their morals, and their bodies. It is one of the most frequent beginnings of sexual vice." It is school-age children who begin "to ponder over the use and abuse of their genital organs."[72]

Masturbation was implicated as both one of the likely causes and one of the indicators of homosexuality. Combining the epistemic authority of truth production with the juridical power of the state, a "diagnostician" for the Juvenile Court System of Seattle, Washington, reported incidents of "habitual pathological functioning of the sexual mechanism" among one hundred delinquent boys. He reported that seventy-one were habitual masturbators and thirty-one of these "presented a history of fallatio [sic] relations." Most of the boys "indicated that there was more or less mutual interest in the acts which generally occurred in their play associations."[73] This doctor possessed an amazing amount of information about these boys' intimate habits, revealing that thirty-one of the "auto-eroticists" engaged in masturbation nightly.[74] Concern over preserving innocence and preventing masturbation guaranteed that greater attention would be given both to childhood and adult sexuality, increasing the level of regulation and investigation of an individual's sexual practices well beyond the level achieved by the church at its zenith of power.

The use of "masculine" descriptions for homosexual women and "feminine" descriptions for homosexual men spread beyond the pages of medical journals, helping to reinforce acceptable and unacceptable behavior for everyone in the culture. This descriptive system of classification not only served to distinguish perversion, thereby providing a way of identification, but it also reinforced cultural values about the proper, correct, and socially sanctioned ways to behave for anyone wishing to escape the designation of "deviant." Rather than being "scientific breakthroughs or original discoveries," these theories were more of "an ideological response to a new way of organizing one's personal life."[75] This descriptive taxonomy became a standard by which a person could measure his or her own behavior and the behavior of others, a threshold over which he or she crossed only at the risk of being labeled "diseased," medically and morally "degenerate," and culturally dangerous.

As these standards of acceptable and unacceptable behavior were deployed in the culture, such practices as passionate expression of male friendship, common between men only a century earlier, disappeared. A more rigid and regulated system of behavior took hold with the result that everyone—heterosexual and homosexual, adult and child—came under wider scrutiny, attention, and regulation. Women, too, faced a constricted number of acceptable patterns of gender behavior. For example, the suffragettes of the late nineteenth century, who pressed for rights that were considered the natural province of men, were labeled "sexually abnormal" by many in the medical profession. They were "militant" according to Horace Frink, who called them "neurotics who in some cases are compensating for masochistic trends, in others, are more or less successfully sublimating sadistic and homosexual ones."[76]

Physical descriptions of the homosexual subject/suspect, as it turned out, were not the only powers of detection brought into play in the policeman's "Hey, you there." As psychiatry and psychology fought to gain acceptance and prestige in the United States, practitioners in these fields joined the search for causes, symptoms, and cures.

The Psychiatric Model(s) of Homosexuality

Congenital illness models of homosexuality narrowed the range of acceptable behavior for men and women and the scope of intra-gender relationships and increased the search for signs of abnormality. The search for the causes of this abnormality sometimes led to genetic explanations, sometimes environmental explanations, and sometimes a mixture of both. But often just beneath the surface of scientific explanations circulated earlier religious condemnations of sodomy as indicative of moral depravity, licentiousness, and weakness.

Explanations of homosexuality still contained the moral quest for and concern about responsibility. In their attempts to "liberate" sodomites, the early sexologists, Ellis, Hirschfield, and Ulrichs, had attempted to draw a line between inherency and responsibility. Many felt that, although homosexuality was a "pathological perversion," some who engaged in sodomy were motivated not by a medical disorder but by "vicious lust."[77]

Psychiatric and psychological models did much to reinforce the behavioral and environmental explanations of homosexuality. The seeds of these explanations can be seen in earlier researchers' attention to "damaged genes," soil, water, and air as possible causes of homosexuality, but psychiatry gave the old environmental theme a new twist. What they never did was question the Althusserian hail of identity, the medical policeman's "Hey, you there" that had made homosexuals subjects/suspects of science and the State. Instead, psychiatrists and psychologists added considerably to the all points bulletin issued to help society learn how to identify lesbians and gay men.

The failure of congenital theories to provide concrete and verifiable causes had opened the door to psychiatric theories. Psychiatric explanations for homosexuality, which had been a part of the medical models of homosexuality dating from the mid-nineteenth century, increased in the pages of twentieth-century medical journals. By the mid-twentieth century, the study of homosexuality would be almost completely the province of psychiatrists and psychologists.[78]

Developmental models of homosexuality, perhaps more than others, reinforced environmental explanations and the idea of parental responsibility for children's development of a sexual object choice. Freud's developmental model of homosexuality was perhaps the most widely cited, adopted, addressed, and amended by clinical psychiatrists. Freud's theory of sexuality maintained that the libido is polymorphously perverse in children but undergoes change as children develop toward their mature sexual level: heterosexuality. Along the way toward this mature sexual expression, the individual passes through a homosexual phase. In Freud's understanding, the adult homosexual is arrested in this immature phase of sexuality.

Freud's ideas about the possibility of redirecting this homosexual object choice changed over the years. In the early manifestation of his theory, he argued that "the connection between sexual instinct and sexual object choice is not as intimate as we have often believed." They were merely "soldered together."[79] This view suggested that the link between sexual instinct and sexual object choice could be changed. But in an April 9, 1935, letter to a U.S. mother concerned about her child's homosexuality, Freud wrote:

> Homosexuality is assuredly no advantage but it is nothing to be ashamed of, no vice, no degradation, it cannot be classified as an illness; we consider it to be a variation of the sexual function produced by a certain arrest of sexual development. . . .
> By asking me if I can help, you mean, I suppose, if I can abolish homosexuality and make normal heterosexuality take its place. The answer is, in a general way, we cannot promise to achieve it. . . . In a majority of cases it is no more possible.[80]

While Freud was rethinking the possible success of severing this link between instinct and sexual object choice, his earlier ideas were shaping the work of his contemporary psychiatric colleagues in Europe and the United States. Wilhelm Stekel, a disciple of Freud's, argued that "by nature all human beings are psychically bisexual." Echoing early Freud, he argued that "fixed homosexuality" resulted as a "disturbance" in the development toward heterosexuality.[81] Constance Long, one of the few women in a still male-dominated field, argued similarly that homosexuality was "a problem indicating a block in the development to mature heterosexuality, caused by social conditions."[82]

Other psychiatrists claimed that homosexuality was "learned behavior"[83] or could be explained by "the developmental history of the individual."[84] Some believed that homosexuality was the product of a fear of the opposite sex[85] or narcissism[86] or, in the case of gay men, the desire "to regain . . . lost or endangered masculinity through an oral attack on the partner's penis in order to acquire it."[87]

The introduction of environmental explanations of homosexuality opened the way to laying blame for a child's "deviant" sexuality on the doorstep of the parents. Many psychiatrists, including Carl Jung, argued that "passive homosexuality" in both women and men was connected to the child's experience of incest.[88] Others posited that adult homosexuality was caused by early childhood trauma.[89] Today only the rarest of parents do not question their own role in their child's homosexuality.

During the 1960s, gay men and lesbians began to challenge these psychiatric views of homosexuality, arguing that the problem lay not with homosexuals themselves but with the heterosexist society. Just as the psychiatrists never really challenged the policeman's hail that first created the homosexual subject, however, these activists never really challenged the development of sexual identity as a new form of person. Still, the resulting debate led the American Psychological Association to declassify homosexuality as a mental disorder.[90] Although many mental health professionals turned away from mental and medical explanations for homosexuality in the 1970s, others have continued to maintain that homosexuality is something to be medically regulated, treated, and cured. Charles Socarides, for example, writes that homosexuality represents "the unconscious manifestations of hate, destructiveness, incest and fear."[91] Socarides ignited a round of protest from the readers of the Jesuit journal *America* in 1995 when he argued with renewed vigor that homosexuality is a choice that can be avoided and an illness that can be cured.[92]

Psychiatrists have been at the forefront of the effort to recognize and identify homosexuals, adding another layer of complexity to the evolving mechanisms of identity construction and regulation.[93] One device that is still deployed to "detect" homosexuals is a subset of questions in the Minnesota Multi-phase Personality Inventory (MMPI), a test that attempts to assess people's personalities through their responses to 550 true-or-false statements about themselves. A scale on the MMPI is designed to identify male homosexuals; that is, male homosexuals are said to respond a certain way to a subset of the statements. "I like poetry," "I would like to be a journalist," "I like science," and "I am entirely self-confident" are examples of these statements.[94]

Twentieth-century psychiatrists, no less than the medical researchers who came before them, did little to "liberate" or even change the social and cultural hostility toward sodomites or homosexuals. In many cases, in fact, their efforts led to much more sinister forms of regulation.

Medical Science and Its Cures

If it is true that the term "homosexual" was first coined as a weapon against the religious, legal, and medical forces that were brought to bear on sexual difference in the nineteenth century, we can conclude only that the success of this strategy has been mixed at best. The efforts of many of the early sexologists who were sympathetic to the plight of those incarcerated for sex crimes helped create an alternative way of viewing sodomitical acts. But they did so by offering medical theories that postulated that sodomitical acts stemmed from deep within the mysterious and incomprehensible world of genetics, disease, and biology.

Medical science succeeded in usurping, at least epistemologically, the church's claim to the exclusive right of "truth production" in the matters of the flesh. By arguing that desire for those of the same gender was an "inborn characteristic" or a "congenital condition," beyond the control of the individual, sexologists helped to illustrate that the State had nothing to gain from the punishment of sodomites, as punishment would not be a deterrence. But medical science succeeded in neither replacing the moral stigmatization attached to sodomy nor decriminalizing these acts.[95] In fact, the medical incitement did much to increase the regulation of homosexuals, adding new dimensions to the way that sexual difference was problematized. Physicians set out to quantify, objectify, define, describe, categorize, medicalize, identify, and inscribe this new phenomenon of homosexuality. By the end of the first years of the twentieth century, the words "homosexuality" and "homosexual" were both used widely in the medical literature.[96] The adjective had become a noun, and undifferentiated individuals had become homosexual subjects.

Arguing against contemporary institutional psychiatry, Thomas Szasz makes a case about schizophrenia that could well be applied to the medical "liberation" of sodomy. Szasz argues that if schizophrenia is shown to have a biological component, then the State could legitimately enforce compulsory medical treatment, but if it remains a "disorder of the spirit with no clear biological component, then the individual should decide whether to visit his or her psychiatrist."[97] If homosexuality could be portrayed as a degenerative, biological, evolutionary threat, then, the greater the moral and scientific justification for State regulation.

Moving the problematization of sexual difference from the realm of moral weakness (where individuals could still be judged, blamed, and punished) to a new realm of "instinctual drives" and "congenital conditions" may have freed sodomitical acts from the oppressive forces of moral condemnation created by the church/ State web of power. But this attempt at liberation from one oppression traveled the same cultural condemnatory path that had made sodomy a problem in the first place. This "scientific" path not only further limited the freedom of the individual to imagine his or her own sexual identity; it subjected this new phenomenon—the homosexual—to new forms of physical and mental regulation and abuse. As Szasz has pointed out, sickness, disease, or medical models become subject to the "correctional zeal of the doctor."[98]

The medical and psychiatric explanations of homosexuality offered in the late nineteenth and early twentieth centuries were voluminous, as we have seen, and the "cures" or "prescriptions" for the "disorder" were no less abundant. Often, a single doctor would prescribe several different courses of treatment simultaneously. One physician prescribed "association with virtuous women," "severe study of abstract subjects such as mathematics," "cold baths every morning," and "plenty of outdoor exercise," in addition to cauterization of "the nape of the neck and lower dorsal and lumbar regions . . . every ten days." The doctor's claim that his "patient improved after three months" is no doubt true if improvement meant a diminution of sexually aberrant behavior. In the clutches of such a rigorous medical regimen, it would be all but impossible to find the time and energy, not to mention the opportunity, to engage in sexual acts.[99] Another physician declared that although female homosexuals could not be "cured," their feelings could be controlled. He sought to help them in this effort with "anaphrodisiac," "cold sitz baths," and "a course of intellectual training."[100] Graeme Hammond claimed to have "successfully treated" a twenty-four-year-old man who "had observed for the past year a gradually increasing desire for members of his own sex." Hammond's solution was a bicycle ride, along with medicinal treatment. Hammond found that a "hard ride would invariably abolish all sexual desire, even if the appetite was at its strongest just before the ride was taken."[101]

But often the prescriptions, proscriptions, and "cures" were worse than the terms of imprisonment that state sodomy laws had imposed. Imprisonment for sodomy might be a better alternative than institutionalization in an asylum and subjection to doctors' correctional zeal. Many physicians believed that a suspected homosexual should be "submitted to a most thorough examination to determine responsibility," and then "removed from the community" and put in his or her proper place: "the asylum."[102]

Psychiatrists were not without their own attempts at cure. Until the 1960s, in addition to the use of psychotherapy to modify behavior, mental health clinicians in the United States and Europe often turned to two widely used forms of therapy, hypnotherapy and aversion therapy, in their treatment of homosexuals.[103] Aversion therapy consisted of electric shocks administered to patients as they looked at pictures of same-sex individuals to whom they were attracted or same-sex individuals making love. Electroshock therapy was also used to induce epileptic seizures in an attempt to erase the part of the memory that affected sexual object choice.

Perhaps the worst "treatment" that homosexual men faced was castration. Arlo Karlen reports that in a Kansas asylum in 1898 alone, forty-eight men were castrated.[104] Weeks reports that, after the turn of the century, castration was used widely throughout Europe as a "cure" for homosexuality. In Denmark, more than six hundred men were castrated between 1900 and 1956, when the practice was finally abandoned.[105] Castration, noted Dr. Emil Oberhoffer, was a successful cure for pederasty, since those who were castrated were "never aroused by the sight or thought of boys." Oberhoffer noted that one subject, however, did feel "anxiety he had never experienced previously."[106]

Castration—called the "radical asexualizing surgical procedure, such as the father of Heloise visited on Abelard"—became a common prescription for "sexual perverts." The doctors who recommended castration thought it more humane than the law, which was "inspired only by vengeance" and by "punishing the criminal." Castration, it was argued, "would mercifully protect both society and the maimed victim of a sexually and mentally degenerate organism."[107] This dialogue with the law represents a new discursive interaction between medical epistemology and the power of the State, as turn-of-the-century physicians and psychiatrists attempted to solidify their alliance with the State by putting themselves forward as *the* experts on sexual crime and "dysfunction."

Courting Power: Putting Medical "Knowledge" to Work on Society

As we have seen, the interest of nineteenth- and twentieth-century physicians and psychiatrists was more than just academic. Seeing their chance to expand the scope of their authority and prestige, they sought and found an audience with the formal institutions of State power.

Many books and articles were published with just this State audience in mind. As the medical professional succeeded in changing sodomy into homosexuality, old laws would need to be examined and new ones written. The medical profession claimed to be uniquely qualified to offer insight into this new phenomenon called homosexuality. According to Hirschfield, one thousand works on homosexuality appeared between 1898 and 1908 alone.[108] Most of these were directed at the legal profession, the main impetus being a desire to address the demands of the new criminal codes that were developing in urban centers at this time.

It is important to remember that the authors of some of these books sought to reform the law so that sodomy would no longer be prosecuted by the State. Ellis's *The Criminal* clearly falls into this category, as do the many works of Hirschfield and Krafft-Ebing. Krafft-Ebing argued that homosexuals should be "excepted from legal penalties and allowed to follow their inclinations when harmless and not violating public decency."[109] Italian criminologist Caesar Lombroso was actually successful in changing the sodomy laws of Italy in 1889.[110]

Other doctors had a different agenda concerning the regulatory umbrella of the State: They wanted to create a State role for their expertise in the identification of "disease" and the determination of the "culpability" of "sexual deviants." This was clearly the goal of two of the leading European medicolegal experts of the nineteenth century, Drs. Johann Casper and Ambrose Tardieu.[111] Both were "chiefly concerned with whether the disgusting breed of inverts could be physically identified by the courts, and whether they should be held legally responsible for their acts."[112]

U.S. doctors, too, found justifications for a greater role in monitoring and regulating public morality. Edited volumes such as Allen McLane Hamilton and Lawrence Godkin's *A System of Legal Medicine* and new academic journals such as *The Medico-legal Journal* provided physicians with new opportunities to plead their case for an expanded role in making legislation and in acting as expert witnesses in court hearings and criminal prosecutions.[113] One such physician argued that his involvement was absolutely necessary because, after all, it was physicians who had "demonstrated that conditions once considered criminal [were] really pathological" and should "come within the province of the physician." Therefore, "the profession can be trusted to sift the degrading and vicious from what is truly morbid."[114]

As the new epistemological authority, physicians contended that their skills were needed because "ignorance on such matters [as homosexuality] is very general among the laity and it would seem an urgent duty of physicians to offer advice in similar cases." One doctor even argued that physicians should seek out opportunities to render advice "even though it may not be specifically requested."[115] So great was the danger of unregulated homosexuality that, whether or not policymakers saw the need, it demanded the establishment of a link between policymakers and physicians.

Many of the justifications for this increased medical and State regulation of homosexuality crossed well into the arena of fullblown polemics. For example, C. H. Hughes argued that "society, organized into government, for the better security of person and property and personal and collective happiness, is specially concerned in the maintenance of chastity and morals. The State . . . cannot be too careful as a protector of morality . . . for sexual crimes are on the increase in our modern civilization. . . . Considerations of psychical sanitation demand alert attention to this subject from physicist [physician], moralists and jurists. . . . The moral pestilence is in our midst, Sodom and Gomorrah are revived and surpassed."[116]

There were those who believed that the homosexual represented "an active hostility toward society," his actions being "contrary to the requirements of social life."[117] Having originally argued for the medicalization of sodomy and homosexual acts, many nineteenth-century physicians turned to this same medical model to characterize homosexuality and homosexuals as threats to society. These threats, they contended, had to be met head on before the rising costs of intergenerational degeneracy were out of control. One psychiatrist, a Dr. F. E. Daniels of Texas, wrote that in fifty years time it would cost too much "to provide asylum and medical treatment for the many offspring of those in whom insanity is latent."[118] His recommendation was that those who committed sexual sins, including "confirmed masturbation," should be "rendered incapable of a repetition of the offense, and the propagation of his kind should be inhibited in the interest of civilization and the well being of future generations." Noting that "hanging, electrocution" and "burning at the stake did not prevent sexual crime," Daniels proposed castration, as it prevented "the hereditary transmission of either disease or vices of the constitution." Included in his plan to halt this hereditary degeneration was the removal of lesbians' ovaries.[119]

Daniels had courted and obtained his dialogue with power. He reported his conversation with James Stephen Hogg, then governor of Texas, who assured the psychiatrist that an asylum superintendent had the "legal right" to "castrate a patient for mental trouble" or as a "therapeutic measure." Daniels also argued for the expansion of the castration solution to those imprisoned for sexual crimes. In the United States and Europe, many prisons heeded this call.[120]

Edward J. Kempf, another psychiatrist, understood the blatantly political role that psychiatry occupied with regard to the homosexual. "Much of the future work of psychiatry," he claimed, "will be concerned with the reconstruction of the personality [of the homosexual] in the sense of shifting the values of undesirable forms of stimuli, which have become adequate for the primary sexual reflexes, to such forms and zones of receptors as meet with the approval of his race."[121] In plain English, this meant that the role of psychiatrists in the future would be to reeducate homosexuals into conforming to more socially acceptable forms of behavior.

The influence of medical experts spread beyond the walls of the asylum and the examination room, as medical professionals sought a wider audience and expanded authority by claiming that they alone had the knowledge that was necessary for the safety and health of society. Soon their influence permeated the halls of such public institutions as prisons, schools, and even juvenile courts.[122]

Medicine, Religion, and the State

Medical attention to homosexuality draped itself in the "objectivity" and "value neutrality" of science, but in reality it was imbued with the earlier moral concerns and condemnations of the religious epistemology. As R. C. Lewontin, Steven Rose, and Leon Kamin argue in *Not in Our Genes,* the pursuit of science always takes place within and is influenced by a social, cultural, and political milieu: "One of the issues we must come to grips with is that, despite its frequent claim to be neutral and objective, science is not and cannot be above 'mere' human politics. The complex interaction between scientific theory and the evolution of social order means that very often the ways in which scientific research asks its questions of the human and natural worlds it proposes to explain are deeply colored by social, cultural and political biases."[123]

Never had this seemed truer than in the exploration of human sexuality. The consequence is that, whether they acknowledged, admitted, or were even aware of it, the medical researchers of the late nineteenth century, like medical scientists today, reflected the values and epistemologies of the culture in which they worked.

The nonprocreativity of sexual acts, originally the church's concern, became the focus of one of the fastest-growing areas of research during the last half of the nineteenth century. Since this was "a time when leaders of the medical profession were trying to upgrade its respectability," it was "in their interest to associate themselves with a conservative sexual morality."[124]

This conservative sexual morality meant a reliance on earlier moral execrations, and as Greenberg has noted, "though the terminology and scientific scaffolding were new, the fundamental opposition between normal sex and abnormal paresthesias was largely based on traditional oppositions. Sex was perverse if reproduction was not its goal."[125] Or, as one doctor put it, "normal and natural love" was linked with "reproduction physically and psychically."[126] One physician made this link even more explicit, offering medical explanations to cover all the same territory that the former religious problematization had encompassed. Calling homosexuality "a sad deplorable, pathological phenomenon," he claimed that every "sexual deviation or disorder which has for its results an inability to perpetuate the race is *ipso facto* pathologic, *ipso facto* an abnormality."[127] This would presumably include masturbation. Some physicians recognized that medical science's focus on homosexuality stemmed from the moral problematizations expressed by society and culture. They argued that "as long as the moral ideas of the majority of the people are opposed to homosexual acts and the law gives expression to these ideas, the so-called contrary sexual persons must control their impulses."[128]

Irving Rosse's comments were much more representative of the fin de siècle medical establishment in both tone and essence. He wrote, "The uncleanliness forbidden by God and despised by man calls at the present time for more earnest attention from the physician. . . . While the moral point of view does not concern us as Physicians, bodily and intellectual welfare is very much within our province. Medical men are clearly the only persons qualified to give trustworthy information in regard to sexual matters. There is no other subject about which people are more anxious to be correctly informed."[129]

Rosse's statement brings together in one paragraph many of the themes examined in this chapter. It illustrates the expanded scope that medicine had achieved in the United States by the end of the nineteenth century. It lays out what was and was not the proper "province" of physicians' investigations, making it clear that these same physicians were assumed to have access to a truth, an authority, a knowledge that no one else had. It justifies the need for medical attention to sexual matters on the basis of the anxiety and consternation that they cause among the populace. Rosse's statement does not, however, admit that medical theorists who posited homosexuality as insanity, degeneration, or a result of masturbation (acting as society's new moral police in issuing the Althusserian hail "Hey, you there") had done much to create this anxiety in the first place. Instead, it manages to reinscribe moral culpability and religious indignation onto a medical model that had originated with the specific intention to end both.

Homosexual Identity or Homosexual Identification?

The early years of the twentieth century witnessed the completion, although not the finish, of an ontological process that continues to shape the way that we think about gay men and lesbians. The increasing abuse that individuals suffered as a result of the view of sodomy as a moral wickedness and a criminal vice was met with a response that was crafted specifically to rescue those who committed acts of sodomy from moral repugnance, social persecution, and ecclesiastic and civil prosecution.

With the full force of Enlightenment rationalism, the homosexual person answered the Althusserian hail of "Hey, you there" and emerged from the pages of the scientific study of sexuality as a personage, albeit not a fully functional one. This new "type" of person came complete with Genesis-like theories of origins and causation, pathologies diagnosed and circumscribed, genealogies investigated, and societal threats explained, practically requiring his or her delivery into the hands of medical experts for whatever slim chance of salvation he or she might have.

There is some evidence that many people began to accept the medicalization of sexuality in the hope that sympathy or toleration might replace disgust and mistreatment or, in the words of one U.S. physician, in the hope that there might develop a "prevalent tendency on the part of these anomalies to regard themselves as 'interesting invalids' to whom sympathy is due."[130] Referring to a twenty-six-year-old "invert," another U.S. doctor reported that he spent his time "arraigning society for its attitude toward those of his type, and was prepared to ethically justify his characteristics and practices."[131]

Krafft-Ebing reported that one of his Austrian contemporaries, a Dr. G., had defended his homosexuality before the police magistrate of Graz, Austria, claiming that he was deserving of protection, or at least tolerance, for his "mental abnormality."[132] As the study of homosexuality was joined by many more scientific researchers in the nineteenth century, the tone that physicians adopted when they spoke about homosexuals reflected anything but understanding and tolerance. It is clear, however, that homosexuals understood that the policeman's hail was addressed to them.

Establishing the "abnormality" of homosexuals was the task of physicians; meanwhile, the moral judgments of the religious problematization of sodomy continued to reverberate in the medical study of sexual difference. The result was that, although new terminology was created to refer to what were formally known as sodomitical acts, the same moral condemnation, the same system of cultural value judgments reinscribed the moral outrage and inferiority associated with nonprocreative sexual acts on the new medicalized homosexual subject. The scientific discourse would continue to be, as the religious discourse of sodomitical acts before it had been, a discourse of lack, a discourse of moral, physical, and mental inferiority.

Establishing the inferiority of homosexuality served a number of purposes. It amplified perceived differences between sexual "inverts" and their "normal" counterparts, which not only created an epistemological chasm to be avoided by those who wished not to be identified as "homosexual" but also invented, applied, and inscribed acceptable "ways of being" for the rest of society. By addressing those who failed to comply with the "normal," the "natural" roles that God, nature, and society had set forth for their gender, doctors solidified their own positions as the new guardians of public health and morality.

But more important for gay men and lesbians today, the future struggle for liberation—the path, the issues, the arena for struggle —was born with this medicalized identification of the homosexual person. Gay men and lesbians might adopt a different name, a different understanding of their history, their nature, and their future, but the path, the direction, and the goals of a political and social movement based on this sexual identity were always already present, their liberatory agenda predetermined by the very power structures and institutions from which they would seek legitimation. Having been created as subjects by the policeman's hail and having been subjected to the interrogation of the medical authorities, lesbians and gay men were now confronted with the business of being put into the law, where they could be further regulated and called upon to account for themselves. This represented a new arena for the exercise of State power and a new site from which to resist this power.

3

Gays in the Military

Constructing the "Homosexual" Other

THE PROCESS of creating an *official* gay identity, as we have seen, has two parts: (1) the creation of the homosexual subject who comes to understand that it is he or she who is being categorized as "homosexual" and (2) the identification of individuals by the authorities and the requirement that these individuals account for and justify their conduct and demeanor, now construed as misdeeds. It is in the course of accounting for oneself publicly that the process of producing an *official* lesbian and gay identity is completed.

The federal policy that governs participation in the armed services is a particularly fertile area for research questions that concern construction of identity and Otherness. The military is central to the construction of the State in the United States. Providing a common defense, according to the preamble to the U.S. Constitution, is one of the reasons that a government is necessary and desirable. Defending one's country has always been considered a defining characteristic of citizenship. In fact, it has been suggested that the legal disabilities of women in classical Greece with respect to property, marriage, and inheritance rights were incurred because women were prohibited from bearing arms.[1] The prohibition against certain groups serving in the military adversely affects these groups in other areas where rights and privileges of citizenship are involved. The fact that the military is also the largest single employer in the United States is both substantively and symbolically important.

Although aversion to homosexuals is present in all facets of society, in no other area is the hostility toward them as absolute or as codified as in the armed forces. Because federal civil rights laws do not prohibit discrimination based on sexual orientation, the courts have upheld the military's right to exclude gay men and lesbians. In recent years, however, as lesbian and gay activists have successfully challenged cultural hostility and social discrimination, courts have been less inclined to accept the military justification for excluding lesbians and gay men without specific and legitimate reasons.

Historically, the overlapping and changing arguments about homosexuals in the military—arguments generated by courts, policymakers, and even lesbian and gay activists themselves—provide a perfect opportunity to examine how the constructions of homosexuality described in Chapter 2 have operated. Debates about the exclusion of homosexuals from the U.S. armed forces are not so much about "military readiness" and "strategic defense" as they are about the social production of truth concerning who and what lesbians and gay men are and about who is authorized to produce this truth as it seeks intercourse with power. All of the historical discursive tenets of homosexuality are present in this debate, often expressed by military personnel and elected public servants, exploding into the "official" public discourse of the United States. These diverse tenets—often overlapping, sometimes contradictory—come together in a description of the homosexual as one who is "unfit for military service" for reasons that are almost never related to job performance or any objectively verifiable standard of military readiness or effectiveness. By the military's own evaluative standards, gay and lesbian personnel have excelled. But fear of homosexuals runs deep, and despite superior service records, hostility toward and discrimination against gay men and lesbians continues to be tolerated by many in the U.S. armed forces.

Still, neither involuntary separation from the service nor the perceived or actual consequences of this separation for the individuals involved are the most revealing aspects of these policy decisions. Rather, the most revealing aspects are the ways in which these decisions are made, employing the authority and legitimacy of the U.S. government to *officially* identify who and what homosexuals are. The armed services codify in law the identity's hail of "Hey, you there," while they simultaneously construct the homosexual—all homosexuals—in a manner that makes the exclusion appear rational.

The history of the way the military has constructed homosexuals and homosexuality parallels the epistemological models outlined in Chapter 2. Homosexuality is first seen as unnatural, immoral, and criminal vice, then as social and medical perversion, as disease and degeneration, and finally as psychological instability, immaturity, and dangerous personality disturbance. This chapter revisits these epistemological categories, demonstrating that the arguments about homosexuals created within each category of sexual difference have circulated—and circulate still—in the representations of gay men and lesbians in military policy texts and court decisions. The combined effect of these texts and decisions is to *essentialize* homosexual identity in a way that contravenes any claim to the full rights and privileges of citizenship. This is the result whether or not the military claims that homosexuality is a choice.

Sodomy: "Unnatural, Immoral, and Criminal"

For many people, the issue of homosexuals in the military dates only to the 1990s, when Bill Clinton pledged that, if elected president of the United States, he would lift the Pentagon ban against lesbians and gay men in the military. In truth, however, the U.S. military has had a policy of discriminating against homosexuals since the 1920s. In fact, the first appearance of the "homosexual" in U.S. public policy occurs in texts of military policy.

Throughout the eighteenth and nineteenth centuries, the military neither officially excluded nor discharged homosexuals from its ranks, and, until the late nineteenth century, neither homosexuality nor the homosexual *person* existed as a concept. The Althusserian hail of identity was yet to be issued, and those whose desires and sexual practices differed from those of the majority had yet to be defined as a new category of person. Still, from the days of the Revolutionary War, the U.S. Army and Navy prosecuted those who were caught engaging in acts of sodomy, which they defined as anal and oral sex. These acts were criminal for members of the military, just as they had been under British law and in the original thirteen colonies.[2] Any soldier in the U.S. military forces who was convicted of sodomy could be sent to prison. West Point, the first U.S. military academy, ironically, was conceived as a way for its founder to avoid being punished for sodomy.

The military's sodomy law is today contained in Article 125 of the Uniform Code of Military Justice (UCMJ). Part (a) of Article 125, which covers all branches of the armed forces, advises that "any person . . . who engages in unnatural carnal copulation with another person of the same or opposite sex or with an animal is guilty of sodomy. Penetration, however slight, is sufficient to complete the offense." Part (b) directs that "any person found guilty of sodomy shall be punished as a court-martial may direct."[3]

This definition of sodomy is an interesting one. The key phrase, "unnatural carnal copulation," is open to varying interpretations. Indeed, the phrase "carnal copulation" literally means copulation relating to the body or copulation of the flesh. It is difficult, even with a fertile imagination, to think of copulation that is other than carnal, in this most literal sense. But "carnal" also carries a negative connotation, indicating that which is base, animalistic, or lascivious. This understanding of carnal copulation suggests a person who is more concerned with matters "of the flesh" than with the more noble pursuits of the intellect or spirit. If the statute is interpreted using this understanding of carnal copulation, the military's prohibition of sodomy is remindful of Christian proscriptions governing all sexuality that is other than procreative. There are ways of copulating, it implies, that are less pleasing to God than others. The pervasiveness of the Christian construction of sexuality is notable. Anal intercourse and oral intercourse, along with bestiality, are lumped together as activities that are offensive to God because none leads to the only legitimate end of sexual concourse: live birth. If the intention of sodomy laws is to promote live birth, then birth control and masturbation are also problematic. Indeed, this has been and continues to be the traditional teaching of the Catholic Church and many of its Protestant counterparts.

But sodomy, as defined in this statute, also violates the laws of nature, as witnessed by the addition of the word "unnatural" and the inclusion of a prohibition against copulation with animals. In nature, so the theory goes, sex is used as an evolutionary guarantee of survival of species. It follows that sexual activity not represented in nature, sexual acts that are not tied to species survival and evolution, cannot be considered "natural." These justifications that cite sodomy's twofold offense against God and nature are often conflated. They are what John Boswell has described as a "vehement circumlocution," where "unnatural" operates as a coded synonym for "bad" or "unacceptable."[4] That sodomy should be defined by Article 125 as unnatural is an example of not only just such a vehement circumlocution but also how our culture's values and beliefs make their way into the official discourses of the federal government.

The statutory construction of sodomy as "unnatural carnal copulation" does little to explain either the rationale behind the statute or what might be the threat or danger to the military. It does, however, succeed in constructing the sodomite as one of questionable moral character, an offender of Christian doctrine, and a freak of nature. Through violation of Article 125, the sodomite becomes a criminal and can be imprisoned by the military.

Article 125 is the only law regarding sodomitical acts enacted by Congress with respect to the military. It does not apply to homosexuals only. And although Article 125 criminalizes both homosexual and heterosexual sodomy as an offense when a member of the armed services is involved, only a few heterosexuals have been dismissed from military service for sodomy. The effect of this statute, if not its intent, therefore, is to exclude homosexuals from military service.

In one of the rare cases in which a heterosexual was discharged under Article 125, it was clear that it was really homosexual sodomy that was driving the service member's removal. In 1963, the navy seaman in question had engaged in an act of oral sodomy with a female prostitute.[5] But the discharge also cited the seaman's involvement in "four abnormal sexual acts prior to entering the Navy and during his first enlistment." These "abnormal sexual acts" were "as a passive partner in homosexual acts of perversion (fellatio) on several occasions prior to his entry in the service, and on two occasions during his first enlistment."[6] It is telling that the Court of Claims describes the act for which the seaman was discharged as "an act of oral sodomy with a prostitute" but describes his homosexual encounters as "abnormal sexual acts" or "acts of oral perversion." By the court's standard, there is nothing "perverted" about sodomy per se or about prostitution. Only homosexual sodomy is perversion. In 1953, an earlier Court of Military Affairs ruled against another serviceman who contested his discharge. The court stated that sodomy "is one of the most heinous offenses, for few crimes are more revolting."[7]

As unnatural carnal copulation, a revolting crime, and perversion, the construction of sodomy by the military follows a familiar path. Reflecting religious and criminal understandings of nonprocreative sexual acts, sodomy first implicated the individual and then came to completely represent him as the performer of sexual misdeeds. He *became* the perverted person, and the sodomitical acts were only the outward manifestation of a deeper illness. So completely has the undifferentiated individual in pursuit of pleasure answered the policeman's hail of "Hey, you there" that homosexual identity is all but impossible to extricate from the sexual acts that first attracted the policeman's flashlight. In military policy, sodomy and homosexuality have become impossible to distinguish.

Consider, for example, a 1993 hearing of the Armed Services Committee in which Senator Strom Thurmond, the ranking Republican committee member, entered into an angry exchange with Democratic Senator John Kerry, who was arguing that the ban on homosexuals in the military should be lifted:

> *Thurmond:* Homosexuals practice sodomy. The code of military justice and many states have provisions against sodomy. How would you reconcile the situation with homosexuals in the military?
>
> *Kerry:* Make it consistent for heterosexuals and homosexuals; whatever the standard is going to be and apply it appropriately. . . .
>
> *Thurmond:* Heterosexuals don't practice sodomy. . . . Homosexuals do.[8]

There was outright laughter in the hearing room in response to Thurmond's remarks. But the belief that only homosexual sodomy is immoral and deserves punishment is widespread. It is reflected in the difficulty that policymakers have in articulating a view of the homosexual that does not include condemnation of sodomy as religious sin and criminal behavior.

To the extent that prohibiting sodomy is of religious origin, it would seem to conflict with the First Amendment's prohibition against the establishment of religion. However, *in Hatheway v. Secretary of the Army,* the Ninth Circuit Court of Appeals wrote, "[Hatheway] has referred to the religious origins of laws against sodomy, a fact that the Army does not dispute. Whether Article 125 violates the establishment clause thus depends on whether 'it still retains its religious character.'" The court chose to rely on an earlier decision, one that dealt with Sunday closing laws (*Maryland v. McGowen*),[9] as the controlling precedent in *Hatheway.* These Sunday closing laws "had undergone extensive changes from their earliest forms" and were "valid because their present purpose and effect, to provide a uniform day of rest, reflected legitimate secular goals." Setting aside the questions of the suitability and legitimacy of comparing Sunday closing laws with sodomy statutes, the court decided that, like Sunday closing laws, "the secular policies asserted by the Army, such as preventing disruptive conduct, were accepted . . . as legitimate prohibition of homosexual conduct. We therefore hold that in a military setting the proscriptions of Article 125 have a legitimate secular purpose and effect."[10] Regardless of the secular purpose that the military's sodomy law was perceived to have, it was always the homosexual trapped within the Christian epistemological discourse of sin who was defined by sodomy.

In a town meeting held in Jacksonville, North Carolina, to debate the military's ban on homosexuals, the participants clearly connected the military policy with the religious problematization of sodomy as sin. *New York Times* reporter Eric Schmitt described the scene:

> As some people waved bibles over their heads and shouted "Amen," one questioner denounced what he said was a lessening of moral standards in American Society.
> "Is being old a sin?" asked the citizen, who did not identify himself.
> "No!" the crowd yelled back.
> "Is being handicapped a sin?" the man then asked.
> "No!" the crowd screamed, louder this time.
> "Is being homosexual a sin?" he came back.
> "Yes!" roared the crowd, loudest of all.[11]

Members of the military have echoed these sentiments, citing the immorality of homosexuality as the primary reason that gay men and lesbians should be excluded from the armed forces. "Homosexuality is morally wrong and has no place in the United States Marine Corps," claimed one Marine Corporal.[12] A twenty-five-year-old sailor stationed aboard the carrier *Saratoga* said, "There's a general consensus that this goes against the moral grain of what the Navy is about. When you're proud of something, you don't want to see it defaced by something like this."[13]

With all acts of sodomy perceived as homosexual acts, and all homosexuals, regardless of "levels of activity," perceived as immoral sodomites, the tautological reasoning is complete. This circular thinking excludes homosexuals either for homosexual acts or for "being" homosexual. Both are viewed as symptomatic acts, and both indicate a criminal character, a diseased body, a disturbed personality, a medical aberration—any one of which could endanger the mission of the military.

As we have seen, the medical definition of "homosexuality" and the "homosexual" was an attempt to save sodomites from the punishment that Senator Thurmond and the laws of many states would inflict upon them. But the conversion of sexual activities into a medical condition and then into a person who is defined by this condition only widened the stigmatized behavior and supposed immorality that could be grafted onto the homosexual identity. If one is immoral enough to engage in acts of sodomy, then one becomes suspect in all avenues of life.

Joining Knowledge to Power: The Medical Construction of the Official Army Homosexual

Medical doctors in the late nineteenth and early twentieth centuries had many theories for explaining, describing, and detecting homosexuals. The homosexual was seen not only as a proper subject for medical study but also as a medical problem that threatened the very foundations of society. As this definition of the homosexual as a medical aberration quickly found expression in official military policy, the second part of the process of constructing an *official* gay identity—putting the homosexual into the law—was completed.

A case in point is a device that was developed as early as World War I, which was believed to detect homosexuals in preinduction screening. The test, which was intended as a way of disqualifying homosexuals from entering the armed forces, was based on electronic measurement of the naturally occurring radioactivity that emanated from men's testicles. Dr. Albert Abrams, the inventor of the device, recorded the levels of radiation that emanated from "normal" men's testicles and the levels of radiation that emanated from women's ovaries. Scaling these readings, Abrams claimed that he could detect homosexuals by their "ovarian reactions" on his scale. In an article entitled "Homosexuality—a Military Menace," Abrams cautioned that "in recruiting the elements that make up our invincible army, we cannot ignore what is obvious and which will militate against the combative prowess of our forces in this war. . . . From a military viewpoint, the homosexualist is not only dangerous, but ineffective as a fighter." Despite the fact that Abrams's experiment was conducted on only six homosexual men, he was convinced of the accuracy of his results. He claimed that in four of the six men with anatomically perfect testicles, an ovarian reaction was found. The other two test subjects had a mixed "testicular/ovarian" reading but with the "ovarian predominating by measurement."[14]

Despite Abrams's insistence on the stupendous importance of these results, there is no record that his device was ever used in the recruitment process. Still, the presence of the device and Abrams's intended application for it illuminate a number of interesting points. First, the very existence of the device illustrates the expansion of the medical model of homosexuality into the arena of public policy and the expansion of the role of the scientific or medical "expert" in the formulation of national public policy. As Abrams saw it, his device was useful to the military because homosexuality constituted a threat to the security of the United States—a threat that only the medical profession had the knowledge to combat. Second, the intended use of the device points to the cultural persistence of the justifications that the Pentagon employed to exclude homosexuals. Indeed, almost forty years later, a Court of Military Appeals had lamented the absence of a medical test to detect homosexuality, stating, "It seems fairly clear that science has found no ready agent for the isolation of the sex pervert. . . . Were the converse true, the Armed Forces presumably would avoid the homosexual offender through pre-induction screening."[15]

In 1921, the army issued expanded screening standards that remained in effect until the eve of World War II.[16] These interwar standards reflected the epistemology of the nineteenth-century medical model of homosexuality, which argued that homosexuals were the product of physiological degeneration. Characteristics that deviated from white, heterosexual, male norms were considered a product of a constitutional disorder. Feminine characteristics were among the telltale signs of "degeneration" that made a man unfit for military service. Taken almost word for word from the pages of the medical journals that first summoned the homosexual into being, these standards cautioned that men with a degenerative physique might present the general body conformation of the opposite sex. Characteristics to watch for included sloping shoulders, broad hips, excessive pectoral and pubic adipose tissue, and lack of hirsute and muscular markings.[17]

In addition to these anatomical signs of homosexual degeneration, the interwar standards included "oral and anal sex between men" as one of many "behavioral" cues of "sexual perversion," thus repackaging religious and moral condemnations against sodomy and the sodomite in a medical model. The army standards also listed "sexual psychopathy" as one of many "constitutional" psychopathic states, reflecting early inroads made by the psychiatric model of homosexuality that would later become the accepted definition of homosexuality in the United States.

By World War II, new army standards were issued to instruct doctors how to detect homosexuals. The 1942 guidelines read, "Persons habitually or occasionally engaged in homosexual or other perverse sexual practices are unsuitable for military service and will be excluded. Feminine bodily characteristics, effeminacy in dress or manner, or a patulous [expanded] rectum are not consistently found in such persons, but when present should lead to careful psychiatric examination."[18]

Although it was acknowledged that these physical manifestations would not be found in every homosexual, they were nevertheless included in the standards for exclusion. The assumption was that these physical markers, because they might indicate homosexuality, made further examination necessary. It is striking how closely these guidelines follow the fifty-year-old assumption by medical scientists that homosexual detection was possible. It is in these new guidelines based on old assumptions that we find the link between knowledge and power, epistemology and the State.

Implicit in the 1921 and 1942 military standards of admission, and quite a bit more explicit in the Abrams test for testicular radioactivity, is the understanding of homosexuality as a biological failing that produces "dangerous," "ineffective fighters" who are "unsuitable for military service." But these attitudes reveal more than society's distaste for homosexuals. Because gay men are excluded based on effeminacy in manner or dress or on testicular radioactivity levels that compare with "ovarian" levels, these attitudes also signal the culture's undervaluation of women. The conclusion is clear: In a culture troubled over the issue of women in combat, the presence of homosexuals, like the presence of women, would "militate against the combative prowess" of the virile armed forces, rendering it soft, ineffective, effeminate.

This conflation of homosexuals with socially constructed gender characteristics of the opposite sex is still evident today. One of sailor Keith Meinhold's navy coworkers, Tom Paulson, told the *New York Times* that he had guessed that Meinhold was gay long before Meinhold had announced it on ABC's "World News Tonight." What tipped Paulson to Meinhold's sexuality? Meinhold's "multi-colored in-box."[19] In the military, and perhaps in the culture at large, a man who is too "colorful" or too interested in his appearance or the appearance of his environment is open to speculation about his "manhood."

A 1942 study of screening procedures at the Boston Induction Station recommended that even a man who is not homosexual be disqualified for service if he "is so effeminate in appearance and mannerisms that he is inevitably destined to be the butt of all jokes in the company."[20] In *Coming Out Under Fire*, Alan Berube describes a form that draft boards sent to high schools asking teachers to comment on their former students' levels of effeminacy.[21]

Lesbians, too, are considered identifiable by their gender inversion. Vice Admiral Joseph S. Donnel's 1992 memo claimed that lesbians are particularly difficult to root out because they are "more aggressive than their male counterparts" and "intimidating" to those who might turn them in to authorities.[22] This is an interesting argument, in that it seems to indicate that "aggression" and "intimidation" make lesbians unsuitable for military service. The same behavior by men would, no doubt, be commended.

But as the 1942 preinduction guidelines make clear, physical signs alone were no longer a reliable indicator of homosexuality. Increased psychiatric screening would be necessary to ensure that homosexuals did not "slip into" the military.

The Psychiatric Model of Homosexuality

During the national mobilization of troops in preparation for the entrance of the United States into World War II, the Selective Service System and the army and navy began to concern themselves in earnest with the sexual orientation of potential soldiers. In 1940 alone, over sixteen million men between the ages of twenty-one and thirty-five registered for the draft.[23] With this great increase in potential personnel, the military could use more "selective" criteria.

Psychiatrists seized the opportunity to expand their influence. The "science" of psychiatry, they argued, could help military officials detect undesirables through psychological and psychiatric screening procedures. In the United States, psychiatry was still treated as the stepchild of the medical professions and had not yet achieved the level of respectability that it had attained in Europe. Psychiatrists could now expand their influence and acceptability throughout U.S. society by becoming part of the military bureaucracy.[24] Taking a role in the screening of potential soldiers gave psychiatrists the opportunity to introduce tens of thousands of physicians and draft board members to the basic principles of psychiatry.

Psychiatrists used persuasive economic arguments to sell the War Department and selective service officials on the importance of psychiatric screening for potential soldiers. Over a billion dollars had been spent caring for the psychiatric casualties of World War I, and by the beginning of World War II, more than half of the beds at the Veterans Administration hospitals were occupied by these psychiatric casualties.[25] Psychiatric screening, it was argued, could reduce these costs. Those who were at risk for mental illness could be identified before they entered the military. Neither the military nor the psychiatrists who sought to gain acceptance through the military argued that the conditions of war themselves might be the cause of what is known today as posttraumatic stress disorder.

The dominant psychiatric theory in the United States in the first two decades of the twentieth century was the brain-disease model of insanity. The brain-disease model classified various mental, moral, and emotional abnormalities, including homosexuality, as symptoms of brain lesions and neurological disorders. These, in turn, might be caused by heredity, trauma, or even masturbation. Interest in Freud's theories of sexuality was growing, however, and Freud described homosexuality more as a psychosexual than a constitutional condition. This new approach took into account a patient's unique life situation, integrating biological and personality factors. Psychiatrists began to believe that they could diagnose severe disorders in their early stages and prevent mental disease.

Two U.S. psychiatrists—Winfred Overholser and Harry Stack Sullivan—were indispensable to the increase in influence of psychiatry. They believed in this new psychoanalytic approach and its merger with the bureaucratic power of the military. Under their influence, the military developed an expanded psychiatric screening process that led to greater prestige and legitimacy for the profession of psychiatry. Ironically, the attitude of Overholser and Sullivan toward homosexuality was not representative of that of the psychiatric profession on the whole. Both men believed that homosexuality was neither an aberration caused by degeneracy nor a symptom of future degeneracy. In fact, Sullivan himself was a homosexual, and Overholser, in his position on the National Research Council, had argued against the military's policy of imprisoning homosexuals. Like the sexologists of the previous century, however, Overholser and Sullivan could not control the use that would be made of their work. Sullivan's initial plan for psychiatric screening contained no mention of homosexuality, but that was to change as it passed through the Washington military bureaucracy.[26]

By 1941, the U.S. Army Surgeon General's Office had created its own screening circular, which made homosexuality a basis for disqualification from military service. The selective service revised Sullivan's draft of the screening guidelines in order to bring it into line with that of the army. Both sets of guidelines included "homosexual proclivities" as a "disqualifying deviation," making homosexuality a disqualification at both levels of the preinduction screening process for those entering the army. Meanwhile, the navy too was developing policies for the exclusion of the mentally unfit.[27]

The psychiatric screening process would introduce a greater scrutiny of sexual behavior, especially homosexuality, and a "psychiatric diagnosis" would become the justification for excluding potential recruits who might be gay. It would also become the basis for investigating those already in service who were believed to be gay. By mid-1941, several months before the United States entered the war, the administrative apparatus for screening out homosexuals was already in place at the Selective Service System, the army, and the navy. It had the full support of the director of selective service, the surgeons general for the army and the navy, and their respective psychiatric consultants.

The great breakthrough that Abrams's 1916 homosexuality detector had promised was the time that it would save in the detection of potential homosexuals. Abrams believed (though the authors of the 1944 army admission apparently did not) that because homosexuals exhibit "no secondary sex characteristics," it could take "months of painstaking psychoanalysis before the inversion was discovered."[28] In practice, psychiatric examinations of recruits were brief: Psychiatrists in the 1940s were developing shortcuts in the "identification" of homosexuals.

By 1943, a group of doctors had developed another test for detecting homosexuals. Called the Cornell Selectee Index, it purported to identify homosexuals by their interest in certain "occupational choices." Men who checked off an interest in such occupations as interior decorator, dancer, or window dresser were excluded from military service because they were believed to have problems with "acceptance of the male pattern."[29]

Current service members suspected of homosexuality were referred to psychiatrists for more thorough examination. None of the military discharges contested in the courts report "months of painstaking psychoanalysis," but almost all report that once homosexual acts or tendencies were suspected or discovered, the service member was immediately sent for psychiatric evaluation. Depending on the result of this evaluation, the soldier's future as a member of the military might be over. The courts have clearly demonstrated their unwillingness to keep homosexuals in the service any longer than necessary. In 1966, one district court in Pennsylvania wrote that it was not willing to "hobble the Army by forcing it to retain even one soldier, for an indefinite period of time, where there are serious questions concerning his emotional health."[30] The court record in this case revealed that these serious questions arose from nothing more than "a letter received by Headquarters, Department of the Army, Washington, D.C., which alleged the plaintiff had homosexual inclinations."[31]

Other psychiatric evaluations presented during court proceedings of contested discharges from the military reveal more about the military's perception of homosexuality as a mental or personality disorder. Abundant in the public record of the military trials of men and women who contested their discharges for homosexuality are such descriptions as "habitual . . . uncontrollable homosexual tendencies in the true psychodynamic sense,"[32] "sexual deviate manifested by homosexuality latent,"[33] "indication of homosexual orientation in the appellant's psychodynamic formulation,"[34] and "personality disorder . . . [homosexuality] of such severity that he cannot be expected to function adequately in the military."[35]

The very fact that men and women can be and were discharged for homosexual *being* is a sinister example of the way that medical epistemology joined with the power of the State and created new and more invasive mechanisms for regulating the lives of individuals. The medicalization of sexuality moved from a regulation of the activities of sodomy to inspection for deviance in the body and personality. With this move came a dizzying array of medical, legal, and administrative apparatuses and categories, complete with instructions. Alan Berube writes, "By 1945 . . . homosexual personnel were identified as either latent, self confessed, well adjusted, habitual, undetected, or known, true, confirmed and male and female. There were homosexual nonoffenders who admitted only tendencies not acts; heterosexual malingerers or homosexual reverse malingerers, normal offenders who were casual homosexuals, first timers, curious, drunk, immature, submissive or regressive; offenders who still possessed salvage value; the aggressors and willing followers, regardless of their sexuality; the sexual psychopath, moral pervert, and sexual deviate."[36] The new medical regulation of identity led to an immediate decrease in the number of court-martials for sodomy; homosexuals were simply given undesirable discharges as sexual psychopaths. The decrease in court-martial proceedings for sodomy was simply replaced by a dramatic increase in the number of individuals forced out of the military. In previous regulatory regimens, the military had to prove that an individual had engaged in *acts* of sodomy; in this new regimen, officials needed only have medical experts declare an individual unsuitable for military service because of *who* and *what* he or she was. Between the years 1941 and 1945, an average of 2,250 servicemen and -women were dismissed each year as a result of the new administrative discharge procedures for homosexuality. In the previous forty years, convictions for sodomy had numbered a mere 25 per year.[37]

In the years following World War II, the line between the category of sodomy as a crime punishable by court-martial and the category of homosexuality as a psychopathology that lead to an undesirable discharge was blurred even further. Often, those who admitted to being homosexual were brought to trial for violation of Article 125 of the UCMJ, despite the fact that there was no evidence of acts of sodomy. Either acts or orientation was used as a means of regulating the homosexual—testimony once again to the way that the deployment of each of these various epistemological systems reinforces the others.

The type of discharge given to those who were declared unsuitable for military service because of homosexuality also proved to be a dilemma for World War II policymakers. Even those military psychiatrists who argued for lenient treatment of homosexuals found themselves acquiescing to a policy that dispensed undesirable discharges to homosexuals. Military officials argued that anything less stigmatizing than an undesirable discharge would encourage men to *become* situational homosexuals in an effort to evade the military service. This argument sheds some light on the seemingly hysterical paranoia that surrounds the question of gays in the military. Evidently, the military itself believes that straight men can willingly become gay; thus, keeping gays out is a way to reduce the homosexual desires of heterosexual soldiers. This argument demonstrates the military's confusion about sexuality as both essence and free choice.

The military's construction of homosexuality as a psychological disorder might perhaps be explained by the position of the U.S. psychiatric community for most of the twentieth century, except that this position was abandoned by the psychiatric community in the early 1970s. Yet the military persists in using it as a reason for the separation of gay men and lesbians. In 1981, in *Rich v. Secretary of the Army*, the Ninth Circuit Court of Appeals noted that "the Army regulations do indicate that homosexuality can be considered as an indication of a personality disorder."[38]

The three epistemological systems presented in Chapter 2, from which the hail "Hey, you there" was first issued, also served as the justifications for regulation, scrutiny, and exclusion—the means by which homosexuals were "put into the law." Both through military regulations that justified the exclusion of homosexuals from service and through military and civil court decisions that upheld these exclusions, these epistemological systems give rise to a host of new justifications for excluding the homosexual.

Regulating Sexual Desire

One common justification for excluding gay men and lesbians from the military is the argument that homosexuals lack the ability to control their sexual desires. Whether because of their gross immorality and bad character, their sexual psychopathology, or their degenerative physical and mental constitutions, lesbians and gay men, it is argued, simply cannot keep their actions or desires in check; therefore, they cannot be trusted. This lack of trust leads policymakers to declare homosexuals and homosexuality—both a type of person and the set of behaviors ascribed to that person— to be "incompatible with military service."[39] Putting homosexuals in sex- segregated barracks, sleeping berths, and showers with heterosexual soldiers is believed to be tantamount to letting the fox loose in the chicken coop. This attitude is evident in the depiction of gay men as corrupt, old perverts who go into the military with the intention of assaulting young boys. One court ruled that describing gay men as chicken hawks, is not unfair.[40] The courts presume a probability that homosexuals will turn to assault in order to satisfy their sexual cravings.[41]

In the 1993 debate over lifting the military's ban against gay men and lesbians, this construction of the homosexual as without control over desires was never far from the focus of discussion. It was obvious in Vice Admiral Donnel's warning that the presence of lesbians creates a "predator-type environment," in which "more senior and aggressive female sailors" exert "subtle coercion" or make "outright sexual advances" on their "young, often vulnerable" female colleagues."[42] Enlisted personnel expressed fear of homosexuals' lack of sexual self-control, holding that showering with them, sleeping near them, or even touching them was unthinkable.[43] "During my Army career," claimed Colonel David Hackworth, "I saw countless officers and N.C.O.'s who *couldn't stop themselves* from hitting on soldiers.[44] Writing in 1975, the U.S. Court of Claims reached the same conclusion in *Augen-blick v. United States:*

> I suppose that in civilian society the sovereign people formerly considered they had a right to prohibit and punish by law behavior they considered infamous, without being required to show the offense had a victim. . . . The old attitude, however, is eroding and we are now told we have no right to punish a victimless crime. Exemptions of "consenting adults" from laws against sodomy, etc. are now frequently urged and sometimes enacted. I suppose such a person who urged such an exemption might still, if heterosexual, think twice about making a long journey with a homosexual.
>
> Civilians can chose their companions but when you join the military you embark upon an extended voyage with persons not of your choice. . . . If persons you regard as undesirable are in the crew, their companionship is foisted upon you.[45]

Even supporters of gay men and lesbians would get drawn into this debate. Testifying before the U.S. Senate Armed Services Committee, Lawrence Korb, the former assistant secretary of state, made the following observation: "There's a body of evidence that shows that not every gay man is attracted to every other man, or the same for women. That's really what we're talking about here. That somehow or another there's a feeling that just because you are a homosexual, you're attracted to everyone who happens to be your same sex."[46] Believing that gay men and lesbians should be allowed to serve in the military, Korb saw the need to inform members of the Senate and the general public that homosexuals can indeed control their sexual desires.

Theoretically, then, this lack of control—this psychological defect that makes gay men and lesbians unable to control their sexual desires—makes their enlistment a threat to the morale, good order, and discipline that is demanded by the military. In reality, of course, there is no evidence that any of these characteristics, immoralities, constitutional defects, or psychological deficiencies is more frequent among gay men and lesbians than among heterosexual men and women.

Following its time-honored approach that "more is better," the military's justifications for excluding lesbian and gay soldiers often moved well beyond the actual or perceived abilities or defects of these men and women. The Pentagon has argued that the military is a special institution. It imposes greater hardships on its members and expects greater sacrifices from them. Therefore, the argument goes, it is reasonable that the military be able to demand of its members a standard of conduct and behavior that would not be tolerated in society.

The Military as the "Exceptional" Community

Attorneys for the various branches of the armed services have spent a great deal of time convincing both military and civilian courts that because the military is a specialized community, it has the right to place restrictions on freedom that are unheard of in civilian life. Until quite recently, almost all courts accepted this argument, sometimes elaborating on the many demands that are placed on the unique military community.[47] Even when they have challenged the military's discriminatory practices, the courts have acknowledged that the "military decisions by the Army are not lightly to be overruled by the Judiciary."[48]

In *United States v. Scoby*, the court stated that the "military community is different from the civilian community," and "within the community there is simply not the same autonomy [on the part of the serviceperson] as there is in the larger civilian life."[49] In *United States v. Brown*, Brown's act of consensual sodomy, said the court, "demonstrates a substantial threat to the military community and creates a distinct military interest without parallel in the civilian community."[50] In a memo to President Clinton, Attorney General Janet Reno speculated on the defensibility of his 1993 Don't Ask, Don't Tell, Don't Pursue policy. She noted that the U.S. Supreme Court had repeatedly stated that decisions by the president and the military commanders must be reviewed deferentially, taking into account the "special needs" of the military society. "As a consequence," Reno wrote, "it is possible to justify in the military setting constraints on individual liberty and choice that might be invalid in civilian society. Because of the extraordinary deference paid by the courts to military service, we are confident that the new policy proposed by the Secretary of Defense will be upheld against constitutional scrutiny."[51]

This "distinct military interest" goes well beyond the way a soldier performs a military duty. A soldier who "engages in conduct that disrupts good order or discipline, or reduces the morale of the other soldiers has failed in one or more of his or her important tasks as a member of the armed forces."[52] In fact, it comes close to justifying any kind of discrimination on the basis of the ignorance and hatred of other service personnel. The homosexual is seen as disruptive to troop morale, which justifies the policy of separating the "offender" from the service. Indeed, in the 1993 U.S. Senate Armed Services Committee Hearings on Homosexuals in the Military, Virginia Senator John Warner argued that homosexuals in the military would constitute such an egregious imposition on other soldiers and would so radically change the conditions of the military environment that if homosexuals were allowed in the military, enlisted personnel should all be given the opportunity to resign without penalty.[53] The chair of the committee hearings, Sam Nunn, a conservative Democrat from Georgia, had twice fired staff members upon discovering that they were gay.[54] In a tense exchange with Senator John Kerry, in which Kerry equated military regulations against adultery with the military ban on gay men and lesbians, he said, "Perhaps the military has a slightly higher standard [than society, and] maybe we ought to welcome that. I am not sure we should go for the lowest common denominator approach."[55] Through these policies, homosexuals have been constructed in such a way that their mere presence appears to violate standards of behavior and codes of conduct that the military demands for members of its specialized community.

One way that lesbians and gay men are constructed as threats to both the military community and its mission is as untrustworthy. This reaction to the revelation of a homosexual identity is familiar to many lesbians and gay men, whose friends, co-workers, and family members are often quick to tell them that they feel that their "trust has been damaged" because they have been "lying" to those around them about who they *really are*. Similarly, the military first makes it impossible to identify as anything other than heterosexual and remain in the military and then constructs as dishonest anyone who attempts to "come out" of the military closet.

There are many examples of doubts about the veracity of a service member arising once the individual has been labeled as homosexual. Even in those unfortunate cases that involve a victim of rape or forced sodomy, it seems that "evidence of [a] victim's homosexual activity [is] relevant as to the issue of consent and the victim's credibility."[56] In *Rich v. Secretary of the Army,*[57] Rich explained that, because he was not gay when he entered the army, he had not lied in answer to the enlistment question "Are you a homosexual?" This argument was rejected by the court, however.

Many young men and women enter the military before they themselves are clear about their sexual identity. For example, James Holobaugh, who had been chosen (no doubt in part for his good looks) by the army Reserve Officers' Training Corps (ROTC) as a poster boy for recruitment advertisements, was asked to repay his ROTC scholarship after announcing in 1990 that he had discovered that he was gay. The army does not usually seek to recover scholarship money from cadets discharged for homosexuality unless there is evidence of deceit.[58] Holobaugh's claim that when he entered college in 1984, he was dating women and had no idea that he was gay was put forth as evidence of deceit. When lawyers for Holobaugh insisted that he would be willing to fulfill his contractual obligation and serve in the army, however, the army dropped the lawsuit against him.

In November 1992, the navy ROTC instituted a new policy that required repayment of scholarship awards upon the discovery that a midshipman was gay. In the military, evidently, a homosexual cannot be believed about his or her past or trusted in the future. Any acts, no matter how distant, are treated as evidence of current homosexuality. Any evidence is seized upon to construct and maintain the homosexual identity. Shane Phelan has described this construction as the rule of "hypo-descent," in which "'even a little" lesbian sexual desire makes one 'really' a lesbian as though desire (and race) were discrete entities, categorized by nature."[59]

In *United States v. Kindler*, Airman Kindler, who vehemently denied the charges of homosexuality, claiming that he was as "normal as anyone," was nevertheless discharged. In upholding the air forces discharge, a Court of Military Appeals relied on "acts of sodomy committed between the accused and his twin brother at the ages of twelve, thirteen and fourteen" to establish that Kindler was, and always had been, a homosexual and was therefore subject to discharge.[60] In the case of *Clackum v. United States*, the court record again reveals that, despite her denial and with absolutely no evidence, the air force dismissed the possibility that Fannie Mae Clackum could be telling the truth about her sexuality and discharged her.[61] Suspicion of homosexual activity in and of itself, it seems, is reason to question the overall veracity of the person accused. Homosexuality is seen as such a blemish, such a weakness of character, that a formerly trusted associate must be reevaluated in the light of this newly uncovered character flaw. In this evaluation, "It may often take corroboration—or strong evidence of good character—to overcome the repelling nature of the testimony" about the "heinous" and "revolting" crime.[62]

Indeed, more than just truthfulness has come into question in the wake of accusations of homosexuality. In 1953, in *United States v. Marcey*, a Court of Military Appeals found that "a person who practices homosexuality is likely to assault for the purpose of satisfying his perverted sexual cravings."[63] In fact, according to the court, all homosexuals are potential perpetrators of assault: "The accused asserts that his motivations were toward consensual homosexuality which would have no probative value with regard to offenses involving violent acts. That is a specious argument when consideration is given to the homosexual who misjudges his prospective partner. If it turns out that his perverted advances are unwanted and the hoped for consent is lacking, the prospect has been victimized by an assault with sodomitical intent."[64] Following this logic, a man who asks out a woman who turns him down is guilty of assault with intent to rape.

Perceived as untrustworthy and likely to assault, homosexuals can also be identified by the company they keep. Another Military Appeals Court allowed testimony that indicated that a serviceman must be a homosexual because he had been seen with other men who had been court-martialed for homosexuality as a part of the same investigation. Although the court claimed not to "accept the principle of 'guilt by association,'" it found nonetheless that "there is much in human experience consistent with the probability that homosexuals are characterized by a stronger tendency to congregate than is possessed by other criminals. Conceivably some special rationale exists in the area of the prohibition against evidence of suspicious associations."[65] Just being seen with a gay man or a lesbian is enough to cause suspicion. The most likely effect is greater policing of one's own behavior and the behavior of others, as every military service member, gay and straight alike, internalizes the policeman's gaze, constantly searching for signs of a manifest homosexuality.

Additional characteristics—physical, psychological, and biological differences—would also be put on the list of ways to identify homosexuals. Given the medical community's overwhelming role in the invention, definition, and regulation of "homosexuality" in the late nineteenth and early twentieth centuries, it is no surprise that medical "experts" would play a role in the military's attempts to describe/inscribe the homosexual. It is, after all, in the intersection with the medical bureaucracy—the link between "truth" and power, "expert" and administrator—that the homosexual becomes a public and therefore a State concern.

Behavior or Identity: Essentialism and the Military's "Identification" of Homosexuals

One of the most interesting (and inadvertent) revelations of the representations of gay men and lesbians in public policy texts and debates about military service has been how little agreement exists over what homosexuals and homosexuality *are*. In public policy debates, those who claim that homosexuality is innate—a product of genetics, biology, or some other deep and immutable property—have been pitted against those who emphasize that homosexuality is an activity. The former opinion, which is held by most members of the gay community, is seen as most likely to lead to an end to the discrimination directed at lesbians and gay men. Massachusetts Senator Edward Kennedy, who is known as a progressive liberal, explained why he believed that the military's ban against homosexuals should be overturned: "It's time for the Armed Forces to stop discriminating against anyone because of who they are."[66] Indeed, asking whether social discrimination against a group is based on some innate condition is one of the first steps that courts take to determine whether the group can be considered a "suspect class" in the eyes of the law. If gay men and lesbians were constituted as a suspect class, then the military would be required to make a more compelling case that its policy is rational and legitimate.[67]

But the gays in the military debate does not break down nicely into essentialists on one side and constructivists on the other. For example, David Hackworth, a retired army colonel, described homosexuality as a "biological impulse." Because the sexual impulse itself "is the strongest thing going among twenty-year-olds," Hackworth concluded, gay men and lesbians should be excluded from the military.[68] As the nineteenth-century sexologists discovered, and as racism makes clear everyday, biological immutability is no guarantee against discrimination. General Colin Powell and others have used behavioralist claims to reject the analogy between the exclusion of gays in the military today and the earlier segregation of African Americans in the military. Powell claimed that skin color was a "benign non-behavioral characteristic while sexual *orientation* is perhaps the most profound of human *behavioral* characteristics."[69]

Powell's merger of behavior and identity is topped only by Judge Richard Matsch in *Rich v. Secretary of the Army*, a 1981 district court case that challenged the military's exclusion of gays. Disagreeing with the plaintiff's claim that homosexuality was a "fundamental matter at the core of one's personality, self image, and sexual identity," Matsch wrote that there was no difference between acts of sodomy and a person's homosexual orientation because "a statement that a person is homosexual or gay . . . refers not to physical characteristics, but . . . to conduct."[70] For Matsch, as for Powell, acts and identities are merged; however, Matsch takes the idea one step farther, making declarations of gay identity equivalent to proven acts of sodomy. The confusion is present too in the current Don't Ask, Don't Tell policy, under which members of the service can be expelled for simple declarations of sexual identity even without proof of homosexual acts. Identity has become acts, and even speech has become identity. Following the mathematical principle "If $A = B$ and if $B = C$, then $A = C$," the military's logic is that speech is tantamount to sodomy! (Who knew? All these years I have been doing it the old-fashioned way.) The fuzzy lines between acts, identities, and behaviors reveal that arguments about homosexual *being* rarely follow the simple academic essentialism/constructivism bifurcation. Behaviors themselves become essentialized into identities, even as identities are used as evidence of sexual behavior. What this clarifies is how little room exists for constructivist arguments in the military policy debate. The silence of constructivist performative claims about sexuality reveals how completely the ground has been ceded to those who make essentializing claims on both sides of the policy debate.

Although many people now accept "homosexual" as a noun that signifies a type of person, an interesting evolution is evident in the military texts and policy debates. The transformation of sexual acts of sodomy and the "medical" condition of homosexuality into the noun "homosexual" failed to rescue the homosexual from State regulation and public abomination as those who had spearheaded the transformation had hoped. Rather, the noun "homosexual" came to describe one who *chooses* to engage in the sexual acts that our culture has anathematized. Described as vice, constitutional degeneration, and mental imbalance, homosexual acts and behaviors have been inscribed onto the body and soul, the very personhood of the homosexual, transforming acts and behaviors into identities. Orientation has become a shortcut for excluding those who might engage in behavior that does not meet with the culture's approval. Rather than liberating the homosexual from these anathematized behaviors, in the next torturous turn of the epistemological screw, orientation *reduces individuals to their anathematized sexual acts,* producing a litany of devices that can help "detect" anyone who might have this problematized orientation. From the examination of testicular radioactivity to the search for "patulous rectums," from "effeminacy in manner and dress" to interest in such "inappropriate" occupations as dancing and interior decorating, homosexuals have become more *detectable,* making more rigorous scrutiny and greater conformity to gender stereotypes the rule of the day.[71]

The hail of identity made possible lesbians and gay men, but the epistemological systems out of which the homosexual was first created circulate still in our *official* representations of lesbians and gay men, framing the way they are seen by the *officials* of the State, often in the face of monumental evidence to the contrary. The constitution of an officially gay person has also meant new levels of invasion, scrutiny, and regulation, as the new gay and lesbian subject has been put into the law.

4

Gays in the Military

Identity as "Official" Justification for Exclusion

BILLY BRAGG'S song "Tender Comrade" provides a provocatively romantic view of an institutionally produced, situational homosexuality that controverts the doom and gloom cranked out by the military itself:

> What will you do when the war is over, tender comrade?
> When we lay down our weary guns?
> When we return home to our wives and families
> And look into the eyes of our sons?
>
> Will you say that we were heroes?
> Or that the fear of dying among strangers
> Tore our innocence away?
> And from that moment on, deep in my heart I knew
> That I would only give my life for love.
>
> Brothers in Arms, in each other's arms
> Was the only time that I was not afraid.
>
> What will you do when the war is over, tender comrade?
> When we cast off these khaki clothes
> And go our separate ways
> What will you say of the bond we had, tender comrade?[1]

Although romantic, Bragg's conception of a tender comrade seeking consolation, compassion, and human warmth in the arms of another soldier is borne out by countless experiences narrated without shame by veterans of this country's wars.[2] Bragg's lyrics about World War II describe a time when the official interpellation of gay identity was not yet complete. Slippage was still possible in the definition of "homosexual," and physical love and affection were still possible between two men who faced possible death in combat without any association with the modern hail of gay identity. But as the process of interpellation that first turned undifferentiated individuals into sexual subjects/suspects advanced, so did greater avenues for regulating the lives of those who came to understand and answer the hail of gay identity. The clearest example of this again comes from the military.

Having helped to create this new category of sexual identity, the military used concern over the physical and mental fitness of soldiers to justify a greater scrutiny of desire. Once the focus of military scrutiny included both sexual *acts* and medicalized sexual *identities*, new regulatory apparatuses were created to deal with this expanding jurisdiction. By 1954, the new regulatory regimens made possible by a merger of science and the State, though imperfect, were firmly entrenched in the operations of military personnel policy and in the courts of military justice.

Since its inception in 1949, the UCMJ has included a provision against sodomy. Article 125 defines sodomy as "unnatural carnal copulation with another person of the same or opposite sex"[3] and specifies that violations of this article are punishable by court-martial. As with much legislation, the military's sodomy law was quite specific, but its enforcement was not stipulated at all. This silence in the UCMJ, which required each branch of the military to devise its own guidelines and policies for administering and implementing violations of Article 125, resulted in an uneven and inconsistent application of the law. For example, in 1954 the regulations under which the U.S. Navy discharged service members found guilty of the military's sodomy law referred only to *homosexual* infractions; the regulations made no reference to the *heterosexual* violations of Article 125. The effect was clear: in the navy, the military's sodomy law as passed by the U.S. Congress could not apply to heterosexuals. Article 125, a law passed by Congress and included as part of the military's own code of justice, a law that refers only to sexual acts and not to sexual identity would be enforced only against a certain category of *person:* the homosexual.

In the court case that brought this discrepancy to light, the heterosexual violation of the military's sodomy law was too outrageous for even the navy to overlook. In one of only two cases in which a consensual act of heterosexual sodomy was prosecuted by the armed forces, Seaman Shawn Doherty, an ensign in the navy, contested his discharge in the Court of Military Appeals, claiming that he was discharged under instructions not applicable to his case. Ensign Doherty had purchased tickets to a navy charity event, during which a female prostitute was called in to perform in public. After the prostitute performed fellatio on two civilians, Doherty, on the urging of his pals, went to the washroom, disrobed, and returned to solicit the prostitute to perform fellatio on him. With navy officers in attendance at the public fund-raiser, it was impossible to overlook the blatant violation of Article 125.

Despite the discrepancies between the generalized military sodomy law and the discharge instructions that point only to homosexual violations of the law, the Court of Military Appeals in which Doherty contested his discharge ruled the discharge valid. In its entirety, Secretary of the Navy Instruction 1620.1 is concerned with "promulgat[ing] a uniform procedure relative to the disposition of personnel in cases involving homosexual tendencies or acts."[4] Describing the gap between Article 125 of the UCMJ (which makes sodomy a crime) and the naval instruction that regulates court-martials for violations of Article 125, the court expressed "doubt that [Secretary of the Navy Instruction 1620.1] covers the type of crime which was committed." The lines of text that follow are notable: "The whole tenor of the letter [Secretary of the Navy Instruction 1620.1] is to project persons with homosexual tendencies into a channel for separation from the military. A homosexual is a person who has morbid sexual passion for one of the same sex and accused's crime was committed with a person of the opposite sex. However, we need not stay by that refined distinction as, for the purpose of the issue, we can assume that accused's behavior brought him within Class II of the letter."[5] A Class II homosexual is defined as "those cases wherein personnel, while in the Naval service, have engaged in one or more homosexual acts or where evidence supports proposal or attempts to perform an act of homosexuality."[6]

Calling differences in the gender of the participants in acts of sodomy a "refined distinction," the court conflated Doherty's oral sex with a female prostitute with homosexuality, suggesting that both indicate a "morbid sexual passion." With the authority of the federal government of the United States, the court declared that all acts of sodomy are *officially* homosexual acts, raising the stakes in the politics of identification made possible by the discovery of this new kind of homosexual person. All acts of sodomy could now be looked at anew, since sodomy, in this court's opinion, was a defining characteristic and symptomatic act of homosexuality.

Not surprisingly, this court decision, applicable only in the case of Seaman Doherty, never achieved widespread practice in the navy or in any of the other branches of the U.S. military. Heterosexual members of the navy could enjoy their "acts of oral perversion" just as they always had. It was only homosexuals, as Secretary of the Navy Instruction 1620.1 made clear, that the military wished to rid itself of.

In another contested discharge, navy procedures left no room for acquittal after allegation of homosexual acts. A form for Administrative Field Board hearings that determined whether a suspected homosexual should be retained by the service contained no provision for a finding of innocence. This Findings of the Board form instructed, "Use one or more of the following: ( ) Sexual Pervert, ( ) Committed Homosexual Acts, or ( ) Homosexual Tendencies."[7] According to the navy, it seems, anyone accused of homosexuality must at the very least manifest "homosexual tendencies."

In *Nelson v. Miller,* the case that brought attention to the Findings of the Board form, Kenneth Nelson succeeded in convincing the Administrative Field Board that he had been a victim of a sexual assault. The form's instructions, however, forced the field report examiner to check the selection marked "Committed Homosexual Acts." Despite an appeal in which board members complained that the form limited their options by not allowing any other possible finding, Nelson was subsequently discharged. The board's recommendation that Nelson be retained in the service was overruled because the form's overriding goal was to identify and separate anyone who was even suspected of homosexuality. Innocence was not a possible finding. Given that an anonymous letter of complaint or a well-placed rumor could, often did, and still can prompt an investigation into a service member's background, this was an unusually punitive measure, even by the military's draconian standards.

Prior to 1982, each branch of the service had regulations much the same as Secretary of the Navy Instruction 1620.1, which designated three levels of homosexual disqualification. Class I homosexuals were defined as "servicemen who have committed homosexual offenses involving force, fraud, intimidation, or the seduction of a minor." Class II homosexuals were "servicemen who have willfully engaged in, or attempted to perform, homosexual acts which do not fall under the Class I category." Class III homosexuals, the most interesting and discriminatory of these categories, were defined as "servicemen who exhibit, profess, or admit homosexual tendencies or associate with known homosexuals."[8] Separation from the military is the prescribed course of action for all three classes.

Both military and federal courts upheld these regulations for many years. In a 1981 case, *Rich v. Secretary of the Army,* the separation of an army man was upheld even though no acts of sodomy were proven. In the *Rich* decision, a U.S. District Court of Colorado admitted its inability to recognize the difference between the act of sodomy and a person's homosexual orientation, writing that "a statement that a person is homosexual or gay is different from a statement of gender identification" because the "latter refers to physical characteristics, but the former to conduct."[9]

Rejecting arguments that army regulations that exclude homosexuals "intrude into fundamental matters at the core of one's personality, self image, and sexual identity," the court ruled instead that although a "male may feel sexually attracted to another male without engaging in orgasm, just as a male may feel sexually attracted to a female without copulation, the justification for the exclusions of homosexuals are applicable regardless of the level of activity involved." Regulations that exclude homosexuals can be interpreted as "equally applicable to declamations as to deeds."[10]

In the *Rich* decision, the court acknowledged that both heterosexuals and homosexuals feel sexual desire for one another, but only homosexual desire is essentialized as an activity that defines the individual and an activity over which he or she will have no choice but to succumb. By equating homosexual desire with the prohibited activity of sodomy, this decision circumvents the First Amendment speech protection issues raised over a person's exclusion from service merely based on declarations of sexual identity or preference. It also posits heterosexual desire as the standard that has been violated.

Most interesting of all is the result of the development of the homosexual as a category of person. Despite the intent to help those who engage in sodomy escape persecution and punishment, *identity* and any acknowledgment of it now stands as a shortcut to proof of homosexual acts of sodomy without the evidence and proof that an accusation of sodomy would require for court-martial.

With all acts of sodomy perceived as homosexual acts and all homosexuals, regardless of "levels of activity," perceived as sodomites, the tautological reasoning is complete. The circularity permits exclusion from the military either for homosexual acts or for homosexual "being," because both are viewed as symptomatic acts; both are viewed as activities that indicate a criminal character flaw or defect, a diseased body, a disturbed personality, or a medical aberration that could endanger the mission of the military.

In light of the various regulations that stipulated different classes of homosexuality, the 1982 Department of Defense move to create one uniform *official* policy that would govern the dismissal of homosexual personnel was less a radical departure than a formal codification at the highest levels of practices and policies that each branch of the military had already written. On January 28, 1982, Casper Weinberger, Ronald Reagan's secretary of defense, issued the Department of Defense regulation that made even *declarations* of homosexual identity grounds for removal from all branches of the military. Department of Defense Directive 1332.14, which is applicable to all branches of the armed services, reads, "Homosexuality is incompatible with military service. The presence of such members adversely affects the ability of the Armed Forces to maintain discipline, good order, and morale; to foster mutual trust and confidence among the members; to ensure the integrity of rank and command; to facilitate assignment and worldwide deployment of members who frequently must live and work under close conditions affording minimal privacy; to recruit and retain members of the military services; and in certain circumstances, to prevent breaches of security."[11]

This Pentagon directive made homosexual orientation and homosexual desire, *regardless of the commission of any homosexual acts*, grounds for removal from the military. A stickler for bureaucratic thoroughness, the Department of Defense also took it upon itself to define homosexuality in the 1982 directive:

> (1) Homosexual means a person, regardless of sex, who engages in, desires to engage in, or intends to engage in homosexual acts;
>
> (2) Bisexual means a person who engages in, desires to engage in, or intends to engage in homosexual or heterosexual acts;
>
> (3) A homosexual act means bodily contact, actively or passively permitted, between members of the same sex for the purpose of satisfying sexual desires.[12]

Part C of the directive advises that "the basis for separation may include pre-service, prior to service or current service conduct or statements."[13]

On the face of it, the directive's instruction that makes a declaration of homosexuality at any time in one's life grounds for dismissal appears to be in blatant violation of the constitutional protection of freedom of speech guaranteed by the First Amendment. The fact that even declarations of sexual orientation made years before military service can be used as the basis for discharge from the military seems a grossly intrusive measure.

Historically, however, the federal courts have upheld the constitutionality of the military's limits on personal freedom, accepting the Pentagon's assertion that, because of the uniqueness of the military mission, the imposition of limits on the freedom of members is justifiable.[14] Even when challenging the military's discriminatory practices, the courts have acknowledged that the "military decisions by the Army are not lightly to be overruled by the Judiciary."[15]

Most important, for the first time in the history of the U.S. armed forces, a declaration of sexual orientation made at any time in one's life became legal grounds for removal from military service, shifting the emphasis from sexual acts to sexual identities in a significant way. Although less today than in the past, discharges from the military can impact life and employment opportunities, since the reason for discharge, shown clearly on the discharge form, is available to all prospective employers.

Beginning with the 1982 policy change, most service members discharged for homosexuality have received honorable discharges, but this was not the case in the past. There are five categories of discharge for military personnel: honorable, general, undesirable, bad-conduct, and dishonorable. The first three are given by administrative action; the last two are given only by court-martial. Only those who are discharged honorably are eligible for veterans' benefits, pensions, and reenlistment. The policy that governs the category of discharge for those who are dismissed for homosexuality has changed over time. In the 1940s and 1950s, homosexuals were either dismissed with an undesirable discharge or were court-martialed and dismissed with a dishonorable or bad-conduct discharge. In the 1960s and early 1970s, gay men and lesbians were most likely to be administratively dismissed, but with a general discharge. Today homosexuals usually receive an honorable discharge, but the discharge form lists homosexuality as the reason for dismissal. Military officials charged with implementing the new policy acknowledged that creating a policy that substituted declarations of identity for proven criminalized sex acts prohibited by the military's sodomy law was a problem. Officials argued against giving gay soldiers honorable discharges, because they worried that this would encourage false claims of homosexuality among troops who wanted to get out of military service.[16]

Discharges given to homosexual soldiers evolved over time, and in 1982 the Department of Defense issued new guidelines that instructed that homosexuals receive honorable discharges when separated from the military. Here we have one of the many examples that demonstrate clearly that power is never complete, never total; resistance springs from the fissures created from within the original relations of power. The military's policy of granting homosexual soldiers honorable discharges evolved as a way to avoid being consumed by the very machinations that the military employed to regulate sexuality. Having spent decades relying on the legal system to reflect society's bias against homosexuality, military policy was now forced to evolve, as gay men and lesbians made social and political advances. For decades, the courts had recognized that a less-than-honorable discharge carried with it a stigma, and, following the growth of the lesbian and gay political movement, the social and judicial climate in the United States had become more tolerant of homosexuality. Increasingly, courageous soldiers began to contest the classification of their discharges, forcing the Pentagon's hand in revising its policy.

However much the military's rhetoric suggests that it is immune to changes in social attitudes and public opinion, the task of proving service members unfit on the basis of little more than the accusations by others and then punishing them with anything less than honorable discharges became increasingly difficult for the federal courts. Scandals about sexual harassment of women soldiers by male superiors and bloated Defense Department budgets brought the military under increasing public scrutiny. These events, coupled with the fact that growing numbers of soldiers were now willing to contest their discharges, forced the Pentagon to try to minimize its chances of suffering a precedent-setting court defeat that would outlaw discrimination against gay men and lesbians. The Pentagon's strategy was to liberalize its discharge policy in an attempt to avoid the federal court system altogether. Until quite recently, honorable discharges were much less likely to be contested than any of the other category of military discharge. By granting honorable discharges to those identified as lesbian or gay, the military could accomplish its goal of separating homosexuals without creating as much risk of having the courts overturn this discriminatory policy. Power creates its resistance; resistance creates social and institutional change, and then power evolves again in attempts to mitigate the effectiveness of the resistance.

Anything less than an honorable discharge from the military might affect future employment prospects and the eligibility for veterans' benefits. It might officially "destroy the reputation of a decent woman"[17] or man. Even an honorable discharge could have a deleterious effect on the prospects for someone who had chosen a career in the military. The federal courts have recognized the power wielded by the armed services in the determination of fitness for continued service. Many court decisions have acknowledged the stigmatization that can result from receiving a discharge that is other than honorable.[18] In *Glidden v. United States*, a court held that "an undesirable discharge carries with it a definite stigma and other unfortunate consequences, such as loss of veterans' benefits."[19] The general discharge can have the same stigmatizing effect. Quoting from the air force's own regulation, the court rejected the arguments that a "general discharge under honorable conditions" was the same as an "honorable discharge." The opinion states, "The air force itself says that a general discharge may be a disadvantage to an airman seeking civilian employment." A general discharge received by a member of the military precludes his or her reenlistment.[20] Throughout the late 1960s and the

1970s, courts were becoming more critical of the military's use of the discharge to politically stigmatize service members in ways that would follow them into their civilian lives. The fear of a dishonorable discharge also worked to keep lesbian and gay members of the service in the closet in much the same way as did Clinton's 1990s Don't Ask, Don't Tell policy.

A 1981 case that concerned the discharge of Perry Watkins highlighted an egregiously political use of the military's policy of discharging lesbian and gay servicepersons that proved too blatantly discriminatory even for courts that have historically supported the military's right to govern itself. In the midst of a downsizing effort, the army had discharged Watkins, a gay man, after sixteen years of service. This, in itself, would not have been unusual; however, Watkins had openly admitted his homosexuality on army enlistment and reenlistment forms from the very beginning.[21] In 1990, Watkins won his lawsuit against the army when the U.S. Supreme Court refused to hear the case, leaving the lower court ruling intact.[22] The appeals court ordered the army to reinstate Watkins, because it had known about his sexual orientation for sixteen years before it began discharge proceedings against him. In a settlement with the army, Watkins agreed not to reenlist in exchange for a retroactive promotion, $135,000 in back pay, full retirement benefits, and an honorable discharge.[23]

The rate of military discharges during wartime provides more evidence of the political nature of discharge procedures. When the United States was at war and in need of troops, the military slowed its investigations and discharges of homosexual service personnel. In the late 1940s, the navy alone discharged more then 1,100 gay soldiers a year. In 1950, at the height of the Korean War, that number was down to 483. But by 1954, when the armistice had been signed at Panmunjom, the navy discharged 1,353 gay sailors.[24] The same was true during the Vietnam War. As Figure 1 illustrates,[25] when the need for soldiers was at its peak in the early 1970s, discharges for homosexual acts dropped off perceptibly, only to increase again after South Vietnam collapsed in 1975. Similarly, when the Department of Defense was looking to beef up its

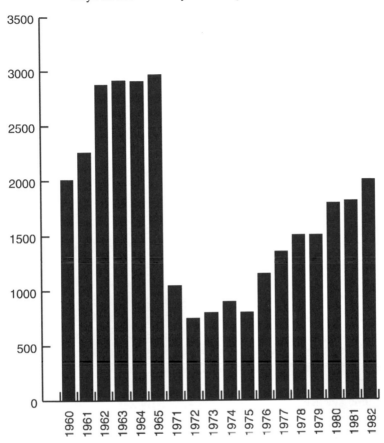

FIGURE 1   Military Discharges for Homosexuality, 1960–1982

troop deployments during the Persian Gulf War, it quietly put aside its decade-old policy of prohibiting gay men and lesbians from enlisting. It is estimated that more than fifty thousand gay men and lesbians served in the Gulf War.[26] Many active-duty personnel and reservists who hoped to test the gay ban "came out" to their commanding officers during this period and were told that they would not be discharged at this time and should prepare to be shipped out to the Persian Gulf. Many were also told that they were likely to be discharged when the war was over.[27] For example, according to Paul Di Donato, director of the gay public interest law firm National Gay Rights Advocates, a woman reported to the firm in mid-February 1991 that she had told her commanding officer she was a lesbian. The commanding officer responded by letter, saying that unless she could produce a marriage certificate to prove that she was legally married, the discharge regulation would not be enforced against her at this time and she should prepare to leave for the Persian Gulf.[28] Similarly, only days after the September 11, 2001, terrorist attacks on the World Trade Center and the Pentagon, the U.S. military suspended all discharges under the Don't Ask, Don't Tell policy.

An examination of military discharges between 1982 and 1992 also reveals the inconsistency with which the ban was enforced across branches of the military service. For example, although the Navy constitutes only 28 percent of the total military forces, navy personnel account for a whopping 51 percent of those discharged for homosexuality during this time period. Figures 2 and 3 show the relationship between the percentage of armed forces personnel by branch of service and the percentage of discharges for homosexuality by branch of service for the decade following the enactment of Department of Defense Directive 1332.14 in 1982.

Because women were already suspect in a military environment, servicewomen were hit particularly hard by this ban. Even a rumor of lesbianism has been known to start an investigation. Although women constituted only 10 percent of all military personnel between 1982 and 1992, they accounted for 23 percent of those discharged for homosexuality. In the marines, the branch of the armed services with the greatest reputation for machismo, women, who constituted only 5 percent of all corps personnel during the same period, accounted for 29 percent of those discharged for homosexuality.[29] There is little doubt that military women face greater scrutinization of their sexual lives than do men. One 1988 investigation at Parris Island, South Carolina, the only boot camp for female marines, resulted in the identification of seventy suspected lesbians.[30] "We've heard a lot of women say, especially aboard a big ship, if they're not willing to put out for sailors, they're accused of being a lesbian, whether they are or

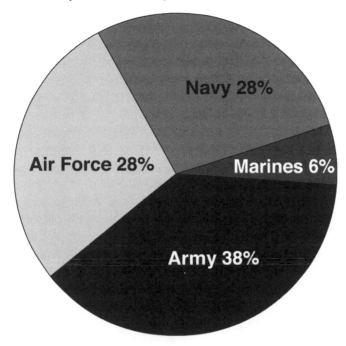

FIGURE 2   Percentage of Armed Forces Personnel by Branch of
Service, 1982–1992

not," commented Gerry Studds, a congressman from Massachusetts. "It's pretty brutal."[31] Lawrence J. Korb, an assistant secretary
of defense in the Reagan administration, echoed Studds's observation: "I think a lot of the initial inquiries about women are a result of their spurning men's sexual advances," he said.[32] It is clear
that the military's shift in focus from prosecuting homosexual acts
to policing gay and lesbian identities has made possible new avenues of investigation and regulation of people's personal lives.

Investigating Identity

Having made greater regulation possible by focusing on identity,
the military needed new apparatuses of control, surveillance, and
scrutiny. As a result, each branch developed its own investigative
arm: the Naval Investigative Service (NIS), the air force Office of

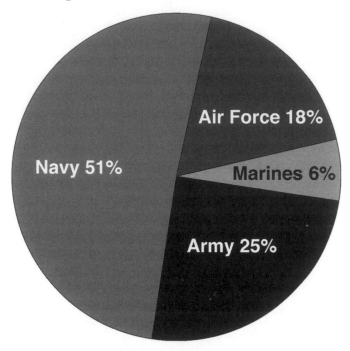

FIGURE 3   Percentage of Discharges for Homosexuality by Branch of Service, 1982–1992

Special Investigations, (OSI) and the army Criminal Investigation Division (CID). In 1990, the NIS alone employed over twelve hundred investigators—many of them civilians—endowed with wide-ranging and often unchecked authority.[33] The enforcement of the 1982 Pentagon policy directed at gay and lesbian identity was almost always not only cruel but also devoid of many constitutional safeguards that civilians take for granted in judicial proceedings. The majority of contested discharges that have involved military investigators demonstrate in the extreme how answering the policeman's hail of identity leads to the practice of identification.

In many of these cases, court documents record routine third-degree harassment of the discharged service member, sometimes involving handcuffing and interrogation under bright lights. As the sexual subject is transformed into the sexual suspect, more regulatory apparatuses are brought to bear in an attempt to extract an admission of *identity*. Often, the officer in charge threatened to reveal the soldier's homosexuality to friends, acquaintances, family members, and sometimes even a hometown newspaper. Others were threatened with the loss of custody of their children. Even civilians associated with military personnel are subject to harassment. For example, military officials threatened Marine Corporal Barbara Baum's civilian girlfriend with the loss of custody of her child. Succumbing to the pressure, she testified against Baum, who was sentenced to a year in military prison.[34]

Everything about a sexual suspect is grist for the identification mill. Air force officials discharged Captain Gregg Greely after they learned that he had led the June 1991 gay pride parade in Washington, D.C. Greely's discharge was put on hold while investigators attempted to force him to name other gay or lesbian air force officers. Greely refused to comply and was discharged on June 25, 1991.[35] Historically, the military has used the discharge as a form of coercion. A service person who agreed to give names of other known gays in his or her unit was promised an upgrade from a dishonorable discharge to a general discharge. Often service members would cooperate only to find that no such upgrade was forthcoming.

Service members identified by others as gay have often been coerced into signing "interview consent" forms, which allow them to be interrogated for hours without breaking for food or rest. In many cases, no legal counsel is provided (or is required to be provided) for those accused of a military crime. Service personnel have been subjected to such humiliations as anal cavity searches in full view of their colleagues. Even worse, during the Gulf War, when Marine Corporal Eric Barker's commander found out that he was gay, he sent him into a war zone without ammunition.[36]

Civilian investigators often frequent gay bars in search of military personnel. Danny Leonard, owner of Friends, a gay bar near Camp Lejeune in Jacksonville, North Carolina, told a *New York Times* reporter that military investigators accompanied by the sheriff regularly park across the street from the bar and pull people over as they leave. A twenty-nine-year-old staff sergeant at Fort Meade, Maryland, reported that after he visited a Texas bar that was popular to both homosexuals and heterosexuals, he was summoned by army investigators. Counting on cooperation between military and civilian authorities, they had apparently tracked him down by jotting down his license plate number while cruising the club's parking lot. "They dumped it on me that I was a homosexual, [that] they had witnesses, and that I should sign a paper saying so," said the sergeant. "I was so scared, I was almost sick. They treated me like I was a criminal, but presented no evidence. It was guilt by association." When the sergeant refused to sign the document, the investigators were forced to drop all allegations.[37] The military's gay bar raids have not always been successful, however. The owner of a gay bar near the naval base in Norfolk, Virginia, reports that surprise visits by NIS investigators stopped several years ago. "Usually we had a call from the base telling us they were coming," said the bar owner. "Homosexuals are everywhere in the military."[38]

Successful or not, the military bar raids raise constitutional questions that have never been fully explored. In 1991, owners of gay bars in San Antonio, Texas, reported that local military police, often assisted by San Antonio city and Bexar County law enforcement officers, blocked exits from gay bars while military police searched the premises for armed forces personnel. Any service members found were arrested for being in an off-limits area.[39] By enlisting the support of civilian authorities to block entrances and prevent patrons from leaving, the military has assumed powers over and denied civil liberties to gay and lesbian civilians in gross violation of constitutional guarantees against search and seizure.

These actions by military investigators make Judge Terry Hatter's 1993 rebuke of the navy seem much more than mere rhetorical ire. When the navy refused to follow his November 11, 1992, order to reinstate Petty Officer Keith Meinhold, pending the outcome of his challenge to the military's gay ban, the angry judge declared, "This is not a military dictatorship." He gave the navy two days to reinstate Meinhold, or be held in contempt of court.

"It is not the former Soviet Socialist Republic," the judge went on. "Here, the rule of law applies to the military."[40]

Even so, the military sometimes appears to disregard the fact that law and justice apply to its governance of personnel. Georges Clemenceau once observed that military justice is to justice as military music is to music.[41] There is much evidence that justice often takes a back seat to more pressing military concerns. In the national debate over gays in the military that raged for months during 1992 and 1993, little was reported about military practices in the identification, investigation, treatment, and separation of gay and lesbian service personnel. And in the years that followed, the investigation of soldiers continued unabated by Clinton's new Don't Ask, Don't Tell, Don't Pursue policy.

In 1999, struck by the failure of his policy to halt the persecution of gays in the military, President Clinton called the implementation of the policy "out of whack."[42] After documenting years of continued harassment under the Clinton policy, Secretary of Defense William Cohen charged the services to prepare training programs that would explain to military investigators the limits of their investigative powers under Clinton's policy. Still, resistance to gay men and lesbians in the military ran deep. In yet another clear indication that power is never total (even when we might want it to be), the Marine Corps took Cohen's directive as an opportunity to create a detailed manual on how to discharge gays from the service under the new policy.[43]

As it turned out, Clinton's Don't Ask, Don't Tell policy, although a failure in almost all respects, focused increased public attention on the abusive practices employed by the U.S. military to find and remove gay and lesbian soldiers. Following the well-publicized murder of Private First Class Barry Winchell—who, after months of harassment, was bludgeoned to death with a baseball bat by other members of his Fort Campbell, Kentucky, army unit—Cohen undertook a study of harassment of gay soldiers.[44] In 1999, the Department of Defense added "Don't Harass" to the description of its policy regarding gays in the military.[45] Although the resulting attention made it increasingly difficult for the military to turn a blind eye to harassment of and by its own personnel, the military was slow to implement any true training to neutralize gay harassment. When it was added at all, as in the case of the army, it came in the form of "two slides in the end of training on the overall anti-gay policy."[46]

Not surprisingly, the military looked inward in its efforts to revive an investigatory apparatus that would be more immune from public scrutiny. Turning again to the new institutions that first officially produced and constructed the "homosexual" as a part of military discourse, the military revitalized a clever apparatus of detection, investigation, and scrutiny. In 1999, for example, despite the new Don't Harass policy and the new training initiative, "psychologists, Inspector Generals, law enforcement personnel, equal opportunity representatives, commanders and others believed that they [were] required to turn in gay people seeking their help."[47] After asking each branch to create training that instructed gay people to seek help when they are harassed, the military enjoined the personnel who were set up to provide assistance to be a part of the disciplinary apparatus to remove homosexuals from the service. Interestingly, the original discourses of sin, medicine, and psychiatry discussed in Chapters 2 and 3 return simultaneously as locations for the recruitment of gay men and lesbians who seek help and as locations for the identification and removal of gay and lesbian service personnel.

Military chaplains, for example, often berated the soldiers who came to them to report that they had been victimized by antigay harassment. Some also advised service members to turn themselves in and face discharge. Similarly, inspectors general, charged with the task of investigating the harassment of gay soldiers for six years after the Don't Ask, Don't Tell policy took effect, took it upon themselves to turn in soldiers for discharge if the harassment investigations showed them to be gay.[48]

Medicine and psychiatry were also brought into the regulatory apparatus. Psychiatrists for the military have also reported that they have been instructed to turn in gay, lesbian, and bisexual military members who seek professional mental health care.[49] In a covert operation that one could find only in the military, officials have allowed erroneous instructions to circulate to mental and medical health care officials. When this was brought to light in 1999, the military refused to inform health care providers not to turn in gay members; in fact, the navy sent instructions to health care providers that they could anonymously submit the names of patients known to be gay, through a web site set up by the U.S. Navy.[50]

Often, the military's practices have been so abusive, intrusive, and disrespectful of human rights that they have threatened the principles of the U.S. Constitution, the same Constitution that members of the military have sworn to defend. These are principles that cannot be taken lightly. The provision of procedural rights to those accused of crimes, the guarantee of civilian control over the military, and the notion of a rule of law that applies equally to everyone are examples of concepts that distinguish a democratic from a nondemocratic regime.

For an example of the military's lack of respect for these principles, we need look no further than the activities of the Joint Chiefs of Staff—the military's top officers who advise the president on military matters—during the early days of the Clinton administration. In what the *New York Times* called an "angry challenge to the administration," which "surprised and dismayed" Pentagon officials with the "intensity of [their] reaction,"[51] the Joint Chiefs openly rebelled against their superior—President Clinton—over his plan to lift the ban that made the presence of gay men and lesbians in the military illegal. Lobbying members of Congress and inviting the public to call the White House and their members of Congress to express their opposition, the Joint Chiefs installed additional telephone lines for the purpose of tallying calls from the citizenry in their own unofficial survey. There were rumors and accusations that the Joint Chiefs leaked these telephone numbers to conservative political organizations days before they were made public, artificially inflating the opposition to Clinton's plan, which they then used to suggest that Clinton's proposal was unpopular among citizens.[52] Once the telephone numbers were publicized, officers who answered the phones in Joint Chiefs of Staff Chairman Colin Powell's offices often attempted to persuade those who called for the purpose of expressing their support for President Clinton that lifting the ban would be "disastrous for the military."[53]

Even more worrisome than the challenge to civilian control over the military was the relative lack of protest and outcry generated by the actions of the Joint Chiefs of Staff. Theirs was a move almost without parallel in U.S. history. Having found a directive from its commander in chief distasteful, the military entered the political arena in an attempt to influence the outcome of a political decision and in the process dauntlessly trammeled the tenuous safeguards that provide for civilian control over the military.

This challenge to the commander in chief—the only elected official in the military command structure and the only direct substantive and symbolic link between the military and the people it serves—would have met with a very different public response had the Joint Chiefs so openly and disdainfully challenged presidential authority on almost any other issue. The fact that gay men and lesbians were the target of this military insubordination made it acceptable in a way that it would not otherwise have occurred.

Indeed, when the media examines the activities of militaries in other countries that challenge their democratically elected governments, it never hesitates to label them "military coups" or at the very least "attempted coups." Back at home, however, the fact that the president of the United States, the commander in chief, together with his secretary of defense, was forced to negotiate with the military over a public policy decision was met with only minimal protest and concern by the public and the media.

Emboldened by the lack of public outcry against its prejudicial and discriminatory practices, the military has demonstrated a dangerous willingness to take on its civilian superiors on this issue. Only days after Clinton's election and a news conference on Veteran's Day in which he reaffirmed his intention to lift the ban against gay men and lesbians, the naval ROTC announced that it would require all ROTC midshipmen to sign a new affidavit agreeing to discharge and repayment of scholarship awards if recognized as homosexual. Although the military services and service academies had for years required their members to report whether they were homosexual and whether they had ever engaged in homosexual activity, the new navy affidavit seemed to reinforce the policy at the moment when the president-elect had pledged again to end the ban. The new policy also surpassed the preexisting policy in its specification that the navy intended to recoup education and training costs for any officer discharged for homosexuality.[54]

Willing to take on their commander in chief, the members of the Joint Chiefs of Staff extended their campaign against Clinton's proposal to end the gay ban, complaining that the presence of homosexuals would undermine military discipline and good order and adversely affect the integrity of rank and command. The Joint Chiefs were nonetheless willing to risk such insubordination themselves in their "angry challenge" to presidential authority. Unconcerned with their own behavior and unrepentant in their attitude of insubordination toward Clinton, one of the Chiefs, speaking to the *New York Times* (on the condition of anonymity) boasted, "We feel we're in a position to convince the President that this would be the wrong decision."[55]

Setting the tone for this debate from the top, the actions of the Joint Chiefs of Staff reverberated through the chain of command, sending the word that it was acceptable for all military personnel to give voice to their fear, ignorance, and hatred of gay men and lesbians.[56] In many ways, the Clinton policy resulted in increased violence toward gay men and lesbians in the military: As the military launched its war to deter the Clinton policy, homosexuals became military targets. The policy that sought to change the practice of discharging gays because of their identity instead made identity the battleground in the military's war against homosexuals.

Challenges to the Ban

In the early 1990s, with voices from within the military testifying to the effectiveness of gay and lesbian military personnel and with discrepancies in the way that the ban was being enforced becoming more widely criticized, the military's antigay policy became one of the sites of normalization where lesbians and gay men could argue—sometimes successfully—that the ban was discriminatory on its surface because it excluded this new form of person: the homosexual. The political response to the ban was, of course, an essentializing one, as critics of the military ban used the same language and understandings of sexual identity to contest the military's policy. Service members were no longer being separated because of what they did but because of *who* and *what* they *were*. In this respect, it would appear, the acceptance of identity's hail and the minority politics that it makes possible have proved to be at least a partially successful strategy.

For the few years before Clinton's attempt to lift the ban against gays in the military, the courts too had been questioning the military's policy. In August 1992, a three-member panel of the Ninth Circuit Court of Appeals acknowledged that "past rulings upholding the ban were based, at least in part, on acceptance of the prejudice of others."[57] Writing for the court, Judge William C. Canby stated that "a blanket policy of discrimination cannot be upheld in the absence of any supporting factual record," and he demanded that the army demonstrate, on the record, that its ban is rationally related to a "permissible government purpose."[58]

In *Meinhold v. Secretary of Defense,* Judge Hatter wrote, "Gays and lesbians have served, and continue to serve the United States military with honor, pride dignity and loyalty." "The Department of Defense's justifications for its policy banning gays and lesbians from military service," he concluded, "are based on cultural myths and false stereotypes. These fictions are baseless and very similar to the reason offered to keep the military racially segregated in the 1940s."[59]

The Defense Personal Security Research and Education Center (PERSEREC), a Defense Department think tank, reached the same conclusion in its 1988 study. It noted that the major justifications for excluding homosexuals "employ precisely the same arguments used against blacks and women before they were integrated into the armed services—namely that their inclusion is contrary to 'good order and discipline.'"[60] A 1940 War Department statement read, "The policy of the War Department is not to intermingle colored and white enlisted personnel. This policy has been proven satisfactory over a long period of years, and to make changes would produce situations destructive to morale and detrimental to the preparations for national defense."[61]

Despite this comparison's resonance with essentialist models of sexuality, many refused to accept it. General Powell, for example, then chairman of the Joint Chiefs of Staff and an African American in an institution where African Americans are still grossly underrepresented in command positions, rejected it.[62] David Hackworth, a retired army colonel and the most decorated living U.S. veteran, agreed with Powell, saying, "It's an insult to Afro-Americans that they're being lumped into this thing. The argument [of those attempting to lift the ban] is 'Look: What you're saying was applied to blacks.' That's mixing apples and oranges. We're talking about a cultural bias vs. a biological impulse."[63]

But, as the 1982 Department of Defense ban made clear, the sexual impulses of on-duty service personnel were not all that the military sought to regulate. *Identity* rather than *behavior* had become the new focus of scrutiny. Opening doors to an *official* examination of deeds, declarations, organizational memberships, or reading material, this shift created new forms of regulation with dire consequences for those who identified with or were identified by the hail of "homosexual." Any supposed sign of this sexual identity would be grounds enough to remove a person from the military, regardless of any proven or committed sexual acts.

Even activists who resisted the ban did so, as we will see, in amazingly essentialized ways, despite the failure of essentialism to bring greater social tolerance and understanding to homosexuals when it was deployed by nineteenth-century sexologists. And despite the lack of success of essentialist arguments in earlier policy debates that governed the military's treatment of homosexual soldiers, essentialist arguments would continue to be deployed by those who sought to overturn the military's gay ban.

5

Gaze in the Military

Competing Perceptions of Gay Performance

HISTORICALLY, the bonds between tender comrades in the service of their nation's military have been celebrated rather than demonized. In 1993, for example, David Cohen instructed *New York Times* readers that although the Spartan armies had been regarded with awe and fear in classical Greece, it was the Thebans who crushed the Spartan army at the battle of Leuctra. The Thebans had been led by an elite troop of three hundred warriors composed of pairs of male lovers and their beloved youths. Cohen explained that it was believed that the presence of erotic love between two soldiers increased morale and combat effectiveness, because neither lover nor beloved would ever break ranks and run away, thereby disgracing himself in the eyes of his lover. "Hundreds of years after Plato and Xenophon," said Cohen, "the historian and moralist Plutarch praised the valor of the Theban unit, the scared Band: 'Some say that this band was composed of lovers and beloved. A band that is held together by erotic love is indissoluble and unbreakable.'"[1]

Plutarch's argument, introduced so many years later to thousands of loyal readers of the *New York Times,* is interesting not simply because it made possible a different reading of a contemporary dilemma regarding lesbian and gay participation in the armed forces. It also presents a different economy of sex, a different set of epistemological discourses that gave order to sexual and romantic pleasures in an ancient civilization, for the lovers and their beloved of Plutarch's account could not be said to be gay regardless of their sexual practices. Identity had not been imposed so thoroughly and systematically on sexual desire and pleasure. It would be left to modernity to issue the summons of sexual identity that would come to surpass acts and practices and cohere around thoughts, desires, and declarations.

The process of interpellation described in the previous chapters has contributed to the creation of, and reaction to, a new type of person: the homosexual. This medicalized category of being provided new sites of regulation as the officials of the State began the serious task of guarding public safety and decency. Simultaneously, it allowed for new sites of resistance. Defined as homosexual by the regulatory agencies of religion, medical science, and psychiatry, the homosexual began to speak for him- or herself, asserting against these regulatory powers a new understanding of identity: the gay male or lesbian subject. These new subjects controverted the terms of the discourse and fought against the epistemological systems that had first given the homosexual birth.[2] Developing new forms of relationship, new cultures and subcultures, even a new political and moral ethos, gay men and lesbians have made great strides as a political and social minority. This transformation into a discrete political minority is based on an understanding of sexuality as identity, and even as the political struggle for rights ensues—attempting to overcome the epistemological systems that have given birth to the lesbian and the gay man —the path to this political equality is always already determined. In each struggle for lesbian and gay equality, the same epistemological systems that first defined the "homosexual" stubbornly cling to the *official* representations of lesbians and gay men. These systems implicitly and often explicitly structure the terms of the discourse for these debates and frame both the way that lesbians and gay men are seen and the path toward liberation that they must take to make any progress toward equality as newly constituted State subjects. The arguments *for* equality will take the form of arguments *against* the discursive constructions of the homosexual as subject to the policeman's hail. Again, the best example comes from the military. The public debate that took place in 1993 when President Clinton attempted to change the personnel policy that prohibited lesbians and gay men from military service demonstrates how a shift from acts to identities, from behavior to being, from choice to essence opens the doors to greater State regulation, even as it opens a path to greater freedom and equality for lesbian and gay subjects.

The debate in 1993 focused on the Pentagon ban promulgated in 1982, which covered all branches of the armed services and declared that "homosexuality [was] incompatible with military service."[3] At this point, however, every branch of the service had had policies that excluded homosexuals in place for nearly 40 years. Department of Defense Directive 1332.14 was thus less a radical new policy departure than a formal codification of existing practices. It made explicit what has always been implicit in the gap between the strict reading of Article 125 (which makes no mention of homosexuals or homosexual identity) and the interservice regulations issued by each branch of the armed services (which do): The making of gay identity has created new avenues for regulation as it allows all homosexuals to be constructed as sodomites, and, by definition, as guilty of criminal violations of Article 125. Still, the justifications for keeping the 1982 policy that bans homosexuals from military service served to focus the debate that took place in U.S. society. The debate distilled the litany of justifications articulated by moralists, physicians and psychiatrists, policymakers, and the military and civil courts that upheld the policies, and it provided the frame through which we were to view the military's justifications. For those opposed to Clinton's 1993 proposal to end the military ban against lesbians and gay men, this was an all-out, no-holds-barred war. To win this war, however, it would be necessary to win the hearts and minds of the U.S. public, and the military's spokespeople focused their efforts on articulating every nuance of the Department of Defense's claim that "homosexuals interfered with the military's ability "to facilitate assignment and worldwide deployment of members who frequently

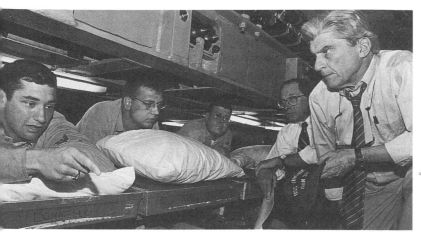

FIGURE 4   Senators John Warner and Sam Nunn aboard the
Montpelier, May 11, 1993 (Jose Lopez/NYT Pictures)

must live and work under close conditions affording minimal privacy."[4] One noteworthy example was the U.S. Senate Armed Services Committee's carefully staged 1993 visit to the navy submarine *Montpelier* as part of the committee's hearings on whether to lift the gay ban. The photograph that subsequently appeared on the front page of the *New York Times* (see Figure 4) made manifest the "close conditions" and "minimal privacy" better than any policy ever could have, even without depicting the area that caused the most persistent fear: sharing bathroom facilities with gays.

This concern over sharing intimate space emerged as a major issue for the public, as local talk shows that held discussions about gays in the military were flooded with calls from people who voiced concern that "straight" soldiers might have to shower with gay men.[5] The discussions also tended to eclipse lesbians, as not a single objection was ever raised by either a woman or a man about the dilemma of having lesbians shower with straight women. This lack of focus on women helped to obfuscate the disproportionate scrutiny of lesbians by the military.

Both the scrutiny and its obfuscation represent the same cultural oversight of women, a virtual inattention to the sexuality of women—an oversight common with many of the physicians who first issued the policeman's hail "Hey, you there" to those who pursued desire that was not sanctioned by society. Often their attention was focused exclusively on male sexual "perversion." But as women asserted rights that men had assumed to be their exclusive privilege, this inattention turned to greater scrutiny. This is understood best by the notion embodied in the practice of "congressional oversight," as greater regulation would ultimately mean greater demonization, which would serve to justify women's exclusion from male privilege. Seen in this light, the intensive efforts by the military to root out lesbians and the exclusion of women from much of the debate about lifting the military ban both rely on the construction of "woman" as Other, ill suited for the rigors of such citizenship duties as voting and participating in military service. So completely eclipsed from the frame were women that they need not be mentioned when discussing the issue of lifting the ban against homosexuals. But this removal of women from the frame also obfuscates one of the military's most offensive abuses of its power, as the lesbian witch-hunts constitute a great part of the efforts to uncover homosexuals and discharge them from the military.

Still, this explains only women's absence from the "bathroom brawl"; it does not explain the irony implicit in the scenario of men—practiced in combat, capable of acts of heroism, and willing to face death in the defense of their country—going to the showers terrified by the prospect that gays may await them there. Showering in front of gays provokes a homophobia that runs deeper than mere modesty; it is a homophobia that subverts the sovereign subject position that most men assume to be their inherent birthright. To threaten this is to threaten their very status as men. In fact, much the same overreaction is present in gay bashing and gay panic episodes in which straight men—and it is almost always straight men and not women—sense that their privilege is at risk.

Psychologists long ago discovered that indiscriminate killing on the scale that war demands requires a dehumanization of the enemy. This process, called objectification, allows soldiers to treat other human subjects, as "objects," alleviating those in combat of the moral and societal strictures against killing. During wartime, entire nations are objectified to facilitate killing. In the early history of our nation, Native Americans were constituted as savages, allowing their genocide and confinement on reservations with only minimal collective cultural guilt. But the creation of Otherness is not limited to wartime. In the not too distant past, slaves were routinely beaten if they dared to meet their masters' eyes. In fact, for years following their emancipation, blacks in the South faced abuse if they returned the gaze of a white citizen.

Today, as many African Americans will attest, white Americans habitually avoid eye contact when they pass them on the street. Without the absolute power to control another human being, the gaze is now transformed into a kind of panopticon of blank stares that seem to be looking at but are often looking past or through those who are different. The original panopticon worked as a form of behavioral control because those submitted to the gaze were never quite sure whether anyone was looking into their prison cells through the two-way-mirror tower posted at the center of a circle of cells surrounding it. On the street, the practiced "blank stare" acts as a kind of two-way mirror, hiding people's feelings, attitudes, even acknowledgments behind a nonseeing stare that refuses to admit respect, equality, or even humanity.

Women, too, have been subjected to the power of "the gaze." Traditionally, deferring to the authority of men—be it the father, the husband, or the stranger—meant diverting one's eyes. To fail to do this even today is seen as a sign of a woman's sexual interest. Whereas a man can stare at a woman without consequence, a woman who stares at a man is considered "loose," morally corrupt, not at all the kind of "girl" you would bring home to Mother.

Sexually, an unspoken agreement exists among men that they should not turn "the gaze" on one another. Men, as the subjects of culture, are not to be objectified. In fact, a man who maintains eye contact with another man for too long renders himself sexually suspect. In the hypermasculine atmosphere of military culture, the hysterical cries of soldiers on the way to the showers has given voice to this fear/desire: the perceived subversion of the privilege of objectification that benefits white heterosexual men at the expense of all who are different. Gays in the shower undermine "morale, good order, and discipline" by turning this process of Otherness creation upside down. The presence of gays threatens the straight serviceman's position as masculine subject—the creator and consumer of objectified images, be they women, slaves, or enemies of the nation. Chapter 3 quotes twenty-year-old airman Jason Alexander, who told a *New York Times* reporter, "We're all crammed together in the showers, and I don't want to worry that some gay guy is staring at me." He recognized the stakes involved in the stare of this "gay guy." So, too, did his fellow airman who lamented to the same reporter, "Now how am I going to feel if I walk into a dormitory and see pictures on the wall from *Playgirl* magazine?" He would feel, no doubt, as many women have felt for years when subjected to the very same objectification. The rhetorical excess in which this debate was mired was not really caused by gays in the military. Rather, it was a struggle over who gets to control the "the gaze" in the military.

Attesting to the persistence of the constructions of the homosexual discussed in Chapter 3 is the military's unswerving insistence that "homosexuality is incompatible with military service," despite overwhelming evidence and arguments to the contrary. Often issuing from the military establishment itself, this evidence usually fully accepts the essentialist understanding of sexuality as identity and, having done so, sets out to make the case that homosexuals are equal to their heterosexual counterparts in every way. The path to equality in this sense is one that demonstrates that lesbians and gay men are every bit as able, competent, and trustworthy as heterosexuals.

In 1957, the *Report of the Board Appointed to Prepare and Submit Recommendations to the Secretary of the Navy for the Revision of Policies, Procedures and Directives Dealing with Homosexuality* addressed one of the principal justifications for the ban against gay men and lesbians: that their sexuality makes them more susceptible to blackmail by enemy agents and spies, who may threaten to reveal their sexuality. Called the Crittenden Report after the chairman of the board, Captain S. H. Crittenden Jr., its findings were, to say the least, a surprise to the navy. The report concluded:

> The concept that homosexuals pose a security risk is unsupported by any factual data. Homosexuals are no more a security risk, and many cases are much less of a security risk, than alcoholics and those people with marked feelings of inferiority who must brag of their knowledge of secret information and disclose it to gain stature. Promiscuous heterosexual activity also provides serious security implications. Some intelligence officers consider a senior officer having illicit heterosexual activity with the wife of a junior officer or [the wives of] enlisted men as much more of a security risk than the ordinary homosexual. . . . The number of cases of blackmail as a result of past investigations of homosexuals is negligible. No factual data exist to support the contention that homosexuals are a greater risk than heterosexuals.[6]

Not finding the conclusions of this study to its liking, the navy suppressed the report for twenty years, until a court order finally forced its release.[7] Twenty-five years after the report was first submitted, and with no new evidence to contradict its findings, the 1982 Defense Department Directive took it upon itself to include the explanation "to prevent breaches of security" among its summary of reasons that "homosexuality is incompatible with military service."[8] By the end of his tenure as secretary of defense, even Dick Cheney would admit that this particular justification for the ban was "a bit of an old chestnut."[9] In fact, in November 1992, Cheney told Clinton (then president-elect) that the Department of Defense's policy was "just a quaint little rule, but we're not going to change it."[10]

In 1988, a second study conceived, financed, and overseen by the Department of Defense reached a similar finding. Conducted by the Defense Personnel Security Research and Education Center (PERSEREC), the study found that homosexuality "was unrelated to job performance, in the same way as is being left- or right-handed."[11] Like the Crittenden Report before it, the PERSEREC report was suppressed by the Pentagon. In fact, the report was not made public until Congressional Representatives Gerry Studds of Massachusetts and Patricia Schroeder of Colorado received copies anonymously and released it to the press in October 1989. Included with the report were Pentagon memos that chastised the PERSEREC researchers for their findings. The memos directed PERSEREC to rewrite the report to remove all claims that homosexuals are suitable for military service.[12] A second PERSEREC report, released by Studds and Schroeder at the same time, found that "homosexuals also showed better preservice adjustment than heterosexuals" as well as "greater levels of cognitive ability than heterosexuals."[13]

A fourth report, a $1.3 million study conducted by the Rand Corporation, also concluded that the ban could be lifted without adversely affecting the "order, discipline and individual behavior necessary to maintain cohesion and performance."[14] Commissioned by the Pentagon, the Rand Corporation study was completed in the Spring of 1993 but, again, was withheld by the Pentagon until Democratic senators threatened to hold up the following year's defense appropriations bill if the study was not made public. The report was released in August, apparently timed carefully to ensure the least publicity. As one National Gay and Lesbian Task Force spokesperson claimed, August is the month when "no one in government is around."[15] Also, by August, the highly sensationalistic U.S. Senate Armed Services Committee hearings on the issue of allowing lesbians and gay men to serve openly in the military had wound down, having culminated in a committee tour through the cramped quarters of a U.S. Navy warship.

Each of the four reports, authored by officials from within the Department of Defense, cast doubt on the Pentagon's assertion that "homosexuality is incompatible with military service." In fact, the last report indicated that homosexuals made better soldiers than heterosexuals.[16] This opinion was echoed, albeit at cross-purpose, by Vice Admiral Joseph S. Donnel, commander of the navy's surface Atlantic fleet. In a 1990 memorandum to the officers in charge of nearly two hundred ships and forty shore installations in the eastern half of the United States, Donnel characterized lesbians as generally "hardworking, career-oriented, willing to put in long hours on the job, and among the command's top performers."[17] Ironically, Donnel's description was not intended to endorse lesbians who served in the navy. Rather, it was formulated to help senior officers identify lesbians among their crew for the purpose of investigation and discharge from the service. What each of the four reports has in common is its acceptance of the category of "homosexual being," a category of people whose performance can be measured and compared to that of their heterosexual counterparts.

In 1992, a General Accounting Office (GAO) report could find no rational basis for the military's ban. The report concluded that "no reasons to support this policy exist, including public opinion and scientific evaluations of homosexuality. If a more tolerant attitude were enforced, it would lead to better functioning of all."[18] The GAO report also attacked the ban as costly and ineffective. Relying on information provided by the Department of Defense, the report stated that between 1980 and 1990, 16,919 servicemen and -women had been discharged for homosexuality. Adjusting for inflation, the cost of recruiting and training replacements for these discharged service members was placed at $498 million.

Documenting an amazing waste of person power and money, the GAO report tells only half the story. The Defense Department acknowledged to GAO researchers that the figures used for numbers of discharges for homosexuality did not include gay men and lesbians who had been separated under other categories of misconduct. Department of Defense officials also admitted that coterminous with the adoption of the 1982 gay ban local military commanders were given greater flexibility in discharging personnel under other categories. The most likely practical effect is that, as a way to avoid being "outed" by the military, many more gay and lesbian servicepersons who were separated because of their sexual orientation were persuaded by commanders to accept discharges under regulations unrelated to sexual orientation.

The GAO's financial estimates are limited as well. The report notes that the GAO was "not able to calculate the original investment cost of training and compensation, the cost of investigating alleged or actual homosexual cases, or the cost of out-processing servicemen and women who have been identified as homosexual."[19] When these estimated costs are added in, the total increases significantly. One estimate puts the cost of the Pentagon policy at three to four times the number suggested by the GAO report.[20] Expenses in military readiness and financial costs aside, if the objective of the Department of Defense policy was to ensure that there were no gay men and lesbians in the military between 1982 and 1993, it was ineffective, as any within the military realize. One navy admiral, speaking on the condition of anonymity, told a *New York Times* reporter, "We know we have a certain number of gays performing extremely well, but they're in the closet, and as long as they stay there we're fine."[21] Having accepted the hail of identity that first made it possible to create new ways to organize life, the regulation of that identity—the way that it was put into the law—now made it necessary to hide that very identity.

Collectively, these *official* studies and reports cast serious doubt on the military's claim that "homosexuality is incompatible with military service." Yet those who opposed lifting the gay ban employed the power of the three previously discussed epistemologies of homosexuality to frame the lesbian or gay man not as the "hardworking career woman willing to work long hours on the job," or as the dedicated serviceman ready to lay down his life for his country, but rather as the uncontrollable chicken hawk, the militant predator, and the diseased pervert.

The justifications for excluding gay men and lesbians from the military have evolved over the past decade. As many of the seven reasons set forth in the 1982 Defense Department Directive that declared homosexuality "incompatible with military service" have been controverted (often by the military's own reports and personnel), new reasons have been contrived to justify the need for this policy of exclusion.

The latest of these was set forth by the Joint Chiefs of Staff in their meetings with the Clinton officials. Maintaining that the presence of homosexuals would wreck morale, they added that gays would undermine unit cohesion and recruiting, force devoutly religious members of the military to resign, and increase the risk of the transmission of AIDS to heterosexual troops.[22] General Powell and senior navy officials complained about lack of privacy on combat ships, where all male crews are squeezed into triple bunks during six months at sea. Other officers opposed to the policy claimed that heterosexual service members would feel uncomfortable sharing group showers with homosexuals or a dance floor at a military social club next to a homosexual couple.[23]

These new justifications suggest that an interesting strategy shift had occurred for those who argued to keep the ban in place. In the past, justifications had focused on the activities of gay men and lesbians and why they were a threat to national security and combat readiness. In 1993, the new explanations focused on how the presence of gay soldiers would affect their heterosexual counterparts.

One interesting explanation offered was that homosexuals increase heterosexuals' risk of contracting AIDS. As recently as November 1991, that justification was not part of the Pentagon's repertoire. In fact, on November 7, 1991, while listening to oral arguments in a case that challenged the Pentagon's policy, Judge Oliver Gasch surprised attorneys by inviting them to quote statistics indicating that the incidence of AIDS among gay men is greater than among the general population. Attorneys for Midshipman Joseph Steffan declined to comment, and the navy's lawyers admitted that concern about AIDS was not part of the Pentagon's rationale for the ban.[24]

That would not stop Judge Gasch, however, from denying Steffan's reinstatement, writing that because of AIDS, "the exclusion of homosexuals from the armed forces constitutes a reasonable step toward the protection of those forces' health." He concluded that the Pentagon ban "is rational [because] it is directed, in part, at preventing those who are at the greatest risk of dying from serving. The interest we have as a nation in a healthy military cannot be underestimated."[25] Fifteen months later, the threat of HIV infection was among the reasons cited by the Joint Chiefs for keeping the ban in place. This claim is made more interesting in light of the fact that the military has mandatory HIV testing for all potential service personnel. Anyone who tests positive for HIV is excluded from enlisting. In addition, all active duty personnel are retested every six months, and those who test positive are reassigned to noncombat positions, where they are not likely to incur injuries that would require emergency medical treatment on the battlefield. These policies are, perhaps, overcautious, since the incidence of HIV infection among military personnel is well below that of the general population.

A military training film shown to all inductees emphasizes the importance of safe sex and the use of condoms to protect them from HIV infection and other sexually transmitted diseases. This film, interestingly, never mentions homosexuality—after all, official policy dictates that there are no homosexuals in the military. Exclusively heterosexual in its safe sex instructions, the military admits in this training film that AIDS is a concern for heterosexuals, and they should therefore take precautions to protect their health. Yet, when the military formulates reasons that gays should be excluded, it cites the increased risk of HIV infection that the presence of homosexuals would impose on heterosexuals in the military. Following this rationale, the military would do well to encourage the enlistment of lesbians, whose statistical risk of HIV infection is much lower than any other group in the population.[26]

By tapping into the stereotypes of lesbians and gay men that were based on the epistemologies of sin, medicine, and personality defect, the military was able to frame the debate in a way that all but guaranteed the outcome. Leaving little "wriggle room" for a president who lacked credibility as a military leader, the result of the national frenzy started by Clinton's campaign promise to lift the ban was his Don't Ask, Don't Tell, Don't Pursue policy, which walked an uneven line between sexuality as *acts* and sexuality as *identity*. This current policy and the way that the "professional" lesbian and gay political movement are implicated in its adoption are the subject of Chapter 6.

6

Don't Kiss and Tell in the Military

Gay Politics and the Clinton Compromise

CLINTON'S ATTEMPT to lift the military ban provided political drama for weeks. Pressure groups, both pro and con, organized White House and congressional telephone and letter-writing campaigns. Even the Joint Chiefs of Staff, in efforts that bordered on insubordination and the subversion of civilian authority over the military, entered the political process unabashedly, lobbying members of Congress behind the scenes and opening up their phone lines for public comment.[1] The organized opposition came from conservative religious groups and other members of the political right. The Reverend Louis Sheldon of the Traditional Values Coalition boasted that his group's numerous calls virtually shut down the telephone lines at the Capitol, and Oliver North made public pleas for money to stop the Clinton plan.[2]

Clinton had underestimated the depth of homophobia. Delighted conservative and evangelical Christian organizations said they could not have written a scenario more to their liking for Clinton's first weeks in office.[3] "It's a bonanza for building organizations and raising money; the fundraising letters are already in the mail," claimed one Christian right organizer.[4] Emotions ran high on both sides of the debate. In an attempt to depict the Democratic Party as the party of "queers," Republican Party Chairman Haley Barbour charged that Clinton had acted "not because of principle but as a political payoff to a very powerful special inter-est group of the Democratic Party."[5]

At the end of the political firestorm, Clinton's now infamous Don't Ask, Don't Tell, Don't Pursue compromise with the mili-tary emerged. Doing little to revise the 1982 Department of De-fense directive, the policy stated that "applicants for military serv-ice will not be asked or required to reveal their sexual orientation" but "service members will be separated for homosexual con-duct."[6] Homosexual conduct, defined by the policy more broadly than ever before, included "homosexual acts, or statements that demonstrate a propensity to engage in homosexual acts, or a ho-mosexual marriage or attempted marriage." According to the pol-icy, statements "by a servicemember that he or she is homosexual or bisexual creates a rebuttable presumption that the service-member is engaging in homosexual acts or has a propensity or in-tent to do so. The servicemember has the opportunity to present evidence that he [or she] does not engage in homosexual acts and does not have the propensity to do so." The policy also directed that "no investigations or inquiries will be conducted solely to de-termine a servicemember's sexual orientation. . . . Sexual orien-tation, absent credible information that a crime has been com-mitted, will not be the subject of a criminal investigation."[7]

What on paper may appear significant changed very little in practice. The new policy left it to military officials to determine what constitutes "credible information" and whether a service member had completely rebutted the assumption that his or her sexual orientation was a statement about his or her intent to com-mit sexual acts. The effect in practice has been continued investi-gation, identification, harassment, and discharge of lesbians and gay men in the military. The biggest change was the elimination from all enlistment and reenlistment forms questions about sex-ual identity. In fact, however, servicemen and -women are often still asked these questions in direct violation of both the spirit and the letter of the regulation.[8] Investigations into the private lives of service members have continued long after the policy change. In-deed, as we saw in Chapter 5, following the Clinton policies, the military has implemented a wider net of detection, often instructing chaplains and medical and psychiatric care providers to violate client confidentiality and turn in service members who report antigay harassment. Lesbians and gay men have always been allowed to serve as long as they were closeted. Clinton's policy did nothing to reduce the hundreds of military and civilian investigators in the military's employ who conduct investigations into any allegations of a service member's homosexuality. It did nothing to curtail the routine military police raids on lesbian and gay bars near military bases.

Recent reports suggest that lesbians and gay men are being discharged at nearly the same rate as before the policy went into effect. Figure 5 illustrates the total number of service personnel discharged for homosexuality from 1990 to 2000. In 1992, the number of military discharges dropped perceptibly as a result of the

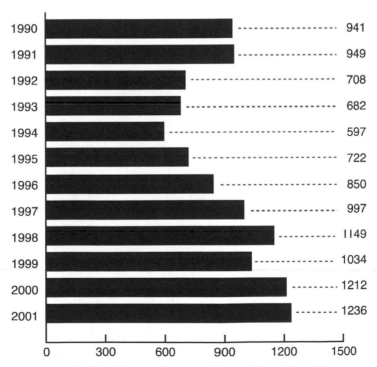

Year	Discharges
1990	941
1991	949
1992	708
1993	682
1994	597
1995	722
1996	850
1997	997
1998	1149
1999	1034
2000	1212
2001	1236

FIGURE 5   Total Lesbian and Gay Discharges from the Military, 1990–2001

Persian Gulf War. Even after Don't Ask, Don't Tell, Don't Pursue, hundreds of lesbians and gay men were discharged from the military despite their apparent compliance with the policy's new guidelines. In 1994, Dixon Osburn—spokesperson for the Servicemember's Legal Defense Network (SLDN), an organization based in Washington, D.C., that provides legal services to lesbian and gay members of the military—observed that "military commanders are finding it very easy to get around the new policy."[9] Indeed, with investigators striving to ensure that they have all the evidence necessary to prove that a service member has committed homosexual acts before bringing up charges, the witch-hunts and persecution of lesbians and gay men have only intensified.[10]

Under Don't Ask, Don't Tell, Don't Pursue, women continue to be subjected to a disproportionate share of the discharges. Constituting 13 percent of the present military force, women represent 21 percent of the discharges for homosexuality from 1993 to 2000. As illustrated in Figure 6, the biggest changes under the Don't Ask, Don't Tell, Don't Pursue policy are the increased number of air force discharges compared to the decreased or relatively stable numbers of discharges in the other branches of the service. The air force, once known as the least homophobic branch of the military, was responsible for an increasing percentage of all gay discharges in the 1990s. By contrast, discharges of lesbian and gay navy personnel dropped over the same time period. Following the murder of Barry Winchell by fellow service members, discharges in the army skyrocketed, as many gay men and lesbians who were frightened for their lives reported incidences of harassment, only to become the subjects of investigation themselves. The cost of these discharges to taxpayers is estimated at more than $200 million between 1993 and 2000 alone.[11]

Most disturbing of all has been the military's violation of its own policies as set out by Don't Ask, Don't Tell, Don't Pursue. The SLDN has documented hundreds of abuses in the years following the policy's enactment.[12] Military officials continue to question those under investigation about their sexuality (in violation of Don't Ask), continue to discharge individuals based on

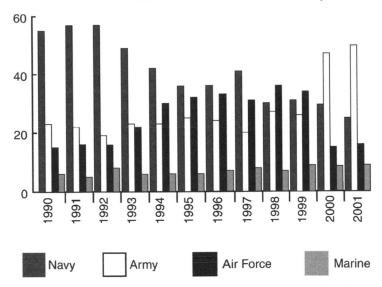

FIGURE 6   Percent Share of Discharges under Gay Policy for All
Services, 1990–2001

confidential statements to chaplains and physicians (in violation of
Don't Tell), and continue to initiate witch-hunts against lesbians
and gay men, launching investigations into service members'
backgrounds without credible evidence that they are lesbian or
gay (in violation of Don't Pursue).[13]

Do as We Say, Not as We Do

In 1999, a fourth piece—Don't Harass—was added to the Penta
gon's Don't Ask, Don't Tell, Don't Pursue policy. Following a period in which the military fought long and hard to keep gay and
lesbian servicepersons out of the armed forces, the increased attention directed new waves of hatred at anyone in the military
who was suspected of being gay or lesbian. As previously indicated, little positive change resulted from the 1993 policy. What
did change was that enlisted personnel and officers both understood that their commanders did not want gay men and lesbians

in the military. Seen as political rather than military, the national debate over lifting the ban against gays in the armed forces had the long-lasting effect of making any service member who was suspected of being gay or lesbian an even greater target than before. Often targets of investigations, now gay men and lesbians were increasingly considered fair game by fellow soldiers.

After two vicious murders of military men by fellow service members, one in 1992 and one in 1999, it seemed evident that, having more than failed to create real change, the Clinton policy had seemingly created a more dangerous environment for gay men and lesbians in the military. On July 5, 1999, as we recounted in Chapter 4, Private First Class Barry Winchell was beaten to death with a baseball bat by a fellow soldier with whom he had had an altercation. Winchell's murderer was motivated to kill him because he believed that Winchell was gay. Although testimony from fellow soldiers indicated that Winchell had faced gay harassment daily from both peers and supervisors, the army suggested that the murder was not a gay hate crime. Having been routinely called "fag," "faggot," and "queer," Winchell had been asked by his supervisors, in direct violation of the Don't Ask policy, whether he was gay. In fact, Winchell was asked "if he took it up the ass or in the mouth," and one of the men responsible for his death told him, "I will make you my bitch."[14]

Winchell's murder was directly responsible for Secretary of Defense Cohen's addition of Don't Harass to the Clinton policy. But, again, with no real will to enforce the policy, harassment continued unabated. In the years from 1999 to 2000 more than fourteen hundred documented cases of antigay harassment were reported.[15] And although the policy was initiated in August 1999, it would be a full year before each of the branches of the service began to implement Don't Harrass.[16]

The federal district courts have been divided in their opinions regarding the new policy. In the early 1990s, two struck it down as unconstitutional and two upheld it. The appellate courts, however, have been unanimous in their support of the new policy, reversing district courts when necessary to uphold the policy. Similarly, the U.S. Supreme Court, demonstrating its agreement with the appellate courts' decision to follow the tradition of allowing the military a wide berth in its regulation of personnel issues, has refused to hear a number of these appeals.[17]

The Gay Politics of the Military Ban

Clearly, a place in the military is not at the top of the wish list for most people in the gay community. Greater funding and awareness for AIDS; the Employment Non-discrimination Act; and a federal civil rights law for lesbians, gay men, and other sexual minorities are all issues with the potential to generate more excitement among the movement's grass roots. Although a "military project" has for years been part of the organizational structure of the National Gay and Lesbian Task Force, the decision to make this issue part of Clinton's compensation for the gay community's support in the 1992 election was not made by the gay community. Indeed, it was not even made by the leaders of the nation's lesbian and gay political organizations, most of whom realized that the gay community's support for lifting the ban might be a mile wide but was only an inch deep. The decision was made instead "by gay people inside the Democratic Party and businessmen who came out only recently and positioned themselves as power-brokers for a community they do not know and cannot represent. But, as 'Friends of Bill' they have access to the White House and an inordinate influence on policy."[18] These political insiders—called Homocrats by lesbian activist Sarah Schulman—were, like many others in the early days of the Clinton administration, virtual political newcomers to Washington. In an interview following the publication of his book *Conduct Unbecoming*, journalist Randy Shilts recounted a conversation with some of these Homocrats: "I talked to people who were involved in the Clinton Campaign—and these are relatively sophisticated people—and I remember right after he got elected in November, I said, "Well, of course this is going to be a very big deal," and they said, "What he's going to do is to come in January and issue his five or six executive orders and slip this in the middle of the pile and nobody will notice." And I just thought, My God, what planet are you people living on? It's such an archetypal conflict, of course it's going to be a huge deal!"[19]

Although they did not control the political agenda, the lesbian and gay political organizations share responsibility for the failure that became Don't Ask, Don't Tell. Their enthusiasm for candidate Clinton seemed undeserved, given his lackluster support of lesbian and gay issues prior to his election, and that enthusiasm translated into greater trust and a greater benefit of the doubt than Clinton deserved. For example, in his June 1992 letter to Human Rights Campaign Fund (HRCF) members, Executive Director Tim McFeeley explained his organization's decision to support Clinton for president despite the fact that the HRCF had ever endorsed a candidate for president before: "Bill Clinton and Bill Clinton alone has clearly and unequivocally articulated positive stands on the issues. . . . In the past several months, Bill Clinton has met with lesbian and gay groups and AIDS activists. He has incorporated our agenda and our goals into his own." If elected, the letter suggested, Bill Clinton would be a president who would use "whatever means necessary" to eradicate AIDS, a president who would advocate for the national lesbian and gay civil rights law, and a president who "with the stroke of a pen" would not only "end the exclusion of gays and lesbians from the U.S. Military [but also] end discrimination in federal employment based on sexual orientation."[20] Having naïvely built up Clinton as the president who would lead lesbians and gay men to the promised land, McFeeley and other political leaders of the lesbian and gay community were caught up in a political drama for which they were ill prepared. Having placed almost idealistic hope in Clinton, they were slow to warm to the task of countering the massive grassroots lobbying campaign initiated by those who supported the ban.

As late as March 26, 1993, only days after Clinton suggested that he would be willing to accept restrictions on the kinds of duty lesbian and gay servicepersons could perform, Tom Stoddard, director of the Campaign for Military Service (CMS), excused the president's comments. Still steadfastly clinging to his belief that Clinton would lift the ban, Stoddard said, "In the end, the motivation for and circumstances of Clinton's comments don't matter. What does matter is that the president reaffirmed his commitment."[21] A fledgling organization formed specifically to help overturn the ban, CMS was long on flash and short on grass roots. Although it helped transform the 1993 March on Washington into the "khaki" siege of D.C.—its posters, volunteers, and petitions could be found throughout the city during the weekend of the march—the signatures of marchers did not translate into real political heat in the form of letters and calls to members of Congress.

In May 1993, Congressman Barney Frank, who had been admonishing the gay community for weeks that the activist efforts of its members were falling short on Capitol Hill, infuriated the Washington gay rights organizations when he proposed his own Don't Ask, Don't Tell, Don't Pursue compromise. The compromise suggested that the military refrain from (1) asking service members their sexual orientation, (2) investigating their sexual orientation, and (3) following up on the activities of servicemen and -women while they were off base, off duty, and out of uniform. "With less than two months to go before Congressional committees begin voting on this," Frank explained, "I believe we have to face a stark fact: if the choice before the Congress is instant equality or a statute which enacts the complete ban into permanent law, Congress will choose the latter."[22]

Frank's compromise drew sharp criticism from the National Gay and Lesbian Task Force, the HRCF, and the CMS. He had formulated his proposal without consulting any of them. Stoddard was especially displeased, claiming that Frank's proposal undermined the CMS's fundraising and lobbying efforts: "Barney has created the impression on the part of gay people that we can't possibly get what we want on this issue anymore and that leads to a sense of despair. The danger is that people will stop giving money and lobbying their members of Congress because they will think we can't possibly get any more out of Capitol Hill."[23]

Although Frank's methods left much to be desired—splitting the gay community away from the political organizations responsible for the bulk of the lobbying on the issue—his instincts were probably correct. The national gay and lesbian organizations are incapable of creating the kind of constituent pressure required to counter their better-organized opposition. A spokesperson for the HRCF admitted that whereas that organization is able to generate a maximum of thirty-five thousand letters, Pat Robertson's Christian Coalition regularly generates more than one hundred thousand letters.[24]

Even if the Washington political organizations had been better organized and better prepared, had had a role in setting the agenda, and had been able to keep the squabbling among themselves to a minimum, they could have accomplished little more on the issue. Clinton, after pledging his support, dropped out of sight, leaving the lesbian and gay community to lobby both Congress and the U.S. people simultaneously, a task that proved too difficult for a still young and underfunded political movement. Attempting to change the military industrial complex and its congressional allies, one of the strongest iron triangles in the national government, would challenge even the most powerful and sophisticated political movement. Without the committed and active support of the president, there was never much chance that lesbians and gay men alone could bring about this change.[25] Clinton's refusal to expend presidential energy on this issue aside, most lesbians and gay men did not consider military inclusion the best issue on which to expend valuable political and financial capital. Many in the community quietly grumbled when the March on Washington for Lesbian, Gay, and Bisexual Equality was transformed almost overnight into a demonstration over the military's ban against homosexuals. This was not the march that many people had planned to attend, and the national circus over gays in the military that it became was certainly not the march that had been in preparation for months.

More important, the gay political leadership, and especially the Homocrats, had misunderstood the depth of the ambivalence of many in the community that they purported to represent. Lesbians and gay men on the political left, many of whom had only recently protested against the Persian Gulf War, wanted no part of an effort that had at its heart support for military efforts that they abhorred. Barbara Smith articulated what many leftists felt:

> Given the U.S. military's role as the world's police force, which implements imperialist foreign policies and murders those who stand in their way (e.g. the estimated quarter of a million people, mostly civilians, who died in Iraq as a result of the Gulf War), a progressive lesbian and gay would at least consider the political implications of frantically organizing to get into the mercenary wing of the military industrial complex. A radical lesbian and gay movement would of course be working to dismantle the military completely. . . .
>
> Thankfully, there were some pockets of dissent at the April march, expressed in slogans like: "Lift the Ban—Ban the Military," and "Homosexual, not Homicidal—Fuck the Military." Yet it seemingly had not occurred to movement leaders that there are lesbians and gays who actively opposed the Gulf War, the Vietnam War, military intervention in Central America and apartheid in South Africa.[26]

Many more moderates, gay and straight alike, who believe passionately in equality for lesbians and gay men were uncomfortable with the idea of the military as the organization that would determine and define notions of citizenship and equality. Hence, many in the lesbian and gay community were unsympathetic, although reluctantly so. With a divided gay community and a critically detached progressive straight community on one side and a well-organized, well-financed coalition of antigay conservatives, religious right organizations, and military careerists on the other side, the battle was lost before it had even begun.

In point of fact, this battle is merely a microcosm of the difficulties faced by the lesbian and gay political movement today. Far too easily co-opted by political insiders, the movement's real goals of equality for all sexual minorities and an end to homophobia and discrimination often take a back seat to political insiders' desires for the movement to be clean-cut, respectable, and moderate. Essentialist understandings of lesbian and gay identity are widespread in other policy areas where lesbians and gay men seek legal redress and acknowledgment by the State. The Althusserian policeman's hail of identity, once easily understood as a form of address that was problematic, has been taken up as the cause célèbre of the lesbian and gay community.

7

Becoming Identity

Public Policy, Gay Identification,
and the "Queer" Response

JEAN ELSHTAIN'S 1982 article "Homosexual Politics:
The Paradox of Gay Liberation," one of her only forays into the
area of gay politics, begins as follows: "There is a specter haunt-
ing homosexuality: the specter of gay liberation. For to the extent
that the aims of the gay liberation movement are attained, the
homosexual, as he presently defines himself, will disappear. The
conditions which, for example, place him outside his society and
furnish a basis for critical detachment, will have been washed
away in the flood tide of a new order."[1] Always provocative, Elshtain is also interesting as someone who often represents mainstream public opinion about issues of sexual identity but is
squarely in the liberal camp on issues of gay rights and equality.
In this regard, her work can serve as a foil that illuminates the
many problems of the liberal position with regard to gay equality.
As gay men and lesbians have answered the Althusserian hail, as
they have become subjects of the State and of State regulation,
their identity as a discrete minority has been ensured. It is this
State identification of the category "homosexual" that has helped
make a reverse discourse possible, as members of the category
have begun to speak for themselves and, in doing so, have begun
to remake the category for gay and lesbian subjects. In this remap-

ping of the category, however, one fact seems evident: The acceptable and mainstream gay position—the liberal position—is one that seeks equality as sameness and, in the name of respectability, papers over or jettisons difference.

In this regard, the regulation of homosexual identity is still operating in the discourse that advances the cause of gay and lesbian rights. Bound to that which is rejected, arguments for gay equality often begin with the contestation of the negative discourse that has circulated in society and in the official records of the State. We have seen examples of this contestation when soldiers have challenged the U.S. military's discharge policy, first in military and then in federal courts. The approach of gay men and lesbians who seek inclusion in the military, and in general the approach of many who seek to change discriminatory laws and regulations, has been to make arguments about suitability, professionalism, even normalcy. The problem with this strategy is that the pursuit of such a liberal politics of inclusion makes the objects of the discourse—gay and lesbian individuals—part of the very apparatus for their continued regulation. An examination of Elshtain's article on gay liberation best illustrates this argument.

While I was teaching a course in gender and politics, I became reacquainted with Elshtain's article, which explores the paradoxes inherent in a 1970s gay "liberation" movement that sought to destroy the very society that had given gay politics birth. Elshtain makes many interesting claims, but my renewed interest stemmed as much from student reaction to the article as from the article itself. With amazing unanimity, my students, many of them gay and lesbian, vilified the article and its author. Despite Elshtain's repeated endorsement of equality, civil rights, and protection against discrimination for gay men and lesbians, they dismissed many of her subtle and complicated arguments as "homophobic." But strangely, my students also rejected the liberationist arguments, which brought them much closer to Elshtain's position than they realized or cared to admit. I find myself asking why the liberationist voice presents such a challenge to heterosexuals and homosexuals alike. In its reexamination of Elshtain's arguments against gay liberation, this chapter demonstrates why I believe her arguments to be flawed and why I believe that both Elshtain and contemporary gay men and lesbians would do well to listen anew to the voices of gay liberation and proceed more cautiously with the essentialist-centered strategy that is dominant in gay and lesbian political movements today.

Paradox and Perversity in Gay Liberation

Elshtain's arguments against gay liberation have a familiar ring. The phantom that haunts homosexuality has relatives that haunt other political movements as well. In 1991, a specter haunted feminism: "The specter of difference constructed as a principle designed to trump all other principles, pops up everywhere these days."[2] Indeed, if one accepts Elshtain's accounts, all movements for social change seem to be plagued by wraiths and apparitions out to change the world. The interesting fact is not that Elshtain had been seeing ghosts for over a decade but the way that she conjures up these spirits to frighten us all about the world that we will inhabit should society come to reflect the goals of these social movements. Her rhetoric is always provocative and often disturbing (and in the specific case of gay liberation, sometimes distorted), and it has the effect of demonizing any efforts to question or challenge the traditional institutions of heterosexuality, marriage, and family.

Elshtain's exploration is based on a number of liberationist texts written mostly by gay men, including Dennis Altman, Stuart Byron, Edward Delph, Richard Goldstein, John Murphy, Carl Whitman, and Allen Young.[3] Yet her attempt to distill a single gay liberationist voice from many often misrepresents authors' ideas about what gay liberation means. Elshtain's gay liberationist is a straw man assembled from bits and pieces of many different intellectual and theoretical works. The result is a nightmarish Frankenstein monster that represents her fears about gay liberation rather than the liberationists' own dreams of how to change an oppressive society. Gay liberation rejected the social enforcement of heterosexuality, marriage, traditional gender roles and family arrangements, and sexual privacy and was built on an understanding of sexual identity as something other than fixed.

For example, Young argued that enforced heterosexuality was an evil caused by a sexist culture "to protect the power of straight men."[4] Whitman was less philosophical than Young and more stridently to the point, claiming that "exclusive heterosexuality is fucked up" and adding that "it reflects a fear of people of the same sex, it's anti-homosexual, and it is fraught with frustration."[5] A liberationist group called the Radicalesbians articulated how this enforced heterosexuality affects a typical lesbian who often finds herself in "painful conflict with people, situations, the accepted ways of thinking, feeling and behaving, until she is in a state of continual war with everything around her, and usually with herself." This turmoil "tends to induce guilt proportional to the degree to which she feels she is not meeting social expectations, and/or eventually drives her to question and analyze what the rest of her society more or less accepts."[6]

The rejection of heterosexuality was tied to similar disavowals of marriage, family, and sex roles. Martha Shelly argues that gay liberationists are "women and men who from the time of our earliest memories have been in revolt against the sex role-structure and the nuclear family structure." She asks other gays to get in touch with "the reasons that made [them] reject straight society as a kid," remembering that for her it was a vow never to be like the "vacant women drifting in and out of supermarkets." She concludes that "straight roles stink" and wonders, "Is love possible between heterosexuals?"[7]

Attacks on the sex roles and the social institutions of marriage and family are common in the liberationist literature. Whitman writes, "Traditional marriage is a rotten, oppressive institution . . . a contract which smothers both people, denies needs and places impossible demands on both people."[8] Young continues this criticism:

> The nuclear family, with its man-woman model built in by the presence of parents, is the primary means by which this restricted

sexuality is created and enforced. Gays experience rejection by the family in a society where familial love is considered important. The family oppresses women and children as well as gays. The phenomena of runaway teenagers and increasing divorce rates are signs of the erosion of the nuclear family. Gay liberation is another sign. We attack the nuclear family when we refuse to get married and have a family. We are committed to building communal situations where children can grow strong and free.[9]

Young goes on to say that for gay liberationists the social institutions of marriage and family were suspect, in need of redefinition if not total elimination, because like heterosexuality, they were part and parcel of the society that oppressed lesbians and gay men by rendering their lives and loves invisible.

The enforced privacy that surrounded all discussions of homosexuality in the 1950s made "getting the facts" a "mission impossible" for adolescents. In newspapers and magazines, on radio and television, in the movies, there "wasn't the slightest affirmation of homosexuality" if the "subject ever made an appearance" at all.[10] Mostly, Young tells us, there was nothing. He also criticizes the liberal, straight notion that sexuality is "essentially a private matter," arguing that this has perpetuated "male supremacy and patterns of dominance which are basically sexist and which are in the end anti-homosexual."[11]

The Radicalesbians, too, complained that "often at an extremely early age [a lesbian was] forced to evolve her own life pattern, often living much of her life alone, learning usually much earlier than her 'straight' (heterosexual) sisters about the essential loneliness of life (which the myth of marriage obscures)."[12] In a passage that Elshtain criticizes, Byron summed up best what many lesbians and gay men experience as a result of the rigid enforcement of a privatized sexuality: "One is, after all, oppressed as a homosexual every minute of every day, inasmuch as one is restrained from acting in ways that would seem normal to a heterosexual. Every time one refrains from an act of public affection with a lover where a straight couple would not—in the park, on the movie line—one dies a little. . . . *Everything* in society—every movie, every billboard, everything done as second nature in public—reminds the gay person that what he or she is is unnatural."[13]

Although perhaps somewhat utopian in their outlook, the liberationists merged their personal insights and experiences of oppression with a rapidly expanding body of feminist and Marxist-feminist theory, creating powerful criticisms of the institutions of heterosexuality, marriage, family, and privacy. Many of these criticisms are still relevant today, as many young lesbians and gay men continue to face oppressive home environments and abusive families when their sexual identity is discovered. At least today this sad fact is widely acknowledged as a problem by both straights and gays. What continues to be as radical today as it was in the 1970s is the liberationists' understanding of what it means to be "gay," what constitutes lesbian or gay *being*. Young wrote that "the artificial categories 'heterosexual' and 'homosexual' have been laid on us by a sexist society" and that "every straight man is a target for gay liberation."[14] The Radicalesbians argued that "lesbianism, like male homosexuality, is a category . . . possible only in a sexist society characterized by rigid roles and dominated by male supremacy."[15] Shelly claimed that the "function of a homosexual is to make [heterosexuals] uneasy." Demanding understanding from "straights," she argued that they could provide this only "by becoming one of us." Thus, one of the goals of gay liberation was "to reach the homosexuals entombed in [heterosexuals], to liberate our brothers and sisters,"[16] to "free the homosexual in everyone."[17] This belief that sexuality was the product of a sexist society and that heterosexuality and homosexuality were two equally oppressive social roles was a sophisticated theoretical argument then and remains so now.

Many of the liberationist ideas are contained in the contemporary social constructivist understanding of sexuality. There is an important difference, however, between the theories of the gay liberationists of the 1970s and the theories of the social constructivists of the 1990s: the issue of choice. Although it is all but impossible to find a social constructivist who would equate social constructivism with choice, the liberationists argued that gays and straights alike needed only *choose* to be gay to make it so. Far from simplistic, this position seemed carefully developed to help create anxiety and provoke reflection among the members of the heterosexual majority, who then had to give a second thought to their sexuality and the social institutions that support it. If Elshtain's response to the liberationists is any indication, they were successful in this goal.

Elshtain begins her analysis of gay liberation with the worried claim, "The idea that homosexuality can and should become the basis from which present social institutions are assaulted and through which a new, liberated social order will arise is heady brew on which the organized gay movement appears to be drunk."[18] Attacking this liberationist vision on a number of fronts, she calls gay liberation the nightmarish fantasy of oversexed *men* who wish to make "anonymous sex our individual and social anodyne."[19] No self-respecting woman—lesbian or straight—would accept the politics of gay liberation. More important, however, she argues that the gay liberation agenda is bad for "us" (read: straights) and bad for "them" (read: gay liberationists and, at times, all gay men and lesbians). It is bad for "us" because the liberationists have "no vision of a democratic politics, or a participatory commonweal, no sense of social goods or purposes," which leads to an "over-personalized politics and an over-politicized personal identity being fused to create a situation where everything is grist for the public mill."[20] For gay liberationists themselves, liberation is bad, she suggests, because, if successful, it would "culminate in the withering away of the group in behalf [of which] its efforts are being mounted."[21] These are complex and complicated arguments that need elaboration in greater detail.

In a footnote to her opening salvo, Elshtain tells us that she refers to "the homosexual as 'he' advisedly," as most of the authors she targets for criticism are homosexual men. Despite her disagreement with lesbian feminists elsewhere,[22] here they are posited as defenders of hearth and home and traditional values:

> There are many fewer lesbian liberationists who accept the promise of a future society in which all distinctions have been eliminated, long term relationships repudiated, and polymorphous perversity on demand legislated into existence—utopia according to

the Marquis de Sade. (Though some believe that groovy goodness will reign and all nastiness will have been eliminated.) Lesbian feminists have, with some exceptions, been quick to recognize the Playboy "philosophy" lurking behind much male gay liberation. One also finds in lesbian discussions not only acceptance but endorsement of long term ties, of coupling and creating homes.[23]

Of course, many lesbians joined in the liberationist attack on traditional structures of marriage and family and argued against the very values and institutions that Elshtain credits them with defending. Writers like Shelly and groups like the Radicalesbians developed far-reaching criticisms of traditional social practices and institutions. So, too, did Karla Jay, one of the editors of *Out of the Closets: Voices of Gay Liberation,* a text that Elshtain cites often in "Homosexual Politics." Jay writes that lesbians and gay men are "the negation of heterosexuality and of the nuclear family structure."[24] In addition, many male liberationists who believed that heterosexual marriage and family were problematic concepts did not think that sex on demand was the answer. The liberationists were more diverse and more sophisticated than Elshtain's analysis would indicate. For example, although Young's rejection of heterosexuality includes the declaration that to be gay means to be "sexually free," he explicitly negates Elshtain's characterization of the *male* liberationist position as one driven by sex. Since becoming a liberationist, he adds, he "has [had] sex less often but finds it infinitely more satisfying."[25] He advises that this "sexual freedom is not some kind of groovy lifestyle with lots of sex, doing what feels good irrespective of others. It is sexual freedom premised upon the notion of pleasure through equality, no pleasure where there is no equality."[26]

The ideas for gay liberation described by these authors, all of whom Elshtain includes in her analysis, may indeed sound frightening to those invested in traditional relationships of marriage and family, but they are hardly the writings of the Marquis de Sade. In fact, Elshtain's alarm notwithstanding, the liberationist vision of politics usually sounds both democratic and egalitarian. Elshtain's claim that gay liberation is really a front for other, more pernicious, causes is perhaps the most interesting and the most revealing criticism that she offers.

Elshtain's remaining objections center on two major points: the importance of a clear boundary between the public and the private and the necessity of sex roles and social institutions. Elshtain's attack on the way that gay liberation's political agenda will adversely affect "us" is in significant part an attack on *all* politics that violate her belief in the necessity of maintaining a separation between what we think of as public and what we think of as private. Ever mindful of the liberal commitment to privacy, she writes, "Pseudo politics of the sort I have in mind, and of which gay liberation is but one example, begins and ends in a stance in which private preferences get couched as public imperatives *simpliciter.*"[27]

Because this mingling of the public and the private violates one of Elshtain's fundamental principles, she begins her critique of gay liberation as she always begins, "by affirming some distinction between public and private activities and identities."[28] Her rigorous regulation of this buffer between the public and private is to save politics itself, as well as to save each of us from ourselves and from one another. In *Public Man, Private Woman,* Elshtain writes, "If a thinker incorporates the private realm of family into a total politicized structure of explanation, and flattens out all distinctions between what is public and what is private, the following dilemma necessarily emerges: if all relationships and activities, including our most intimate ones, are political in their essence, if politics is everything and everywhere, then no genuine political action and purpose is possible, as we can never distinguish the political from anything else."[29]

According to Elshtain, the major dilemma presented by gay liberation is that its "key imperative . . . *is* the erosion of any distinction between the personal and the political,"[30] opening the floodgates to greater State control, public regulation, and social coercion. According to Elshtain, the liberationists imagine themselves "a revolutionary vanguard" out to alter human nature itself, leading to a politics that would unleash a "terrible engine of social control." "This quest for absolute freedom," she tells us, "ends in absolute terror."[31]

This Jacobin terror is the bogeyman that always awaits those taken in by political movements haunted by Elshtain's specters,[32] but gay liberation's terror in Elshtain's eyes is uniquely perverse, ending ultimately with the public sanctioning of the sexual abuse of children. Including members of the North American Man/Boy Love Association in her nightmarish vision of who the gay liberationists are, she claims that these "maximal liberationists" seek to end the existence of "laws governing the age of consent . . . or *any* constraints at all on sexual acting out." She asserts that gays will claim that they are oppressed "within this frame of reference, until society provides both the opportunity and the assurance of safety for adult gays—and one must assume heterosexuals—who wish to take young people under sixteen, with no limits, for their sexual partners."[33]

Elshtain's second concern about gay liberation is related to the first. She imagines a paradoxical set of circumstances in which gays will desire to destroy the very society that gave birth to their identity. This is a paradox, Elshtain argues, because gay liberation turns out to be bad for the very group in whose name liberation is sought. This paradox is one inherent in the liberationist ontology. Among gay liberationists, she writes, there is a tacit recognition that homosexuality "exists as an internal margin or boundary in contemporary American society and is called into being *by* that society." Comparing homosexuality to adultery, the allure of which rests at least partly on its status as "forbidden fruit," Elshtain writes that "homosexuality remains an existential choice, a distinctive identity, *only* within a wider social system in which gays provide an identity for themselves and their group by 'negating' the norms, standards, and way of life of the culture's heterosexual majority." Heterosexuality, then, "provides homosexuality with its dialectic opposite and gives homosexuality its special fascination and claims to uniqueness."[34]

The thrust of Elshtain's criticism is that *if* homosexuality is a choice made possible by a certain historical alignment of social institutions and traditional familial arrangements, as is claimed by the liberationists, then an attack on the society that has helped define homosexuality and has made its organization as a political group possible is an attack on homosexuality itself—a kind of collective, subconscious, masochistic cry of mea culpa that renders the political goals and objectives of homosexuals untenable if not nonsensical. Of course, Elshtain believes that this is a big *if* and (revealing her own discomfort with gendered or sexual identities that are anything other than fixed)[35] suggests that sexual identity as well as gender identity "are not only imbedded in ordinary language, [but] they are [also] constitutive of ordinary life."[36]

Privacy and the Liberal Closet

Elshtain's warning concerning the danger of an ever encroaching State regulatory apparatus that threatens any distinction between public and private is worth heeding. Increasing State involvement in all areas of life could well be dangerous to the democratic form of government. With this I have no objection; indeed, I have always found Elshtain persuasive on this point. But no matter how persuasive this insight might be, it does not validate her larger argument. Not only does her attack offer little evidence that gay liberation is likely to bring about the Jacobin terror that she describes but it is also part and parcel of a larger conservative agenda to demonize lesbians and gay men. Liberal privacy—the privacy of the closet—is offered as the only viable political position for queers who seek political change. This, of course, was exactly the course rejected by the gay liberationists, who were "tired of waiting around for the liberals to repeal the sodomy laws."[37] Elshtain is so repulsed by gay liberation that, seeing danger everywhere, she overstates it even to the point of calling upon the oldest argument of all to discredit it: What queers really want is to have sex with your kids. A tired and cheap trick, conflating pedophilia and homosexuality serves her well, effectively halting all consideration of the many insights and proposals offered by the gay liberationists.

Most seriously, Elshtain misses many of gay liberation's concerns about privacy in a number of important respects. First, she ignores the central implication of the liberationist critique—that the private institutions of marriage and family are actually publicly supported, defined, maintained, legitimated, and regulated. This suggests that there always has been significantly more overlap in the categories of "public" and "private" than she concedes and that access to these institutions has less to do with a "natural order" that constitutes everyday life than with the granting of sociopolitical privileges to some at the expense of others.

Privacy has never been a value that everyone shared equally, despite Elshtain's declaration that "the right to privacy, the right for gays to practice their sexual preference without fear of harassment, has been widely acknowledged as part of a protected right to privacy in American Society."[38] Five years after "Homosexual Politics" was published, the U.S. Supreme Court declared that there was no such constitutional privacy that protected the practice of gay sexual preference. In *Bowers v. Hardwick*,[39] the U.S. Supreme Court made explicit what gay men and lesbians had always known implicitly, that they could not expect to be included in the rights and privileges "widely acknowledged" as existing for heterosexuals.

Second, despite Elshtain's assertion that "gays or any other group of citizens have the civil right to be protected from life threatening intrusion of simple harassment under the right to privacy, as well as the right to be free from discrimination in employment, housing, and other areas [as] an ongoing imperative of our constitutional system,"[40] her understanding of what gay men and lesbians *are* travels the same path as the U.S. Supreme Court decision in *Bowers*, which denied these very same rights. When she discusses the supposedly acknowledged right to privacy, Elshtain claims that this right protects gays in "the practice of their *sexual preference.*" Elsewhere in the same article, she rejects the liberationist claim that gays are an oppressed class, because she does not believe that "private *sexual preferences* are sufficient to constitute an oppressed class of persons." She does grant that "one's *sex-*

ual preference—unless they do violence to others—should not affect assessments of one's rights and worth as an employee, a
home-owner, and so on."[41] For Elshtain, the definition of "gay"
and "lesbian" is embedded in what one does in bed. She extends
to gays a right of privacy with which to shield all sexual activities—something the U.S. Supreme Court refused to do—but, in
doing so, defines gays by and through those sexual activities. The
sum of the difference between the U.S. Supreme Court and Elshtain is that one does not protect the right of gays to have sex in
private, whereas the other does; neither, however, believes that
being gay or lesbian is about anything more.[42]

President Clinton's "compromise" that allows gays to serve in
the military as long as they keep their sexuality to themselves is
another example of the way that privacy can be used to apply to
gay men and lesbians sets of expectations that are different from
those applied to their heterosexual counterparts. In the name of
privacy, homosexual behavior or any declarations that acknowledge one's gay or lesbian identity still result in dismissal from the
military, transforming privacy into an enforced silence. Gay men
and lesbians do the work of self-policing, closeting themselves
willingly if they wish to continue to serve. This changes the military's long-standing policy, to be sure, but in a manner that employs privacy to further the interests of the military at the expense
of those to whom this right is supposedly granted. It enables the
military to abandon the ridiculous policy claim of high-ranking
military officials that there are "no homosexuals in the military"
in favor of a more modern and seemingly more liberal policy position. But the presence of lesbians and gay men is tolerated only
as long as no one knows for sure whether any single individual is
lesbian or gay. Under this understanding of sexual identity and the
right of privacy, lesbians and gay men are invisibilized.

This invisibilization need not be the result of only official public policies. Gay men and lesbians often participate in this process
in the everyday way that they police interactions with colleagues
and friends. For example, during a year that I spent teaching at a
small, prestigious liberal arts college, a supportive and sympa-

thetic senior colleague once told me that there was "a certain kind of gay person that [did] well at this college." This kind of gay person turned out to be one who was in what appeared to be a long-term, monogamous relationship; who never uttered the word "gay"; and who, for all intents and purposes, was "just like everyone else." The implication was clear. With books and posters about lesbians and gay men all over my office, announcements for lesbian and gay studies programs posted on my door, and pictures of my latest boyfriend on my desk, I was not the kind of gay person he had in mind. I was free to be gay to be sure—they were all good liberals in this department—but this freedom was to be bought with my complicity in my own invisibilization (a price I was unwilling to pay). By imposing privacy and silence on what we would never want made public in any case, this liberal privacy invisibilizes *all* parts of lesbian and gay life. The idea that gay men and lesbians may encompass more than simple sexual preference is so threatening that liberal notions of privacy and civility must be called upon to help invisibilize them.

This invisibilization occurs too in the media treatment of lesbian and gay issues. As Michelangelo Signorile has argued persuasively, if the media pries into the private and intimate lifestyles of the rich and famous who are straight, to do less when lesbians or gay men are involved is a double standard that screams of the hypocritical uses to which the right to privacy is put.[43] The media does this and more, often reporting on the supposed heterosexual tête-à-têtes of people they know to be lesbian or gay. This is not to say that I agree with the invasive and demeaning intrusions of the tabloid press. It is simply that I agree with Signorile that what rests behind the media's difference in treatment is not a more expansive application of the liberal right to privacy to gay men and lesbians but rather a way to exclude gay men and lesbians from media coverage. What rests behind this difference in treatment is another closet, and a closet lined with liberal good intentions is still a closet.

Much of Elshtain's dismissal of liberationist criticism of traditional child-rearing practices and sex role arrangements builds upon her defense of privacy. Both stem from her uneasiness with any attempts to rethink the sacrosanct family, an institution that she believes is the archetypal private/social institution.[44] The gay liberationists argued persuasively that these central elements of family contribute to the making of a gender order that many of us find oppressive. The heterosexist assumption that all children are straight and will grow up to live in exactly the same model of heterosexual marriage and family as their parents is a coercive power for which even the most oppressive State could only hunger. The high rate of teenage suicide among sexual minorities is testimony to the desperation that many gay men and lesbians feel when confronted with telling their parents that they are not heterosexual.[45] The privatized institution of family as currently arranged simply fails the many children who would rather face death than disappoint their families.

Feminists too have criticized the conjunction of marriage, family, and privacy as a site of gender subordination and one in which wife and child abuse historically escape notice by police and State authorities.[46] Sadly, it is within the very institution of family that Elshtain lauds where sexual abuse most often takes place, and the sanctity of privacy surrounding family serves to prolong, if not perpetuate, the abuse. In fact, it is our cultural shame surrounding sexuality—a value transmitted through the institution of family in most cases—that keeps children from reporting sexual molestation. Thus, the unqualified celebration of privacy that Elshtain undertakes is difficult to understand.

Equally perplexing is Elshtain's second claim—that if the liberationists succeed, then homosexual identity will be washed away/withered away/disappeared. Upon closer examination, the paradox of gay liberation seems not so paradoxical. Putting an end to the way that queers were treated by an oppressive society was exactly what the liberationists deemed necessary. If ending that social discrimination meant that both homosexuality and heterosexuality would cease to play the central role in our collective theorizing of who we are, if sexual identity would no longer be the way we tell the truth of our soul,[47] most of us would say, so much the better. Giving up the privileged status of forbidden fruit seems more than a fair trade for winning a new social order in which children need not fear coming out to their parents and adults can live openly with the person of their choice without fear of physical and economic violence and social ostracism.

Elshtain's fear that this new society will end in a razing of all other social practices and social meanings seems, once again, overstated. If institutions such as compulsory heterosexuality, marriage, and family were somehow shattered, would this result in a blank slate, a kind of social tabula rasa from which all social meaning and identity would have to be fashioned anew? This scenario seems doubtful at best.

Still, it is at this point that Elshtain's arguments provide insight into her greatest anxieties and fears about gay liberation. Should gay liberation succeed, not only would homosexuality disappear; so too would its heterosexual counterpart. In the closing paragraphs of "Homosexual Politics," Elshtain declares that "a viable liberationist project" would be one in which "homosexuals and heterosexuals . . . recognize and accept one another as brothers and sisters. Neither would be driven to deny their respective doubles, or set them up as hostile Others, to be repudiated, overcome, or in the language of open tyranny, 'reeducated' or 'reconstructed.'"[48] Heterosexuality, then, *requires* a homosexual sibling—or more to the point, a homosexual stepsibling—in order to have meaning as a distinct category. As Judith Butler has argued, "If it were not for the notion of a homosexual *as* copy, there would be no construct of heterosexuality *as* origin."[49] Once heterosexuality is revealed to be no less the original than homosexuality, one having no greater claim to being "natural" than the other, then much more energy is required to make heterosexuality *become* compulsory, *appear* natural, and *become* the original. It is this process of essentialization that we see at work in Elshtain's critique of Young's claim that both homosexuality and heterosexuality are the product of a sexist society. Her response is that these categories, like categories of gender, are "constitutive of ordinary life." Elshtain believes that the distinction between the sexes is the "primary social distinction" and that, like gender differentiation, the "distinction between homo- and heterosexuality is, if not so primary, nonetheless vital and important."[50] Ultimately, Elshtain would like to fold sexual identity nicely into the primary social distinctions, like male and female, allowing her to eschew the liberationist's lack of a fixed and firm sexual identity. This lack of fixity constitutes the core of the liberationists' theory and rhetoric, and it is what proves so threatening to Elshtain. It is also what is missing from the gay equal rights approach that she endorses.

Interestingly, today the fixity of sexual identity, its permanence, and the lack of individual choice in the determination of this identity have become the shared territory of both sides of the constructivist/essentialist debate over sexuality. As Daniel Ortiz has argued, the question asked by essentialists, "What causes one to be gay?" is independent of the question "How is gay identity given meaning?" One is etiological, and the other is epistemological, but both kinds of explanations about queer identity posit gay men and lesbians who have little or no choice in the constitution of their own sexuality.[51] In theoretical discussions of sexual difference, as well as in the rough-and-tumble world of sexual politics, Ortiz's two questions are more difficult to keep separate than his analysis suggests. As Michel Foucault, Ann Fausto-Sterling, and Cheshire Calhoun make evident through the example of the hermaphrodite, legal and societal interpretations of what supposedly constitutes biological categories help to blur the line between etiological and epistemological categories of identity.[52] In our own struggles to gain lesbian and gay liberation, etiological arguments over what constitutes gay *being* are often used to constitute a public, social, or even official/legal identity for gay men and lesbians that then contributes to the way that identity categories are maintained and regulated. This makes a simple severing of ontological and epistemological concerns difficult at best and simplistic at worst. But these constructivist accounts join essentialist accounts in the efforts to remove all elements of choice from the explanation of sexuality. The radical element of gay liberation's ontological debates that had caused social conservatives like Elshtain such anxiety, the element of choice, has simply disappeared. But, as witnessed by my students' reaction to her article, it is not only Elshtain who is troubled by the gay liberationists' fluid understanding of sexuality.

My students' response to Elshtain's arguments was that of a collective dismissal. They labeled Elshtain a homophobe whose arguments need not be taken seriously. As they saw it, she was, after all, engaging in the heterosexist practice of speaking for the gay community, telling the gay community its mind, without the slightest understanding of the issues involved. I sympathize with this position, but I saw something more troubling than their dismissal of Elshtain. They did not dismiss Elshtain simply because she was a conservative heterosexual who did not quite comprehend what the liberationists were all about. They dismissed her because they thought that she had invented the liberationist arguments as a way to discredit gay men and lesbians—this in spite of the fact that Elshtain's critique draws extensively from the writings of gay and lesbian authors from the 1970s. It quickly became evident that the source of their discomfort continued to be the gay voices of "liberation" upon which Elshtain had based her criticism. In my students' opinion, Elshtain must not be honest; she simply could not be telling the truth. Quite literally, they accused her of having invented the voices of the liberationists, as no one could really have issued those calls to destroy marriage, traditional family, and heterosexuality.

Smugly, my students retreated into the superior vantage point of the present, from which they could cast aspersions on the past. Throwing the proverbial baby out with the bath water, they dismissed both Elshtain and the liberationists, calling the liberationists simplistic, utopian, and dangerously radical. They found it difficult to believe that anyone could ever have had such strange and antisocial notions. This seemed to me to be a bigger paradox than the one that Elshtain had described.

Through no fault of their own, many of today's young gay men and lesbians find themselves ignorant of much of lesbian and gay history; thus, Elshtain's article and the liberationists themselves seemed hopelessly dated, trapped in a time that was no more. Smarter, more sophisticated, better informed than all who had come before, my students, in their modest assessment, stood at the end of history, the result of a historical process of sexual "liberation." They dismissed the liberationist agenda, which sought to change the social order and challenge the institutions of heterosexuality, traditional family, and cultural and social practices that make participation in these institutions almost "compulsory,"[53] as the radical rhetoric of an "immature," political movement.

Dismissing the claims of the liberationists so completely, they dismissed Elshtain as well; the messenger who had carried the coarse message to their ears must be declared profane. But in their haste to distance themselves from the liberationists' radical agenda, their discomfort revealed another interesting fact: To a person, they also understood their sexuality and its expression as a natural, unchangeable "truth." Rejecting any understanding of their sexuality that was other than "essential," they scoffed at the liberationists' claim that homosexuality and heterosexuality were "artificial categories . . . laid on us by sexist society" just as much as had Elshtain. They and, arguably, most of the gay and lesbian political movement today seek integration not (dis)integration, assimilation with cultural institutions not their obliteration. These young gay men and lesbians interested me because they represent a larger contemporary "truth." Today, the bold claims of choice have disappeared, replaced by a "growing inclination in the gay movement in the United States to understand itself and project an image of itself in ever more 'essentialist' terms."[54]

The connection between an essentialist understanding of sexuality and the quest for equal rights came into sharp contrast with the liberationist agenda, an agenda that was premised on a more malleable construction of sexuality. As I pondered the shift in attitudes that I perceived among gay men and lesbians separated by less than a generation, I was led to some difficult questions. If sexuality were really natural, essential, and "constitutive of everyday life," for example, then why must the liberationists' voices be silenced, dismissed, or subjected to such vehement attack by straights and gays alike? What threat could the voice of gay liberation possibly present if their assumptions about sexuality as a choice are so wrongheaded? What social and political forces have led to the greater essentialization of sexuality among gay men and lesbians over the past two decades, and how has this understanding of gay and lesbian "self" been related to the gay movement's new equal rights political strategy? Finally, what kind of limits do we impose on the possibilities for political change when we accept "essentialist" understandings of homosexuality?

(En)Forcing the Essentialist Moment

Elshtain was not the only one who expressed reservations about the advances of gay men and lesbians during the 1970s. Only months before the publication of "Homosexual Politics," the Pentagon had issued the now well-known Department of Defense Directive 1332.14. The directive made homosexuality officially "incompatible with military service" because it undermined "discipline, good order and morale," adversely affected the "integrity of rank and command," and hampered efforts "to foster mutual trust and confidence among [service] members."[55]

Less than five years later, in the 1986 *Bowers* decision, the U.S. Supreme Court went well beyond the question of the constitutionality of the Georgia sodomy law, ruling that the Constitution did not provide a right to privacy to gay and lesbian people (those who engage in homosexual sex). In the five years following the publication of Elshtain's article, gay and lesbian identity was deployed not as means of "assaulting the institutions of society" but as a way to deny gay and lesbian rights. These legal and military decisions set the tone and the direction for gay and lesbian political activism in the 1980s. The struggle in the 1980s became less one of liberation for gay men and lesbians and more one of access to that which they were excluded by law: equality in employment, privacy, and military service.

At the same time, there was an ever greater essentialization of homosexuality. As we saw in Chapter 2, the argument that gay men and lesbians are born and not made was first developed by nineteenth-century medical practitioners who hoped to lessen social and legal condemnations of sodomy. Over and above the fact that "born and not made" is how many gay men and lesbians perceive their own sexuality, it was also the most viable position from which to appeal for civil rights. If homosexuality is biologically or genetically determined, after all, then it rests outside the sphere of individual control and should therefore rest outside the realm of condemnation and discrimination. For many gay men and lesbians whose sexual identity has been ruled immature or who have been pressured to become heterosexual, an essentialist claim to homosexuality provides more protection than do constructivist claims that "gay" and "lesbian" are textual, historical, or discursive productions.

To the extent that persecution, harassment, and discrimination exist, biological explanations for sexual orientation facilitate the pursuit of equal or perhaps even preferential treatment as a "protected class." For many, essentialist explanations for homosexuality allow gay men and lesbians to challenge orthodox condemnations of homosexual feelings, acts, and identity. If sexual orientation does not depend on human choice, then homosexuals, like heterosexuals, can claim to be the creation of God; thus their form of sexual activity becomes less problematic. If gays are born and not made, then a gay elementary school teacher who serves as a role model for, or in a position of authority over, children presents no threat to the children and no legitimate concern for their parents, since the teacher's sexual identity cannot influence the children's sexual development. Moreover, those who suffer from AIDS cannot be charged as deserving of the illness or, worse, as victims of God's condemnation.

Gay men and lesbians have benefited in some significant political and social ways from this reconstitution of sexuality in terms of fixed, unchanging identities rather than behaviors or more fluid constitutions of identity. The best example of these benefits is the decision in *Romer v. Evans*.[56] In *Romer,* the U.S. Supreme Court overturned a state of Colorado constitutional amendment passed by referendum in 1992, which prohibited all state and local government action designed to protect lesbians and gay men from discrimination. Writing for the majority, Justice Anthony Kennedy declared that Amendment 2 violated the equal protection clause of the U.S. Constitution because it "imposed a special disqualification upon [gay men and lesbians] alone. Homosexuals are [thus] forbidden the safeguards that others enjoy or may seek without constraint."[57]

Justice Kennedy clearly relies on the notion of homosexuality as a category of person, completing the first part of the process of interpellation (calling the subject into being) even as he continues the second part of the process (putting these newly constituted subjects into the law): "Amendment 2 bars homosexuals from securing protection against the injuries that these public-accommodations laws address. That in itself is a severe consequence, but there is more. Amendment 2, in addition, nullifies specific legal protections for this targeted class in all transactions in housing, sale of real estate, insurance, health and welfare services, private education, and employment."[58] Rejecting the language of "special rights" that the advocates of Amendment 2 claimed that it was designed to curtail, Kennedy wrote, "We find nothing special in the protections Amendment 2 withholds. These are protections taken for granted by most people because they already have them or do not need them; these are protections against exclusion from an almost limitless number of transactions and endeavors that constitute ordinary civic life in a free society."[59] The Kennedy decision accepted completely what Justice Byron White had refused to acknowledge in the *Bowers* decision a decade earlier, that homosexuals as *citizens* were entitled to the same protections as are other *citizens*. Already hailed as the lesbian and gay *Brown v. Board of Education*, the Kennedy decision, which is based on an understanding of sexuality as *identity*, was an important step on the path toward equality for lesbians and gay men.

There have been other successes as well. For example, in recent years, major corporations such as Microsoft and the Levi Strauss Company and esteemed colleges and universities such as Stanford, Harvard, Wellesley, and Smith have granted spousal benefits to partners of gay and lesbian employees. Still greater numbers of employers, universities, and city and state governments have included sexual orientation in their nondiscrimination clauses. In 1992, even the staid American Political Science Association created a permanent standing committee on the status of gay men and lesbians in the discipline.

But the 1980s also witnessed a battle over funding for arts that were deemed homoerotic, sadomasochistic, and antireligious—art, it was argued, that appealed to a depraved minority and threatened the nation's belief in traditional "family values." National Endowment for the Arts (NEA) Director John Frohnmayer was fired and replaced with a gay unfriendly lesbian, continuing the cynical game of identity politics that had made possible the nomination of Clarence Thomas to the U.S. Supreme Court.[60] And in May 1992, it was revealed that a top official at the Federal Emergency Management Association (FEMA) had threatened a gay employee with job loss if he refused to help him create a list of all gay FEMA employees.[61] The reason for the compilation of the list was never explained, and the list was subsequently destroyed. Still, with increasing frequency, gay men and lesbians have become the subject of political and legislative discourse. In February 2002, for example, Alabama Supreme Court Justice Roy Moore wrote a concurring opinion in a child custody case that denied a lesbian mother custody of her three teenage children. He described the lives of gay and lesbian people as "abhorrent," "immoral," "detestable," an "inherent evil," and "an intolerable evil." He also condemned homosexuality as "so heinous that it defies one's ability to describe it" and claimed (as Elshtain had claimed of the gay liberationists before) that the consequences of homosexuality were "inherently destructive to the natural order of society."[62]

As people, gay men and lesbians were transformed into perverted demons who sought to undermine the cultural institutions of family and heterosexuality, and equal rights and equality of treatment under law were perceived as "preferential treatment." At best, gays have been represented as just another interest group seeking "special treatment." Acknowledging the cultural, legal, and social oppression of gay men and lesbians becomes the "progressive" alternative to hate mongering. But, in order to be accepted as "just another interest group," their sexuality must be transformed into a fixed identity, both a personal one and a political one.

And these examples are only the tip of the iceberg. Homosexuals have been identified with the AIDS epidemic in this country. They have been targeted in the debate over NEA funding of "homoerotic" art as immoral subverters of public morality and sensibility. And despite the decision in *Romer v. Evans*, which makes the passage of legislation such as Amendment 2 unconstitutional, significant percentages of the voting populations of places as diverse as Oregon, Colorado, Maine, and Florida have seen fit to subject the fate, the future, the very *being* of this new political class of persons to the whims of the referendum process. The politics that have taken shape since the 1980s have made all but impossible a public/legal/official understanding of sexuality that was anything other than essential. Despite the fact that many now claim that *Bowers* helped desexualize lesbians and gay men,[63] this approach is still accepted as the one most likely to help advance lesbian and gay equality.

Essentialism and the Limits of Equal Rights

Today we celebrate the increasing political clout of a gay community. Openly gay and lesbian candidates have won election to local city councils, to state legislatures, and to the U.S. Congress, and gay marriage, gay parenting, and gay adoption promise to be politically charged issues in the future. In January 1997, President Clinton, once seen as the champion of lesbian and gay rights, nonetheless signed the Defense of Marriage Act forbidding any state from giving legal recognition to a marriage between persons of the same sex.[64]

But what the many gay political groups had in common in the 1990s and the first years of the twenty-first century was their equal rights approach to political change. That which Elshtain takes as a given—that "gays or any other group of citizens have the civil right to be protected from life threatening intrusion or simple harassment under the right to privacy, as well as the right to be free from discrimination in employment, housing, and other areas"[65]—had become the contested territory, the social and political battleground for the gay and lesbian struggle. For example, in the year 2000, Nebraska adopted a sweeping prohibition against the legal recognition of gay and lesbian relationships anywhere, whereas in 2001, Vermont passed a law that recognized legal unions between gay men and between lesbians. In the 1993 *Baehr v. Lewin* case, the Supreme Court of the State of Hawaii ruled that the state marriage laws must be subjected to the highest level of scrutiny under Hawaii's constitution, because the state's ban of same-sex marriage might violate the sex discrimination ban.[66]

The argument in *Baehr* was that the subordination of women preserved by the prohibition against same-sex marriage is similar to the subordination of African Americans in the South preserved by the laws against interracial marriage until the 1967 U.S. Supreme Court decision that declared them unconstitutional.[67] This has led Morris Kaplan to argue that gay marriage might well be transformative of the entire institution of marriage, since "whether lesbian and gay families conform to the normalizing regimes of compulsory heterosexuality or act to subvert and challenge its gendered forms remains an open and contested question."[68] But Kaplan also contends that the pursuit of gay marriage "provides a perhaps surprising locus for potential reconciliation with the defenders of traditional community norms" and shifts the ground of the lesbian and gay agenda away from "sexual freedom and [toward] the recognition of lesbian and gay partnerships and families." The appeal of this approach is that it "asserts a commonality with the professed aspirations of the heterosexual majority and undercuts the construction of queers as sexual subversives."[69] Kaplan's objection to the sexual subversives is that he thinks that they delude themselves. "To the extent that opposition to lesbian and gay domesticity invokes an image of sexual outlaws inventing radically alternative forms of life, it underestimates the extent to which even our most intimate activities are implicated in form of social life, even through their interdiction. After all, outlaws, especially, are defined by the law."[70]

So too, it should be remembered, are those who simply seek assimilation into these same legally constituted practices and institutions. In my view, this approach does nothing to significantly alter the way we consider how oppression is generated in our society and how freedom from this oppression is always already determined. For lesbians and gay men to act like good heterosexuals will not change the way that even good liberals think about who and what homosexuals are. Elshtain remains a case in point. In "Against Gay Marriage," she writes that she has "long favored domestic partnership possibilities" but does not believe that marriage should be extended to queers because "marriage has never been primarily about two people—it is and always has been about the possibility of generativity."[71] Putting aside the fact that if Elshtain did not construe generativity narrowly, many lesbian couples with children would qualify, partnership benefits would come to have a specific but quite restricted function. Partnerships would exist as "ways to regularize and stabilize commitments and relationships,"[72] while they left in place all the institutions and social practices that have been used to create sexual difference and oppression all along.

Almost as if following Elshtain's script, today's gay political movement and many of today's gay and lesbian youths have sobered up. The "heady brew" of liberation that intoxicated their radical predecessors has been abandoned in favor of what might be called "Liberation-Lite"—a less filling equal rights alternative, more palatable to the bland taste of the 1990s queer. For them, "We're Here, We're Queer, Get Used to It" constitutes a revolutionary agenda.

The gay political agenda today includes spousal benefits, privacy and employment rights, legitimation of gay and lesbian marriages, and the right to participate in military service. Nothing on this agenda seeks to challenge, to disrupt, or even to fundamentally alter the central institutions of society. Instead, it seeks integration with these institutions. The voices of rupture—the liberationists—have fallen silent. Liberationists raised issues that made the struggle for equal rights more problematic, with their "radical" alternative that sexuality might be informed by society *and* by personal choice. They have now become inconvenient, an excess that the new legitimate gay and lesbian movement can no longer afford. The answer, of course, has been to declare sexuality "essential," an intractable aspect of a person's *being*, determined by genetics, biology, or some other "deep property" over which the individual has no control. In order to free homosexuality from the stigma associated with problematized sexual behavior, a flight into a fixed identity is required. As one's identity, sexuality is inexorable, unchangeable, and not the responsibility of the individual. The fact of my homosexuality, like heterosexuality, is simply "beyond my control."

Currently, gay teen groups question teens to assist in the "discovery" of their authentic sexuality; adults, through therapy and self-exploration, reinterpret events in their lives within the framework of this powerful new truth. The *truth* of sexuality has become so obvious to those who possess this knowledge that gay people "will often remark of someone that he does not yet 'realize' he is gay—a clear indication that the category is not necessarily a self-conscious one in their view."[73] Choice has been removed from this debate. Similarly, in the nineteenth century, hermaphrodites' freedom to choose their sexuality when they reached adulthood was stripped from them and reinvested in the site that brought together medical science (truth) and the State (power). Michel Foucault describes the consequences of this shift:

> From the legal point of view, this obviously implied the disappearance of free choice. It was no longer up to the individual to decide which sex he wished to belong to, juridically, or socially. Rather it was up to the experts to say which sex nature had chosen for him and to which society must consequently ask him to adhere. The law, if it was necessary to appeal to it (as when, for example, someone was suspected of not living under his true sex or

of having improperly married), had to establish or reestablish the legitimacy of a sexual constitution that had not been sufficiently well recognized. But if nature, through its fantasies or accidents, might "deceive" the observer and hide their true sex for a time, individuals might also very well be suspected of hiding their inmost knowledge of their true sex and of profiting from certain anatomical oddities in order to make use of their bodies as if they belonged to the other sex. In short, the phantasmagorias of nature might be of service to licentious behavior, hence the *moral* interest that inhered in the *medical* diagnosis of the true sex.[74]

Today sexuality has gone the way of the hermaphrodite. As Foucault makes clear, there is a State interest and a moral interest in ensuring the fixity of identity, in guaranteeing that we all are who and what we claim to be.

Having the freedom to choose a sexual identity creates anxiety in all of us. It is the same anxiety that Elshtain manifested toward the gay liberationists: "To declare homosexuality a class by virtue of . . . behavior . . . to insist that what makes homosexuals a class is the imposition of social control on a minority; yet simultaneously, to admit that 'homosexual members of the *dominant class* by and large manage very well, moving quite freely between the gay and straight worlds,' seems unacceptably tendentious."[75] Today, we expect our sexualities to be clearly marked and easily read, lest lesbians and gay men have the freedom to move between worlds, spies infiltrating the halls of privilege. Many gay men and lesbians manifest this desire for fixity in their hostility toward bisexuality, rejecting the claim that bisexuals are sexually and emotionally attracted to both men and women. We attribute to bisexuals everything from untrustworthiness to immaturity, thereby internalizing the State's desire that we have our identity papers ever in order and taking up the work of policing our own conceptions of what constitutes a legitimate sexual minority.

The dilemma of a gay equal rights movement is that in accepting the essentialization of personal identity, it also accepts the inferior status that this identity assigns to homosexuals in the heterosexual/homosexual dichotomy. The fact that homosexuals seek State protection is evidence of their present social and political inferiority. But in the struggle for equal rights, equality is defined by the superior partner in the dichotomy; in short, "equality" means "sameness." Gay men and lesbians must struggle and fight to gain access to the *same rights* held by heterosexuals. And, after a long, often bitter struggle, they will no doubt be granted the same formal rights that the State provides for heterosexuals.

The danger of this drive to conform in the interest of equal rights is that it adversely affects our desire to combine "what we regard as the better parts of the alternative; we want equality without its compelling us to accept identity; but also difference without its degenerating into superiority and inferiority."[76] By simply demanding the same rights as heterosexuals and requesting integration into the social institutions of marriage and family, homosexuals do nothing to change the process by which difference was constructed in the first place, leaving intact the cultural and social institutions that produce Otherness. Within the equal rights ethos, the goal becomes integration with that which we do not have. Demands for change become pleas for admission to the privileges held by the dichotomous "self" from which we have been estranged in the process of Otherness creation. Even if successful, equal rights and integration would leave the same bias and hatred toward gay men and lesbians operating within the dichotomy of straight or gay. In order to fundamentally alter this, a rupture in the process of difference formulation is required. This may well require rethinking and rejecting many of the social institutions and practices of our society along the lines of the seventies liberationists.

Although this would be no small feat, one thing is clear: No voice of rupture is likely to be discovered among those who seek "equal rights." By overwhelmingly accepting essentialism as our ontology and its corresponding goal of "equal rights," we limit our ability to reconstitute ourselves and the process that produced the heterosexual/homosexual dichotomy in the first place. Many of the insights of the liberationists were important. Compulsory heterosexuality, traditional sex roles, and the oppression that is too often a part of traditional marriage and family—all of these needed to be changed. Although significant changes have been achieved in these areas, I would argue that more changes are needed. Gay liberation asked us to look beyond lesbian and gay mimicking of heterosexual relationships and to imagine different kinds of personal, family, and social arrangements that were less oppressive, more egalitarian, and more inspired. If we now reject this message, if we buy wholesale into the idea that an equal rights ethos is the *only* legitimate progressive path, then we simply limit our ability to imagine ourselves differently and to differentiate ourselves imaginatively.

Conclusion

Nightmares, Fantasies, and
Sexual Performance

EXPLAINING to a *New York Times* reporter why she was contesting her discharge from the military, Colonel Margarette Cammermeyer said, "What I hope to represent is a part of the normality of being homosexual, of not being in leather or shaving my hair, but rather showing how much we are all alike. If people can see the sameness of me to you, then perhaps they won't have the walls that make it so that they have to hate us."[1] As Cammermeyer's statement makes clear, embedded in the debate over gays in the military, never far from the surface, have been competing notions of who and what lesbians and gay men are. Questions of gay identity have been as much a part of this debate as anything else. But with their justifications for excluding homosexuals challenged and defeated one by one, the military succeeded in making one charge stick: the presence of homosexuals, as a group, will interfere with morale, discipline, and good order because of the hatred and bigotry of straight soldiers, which is manifested in such fears as sharing sleeping quarters and bathroom facilities. The tautology here is not to be missed. The military spent the better part of the twentieth century officially constructing lesbians and gay men in ways that make others fear and loathe them. Now the military uses the homophobia and bigotry among straights—homophobia that they have nurtured and fostered for many decades—as a justification for keeping lesbians and gay men out of the service or, at least, in the closet.

But Cammermeyer's claim that lesbians and gay men are just like everyone else seems part plaintive wish, part self-fulfilling prophecy. When the sexologists of the nineteenth century created the category of "homosexual person," they hoped to alleviate the same bigotry and hatred that Cammermeyer seeks to overcome. The sexologists of the day believed that sexual bigotry would end if it could be demonstrated that homosexuals are born homosexuals—if, in effect, homosexuality could be demonstrated to be an essential part of a person's nature. The result, of course, was not greater tolerance but the birth of a new form of life—the homosexual, a category of being that quickly dichotomized into polarizing categories of identity: gay/straight, homosexual/heterosexual, deviant/normal. From these categories of identity, the gay political movement was born, and although it is demonstrably true that lesbians and gay men today live more openly and freely than in the past, with that hard-won freedom have come greater levels of regulation, scrutiny, and State control. The history of the treatment of gays in the military is witness to this. As the category of gay identity developed, so too did the attention to the personal habits, mannerisms, and personalities of those who sought to enlist. Today any hint of effeminacy in manner and dress has disappeared among the nation's fighting men, so successfully do all men, straight and gay, police their own gender conformity to acceptable models of masculinity. Similarly, lesbians, and indeed all women in the military, walk an even narrower line between appearing feminine (and therefore weak) and appearing tough and hardworking (and therefore lesbian).

Greater tolerance does not come through proving to straights that lesbians and gay men are kinder and gentler versions of heterosexuals. The acceptance of lesbians and gay men will not occur because they are born that way or because they can be just like the rest of U.S. society. Have movement leaders failed to notice the obvious? Life in the rest of the country could stand to change a bit itself. Homophobia, racism, sexism are all the products of the same set of cultural practices that posit straight white men as the standard-bearers of culture and mark everyone else as decidedly Other. Ending this enforced conformity will require a political agenda very different from one that seeks simple and unquestioning integration with the values of such institutions as heterosexuality and the U.S. military.

In 1951, writing in the *Origins of Totalitarianism*, political theorist Hannah Arendt documented the rise of "racism" toward Jews in nineteenth-century Europe. Integral to this racism was the identification of Jews as a "race," as those *born* to a certain inescapable identity:

> As far as the Jews were concerned, the transformation of the "crime" of Judaism into the fashionable "vice" of Jewishness was dangerous in the extreme. Jews had been able to escape from Judaism into conversion; from Jewishness there was no escape. A crime, moreover, is met with punishment; a vice can only be exterminated. The interpretation given by society to the fact of Jewish birth and the role played by Jews in the framework of social life are intimately connected with the catastrophic thoroughness with which antisemitic devices could be put to work. The Nazi brand of antisemitism had its roots in these social conditions.[2]

Realizing that the same transformation was taking place in the arena of sexuality, Arendt argued that "the 'vice' of Jewishness and the 'vice' of homosexuality . . . became very much alike indeed."[3] The medical transformation of criminal *acts* of sodomy into sexual *vice* and *identities* parallels the transformation described by Arendt. If we replace the terms "Jews," "Judaism," and "Jewishness" with "homosexuals," "sodomy," and "homosexuality," in the Arendt quotation, the danger of this parallel transformation to gay men and lesbians today becomes clear.

Until quite recently, historians have overlooked that in the most apocalyptic use of identity politics by the modern State—the Holocaust—the Nazis included gay men and lesbians among those who were to be purged from society. And although many today, even in the gay and lesbian community, remain convinced that "it can't happen here," the political success of such candidates as Pat Buchanan and David Duke and the violence directed at

Allan Schindler, Matthew Shepard, Brandon Teena, and Barry Winchell should give us all pause.

So should medical research such as Simon Levay's hypothalamus study and Laura Allen and Roger Gorshki's anterior commissure study,[4] both of which claim to find differences between the brains of homosexuals and the brains of heterosexuals. Although the intention of these researchers is to "prove" that gay men and lesbians are born that way and therefore should not be persecuted, they have no more control over how their research is used than did the early sexologists who formulated similar theories more than a century ago.

The current essentialist embrace of a medicalized homosexuality might sever the connection between sexual pleasure and procreation in the minds of many who still would like to bring religious condemnations upon gay men and lesbians. But it also contains possibilities for more rigid regulation than ever before imagined. For example, the notion of sexual identity has trapped gay men and lesbians in the statistical game that science plays. Both the medical and psychiatric communities have now determined that homosexuals represent about 10 percent of the citizens of the United States. Gay men and lesbians have also accepted this approach to statistical identity, claiming that one person in ten (or sometimes one in seven, or even one in twenty) is "naturally" homosexual, born to an unchanging sexual identity. But if this homosexual identity is innate, natural, predetermined, how do we explain the practice of man/boy love among the ancient Greeks? Clearly, many more than 10 percent of the Greek male citizens engaged in this practice. Without recognizing that homosexuality is socially constructed—madness invented to combat a madness, as Gore Vidal has described it[5]—how do we explain the difference between the percentage of "homosexuals" in fourth-century Greece and the percentage of gay men and lesbians today?

One insidious way that this problem might be rationalized is through the lens of a Darwinian epistemology of natural selection. Darwinian explanations have often been employed well outside of biology, Charles Darwin's own field of study; indeed such explanations are inherent in the debate over the nonprocreativity of homosexuality discussed earlier. Accepting an explanation of sexual identity as biological and then projecting it, unchanged, backward into history could lead to a Darwinian explanation of survival of the sexual fittest. We could argue that gays are demonstrably fewer today than they were in fourth-century Athens because the "deep properties" that give rise to their homosexual condition predestines their evolutionary extinction, the homosexual "gene" growing weaker and weaker as the centuries pass. As the last vestiges of a stubborn atavistic abnormality, homosexuals could again be subjected to the correctional zeal of medical science. Clearly, this vision of the enforcement of "normality" is as frightening as the theories that the nineteenth-century sodomite faced.

In fact, all the pieces for this justification are already in place. A 1993 study by the Alan Guttmacher Institute found that only 1 percent of U.S. men were gay. Despite the fact that the data for this study were collected in face-to-face interviews, where few are likely to admit their homosexuality, the study has been used by religious and conservative political organizations to undermine the "need" for equal rights protections for gay men and lesbians, since science has demonstrated that they constitute only a tiny group of sexual deviants undeserving of legal protection.[6] Three years later, gay conservative Andrew Sullivan would accept this view, adding his own unscientific opinion that gays actually constituted 2 percent of the population.[7] If we try to export these notions of sexuality to other cultures, other historical epochs, other regions of the world, their shortcomings are revealed; even so, the power of numbers, the pull of nature, the desire to fix identity in some completely stable form remains strong.

Sexual Orientation and the Power of Life and Death

The final chapter of the first volume of Michel Foucault's *History of Sexuality* suggests that the scientific power to invent sexualities and the power of the sovereign over life and death have merged in the modern State.[8] The alliance between sexual difference, medical epistemology, and the State has resulted in the conception of possibilities for regulation that are new in the history of the world. Because I share Foucault's uneasiness about the future and his dread of the possibility of a sexual apocalypse, I wish to give shape to this potential apocalypse that haunts gay and lesbian identity.

Gay men and lesbians, believing that they are fighting the medicalization of the homosexual, are now ensnared in the same discourse of origins and causes that invented the homosexual. In reaction to the psychological explanations that events, traumas, immaturity, or lack of development cause homosexuality, it has become politically expedient, if not absolutely necessary, for gay men and lesbians to claim that homosexuals are born and not made. First, an understanding that sexuality is unchanging and innate provides a weapon with which to question the appropriateness of psychological explanations and psychiatric intrusions into the personal and intimate details of people's lives.

Second, discrimination against those whose sexual "orientation" is predetermined becomes simple prejudice, since gay men and lesbians can argue that their presence in the military, in schools, even in day care centers constitutes no threat to those around them. This argument is, I believe, both unsound as a political strategy for liberation and potentially very dangerous. It is, however, a good example of the way in which an epistemological system comes to dominate even those who believe that they struggle against it.

It should not be forgotten that the discourse of sexual identity was born of the earlier desire to find causes and cures for homosexuality and has never fully escaped it. The search for causes and cures has been waiting for the next opportunity, the next level of medical miracles to be invented. Once they are invented, new forms and methods of scrutiny will again be brought to bear on this stubborn problem, which medical science has always failed miserably to explain. The latest shift in the medical epistemological system of truth creation is already underway and has been for some time. Today science has the technology to identify which genes determine such characteristics as eye color, hair color, and baldness. It is only a matter of time before medical science, having invented the technology, "discovers" the gene that determines "homosexuality" and then attempts to use the discovery to solve the lingering problem of sexual "abnormalities." Scientists will find the gene they seek, just as they found that homosexuality was contagious and resulted from too much masturbation and that homosexual men could be detected by their low levels of testicular radioactivity. These new Drs. Frankenstein already claim to have "discovered" the gene that causes alcoholism, a problem similarly constructed by the medical epistemology.

The danger to gay men and lesbians lies in whatever latest cures for homosexuality might follow these "discoveries." Will carriers of the offending gene be allowed to marry? If so, will they be allowed to have children? Will homosexual adults be "cured" through genetic surgery? Or will these "scientists" be satisfied to help Darwinian evolution along by altering the genetic makeup of fetuses who carry this atavistic gene? These concerns may seem extreme, even ridiculous, and I hope that they are. But I believe that they are real possibilities as the next generation of medical epistemologies is reflected in the law.

Regulation of our lives need not come in the form of the Orwellian totalitarian State; it is not only in complete domination, not only in being ordered to report for genetic surgery that I believe the present danger lies. The most insidious regulation occurs at the very point where we believe ourselves to be free. In a liberal democracy where social opinion makes the drive to conformity absolute, this new knowledge will be offered as choice. Marital blood tests or amniocentesis may emerge as ways in which this new power is used to regulate the intimate affairs of our lives. Many parents, given the knowledge and the choice, would not choose to carry a child to term if they knew that child would grow up to be gay or lesbian. Under the rubric of greater knowledge, greater truth, expanded choices, we are unwittingly enslaved.[9]

Homosexuality as a Stage: Performing Sexual Identity

Both constructivist and essentialist conceptions of homosexuality circulate within the policy texts and debates of the United States today. Often justifications for discrimination against gay men and lesbians include both essentialist and constructivist explanations. This is true of arguments proposed by the opposite camp as well, although, as essentialist conceptions of identity have been embraced as the liberatory mantra for all gay men and lesbians, these voices have become increasingly one-sided. Still, Diana Fuss's question cited earlier is still relevant. In any discussion of gay and lesbian identity, politics, or community, the question should not be whether identity is "essential" or "constructed" but rather *What motivates the deployment of each of these conceptions of identity?*[10]

From this vantage point, the recent rush to an essential gay identity can be seen as the quite sane response to the epistemological, philosophic, moralistic, and political attacks launched against the homosexual in the past hundred and fifty years. But for this response to be rational and useful, I believe it must be strategic and therefore flexible. Strategically deploying essentialist arguments makes sense in some debates but not in others. As we have seen, the enemies of gay men and lesbians certainly are willing to deploy both kinds of arguments in their efforts to keep gay men and lesbians from achieving equal protections under the law and in society. As a possible alternative to this dilemma and as a starting point for future investigations, I offer the concept of sexuality as performance.

"You're just going through a stage" is a familiar phrase to many gay men and lesbians. Psychiatrists and psychologists often suggest that homosexuality is just a "stage" or "phase" of development, through which "normal" people may pass. But "stage" is meaningful to this discussion for another reason. Fleeing abusive families and oppressive towns, many gays have historically taken refuge in the theater, where they have found acceptance and created new families and where activities that were unacceptable in almost every other environment were tolerated. Theater companies, once composed entirely of men, gave birth to the modern practice of cross-dressing, since male actors had to perform all the female roles. The modern descendant of this theatrical transvestism—"drag" performances—flourishes today in the gay bar culture.

The butch/femme dichotomy that is customary among many lesbians and the inversion of gender and sexual stereotypes that are common practice among gay and lesbian sexualities within gay and lesbian communities provide another example of sexual performance. But when they move outside these communities, many gay men and lesbians must perform identity differently, "passing" as straight when they visit their families, go to work, or even just walk down the street. To do otherwise means to risk alienating family members, being fired from their jobs, or even becoming victims of violence.

Common to each of these experiences is the practice of performance. Lesbians and gay men, moving between roles and performances of identity out of necessity, have become quite accomplished actors. However oppressive having to pass as straight may feel to many men and women, it is no less a performance, no less "socially constructed" than the many mannerisms, behaviors, and presentations of self as gay or lesbian that exist within gay and lesbian communities today. Indeed, the fact that gay men and lesbians have constructed whole communities in which they give their identities expression—world stages on which they openly and freely perform—is in itself an admission of the constructivity of sexuality. In much of the military debate, lesbians and gay men have stressed that they wanted to be judged on their performance. Perhaps we should take their advice.

In *Gender Trouble,* Judith Butler argues that gender is a constructed category with no essential characteristics: "Acts, gestures, and desire produce the effect of an internal core or substance, but produce this *on the surface* of the body, through the play of signifying absences that suggest, but never reveal, the organizing principle of identity as a cause. Such acts, gestures, enactments, generally construed, are *performative* in the sense that the essence or identity that they otherwise purport to express are *fabrications* manufactured and sustained through corporeal signs and other discursive means. That the gendered body is performative suggests that it has no ontological status apart from the various acts that constitute its reality."[11]

The effect of thinking of gender in this way is that "if true gender is a fantasy instituted and inscribed on the surface of bodies, then it seems that genders can be neither true nor false, but are only produced as the truth effect of a discourse of primary and stable identity."[12] If gender can be revealed as a truth effect, a construction of various discourses of power, then so can sexuality. In fact, sexuality is even better suited to such "revelations." Gay men and lesbians already choose consciously to perform sexual identity differently in different situations.

The future task of gay and lesbian politics lies in an understanding of the forces that have come together to inscribe on the bodies of homosexuals their unique sense of identity. Partly chosen, partly responses to forces not of their own creation, gay and lesbian identities do not preexist, fully developed, as if queers were a single people waiting to be granted the same rights and privileges as other social groups. Rather, gay and lesbian identities are constantly evolving in response to such factors as State identification and the struggle for equal civil and social rights.

No less than heterosexuality, homosexuality needs to be studied as an institution, as a commingling of discourses of power, epistemologies of science and identity, and a politics of social change and political (r)evolution. In this way, gay men and lesbians can begin to turn the forces of history, philosophy, science, and politics on these institutions. They can begin asking, and answering, questions like the one posed by Adrienne Rich in her pathbreaking 1980 *Signs* article, "Compulsory Heterosexuality and Lesbian Existence": "Why species-survival, the means of impregnation, and emotional/erotic relationships should ever have become so rigidly identified with each other; and why such violent strictures should be found necessary to enforce women's total emotional, erotic loyalty and subservience to men?"[13]

This approach would enable lesbians and gay men to ask what forces have driven their heterosexual counterparts into such a rigid and narrow expression of their sexuality when examples in

history suggest that men were able to move freely between relationships with their wives and relationships with their male "be-
loveds" and women were able to live together in romantic friend-
ships and successfully resist the cultural imperative to marry and
have children. Enlisting the full power of scientific investigation,
lesbians and gay men could then ask what has happened to
heterosexuals. What biological or genetic forces have rendered
them so uncultured, so narrowly "straight," so unable to realize
Greek eros or Victorian romance in this modern period, parody-
ing the questions that are used to shame, silence, and demonize
gay men and lesbians today? This approach also gives lesbians and
gay men the ability to resist the State's attempt to legislate their
relationships into "normality," imposing a heterosexual model
onto gay and lesbian relationships, defining their political liberation as a banal integration into the universe of the "same."

Adopting an understanding and a political strategy that recog-
nizes identity as performance, we expand the opportunities both
to imagine ourselves differently and to differentiate ourselves
imaginatively, ushering in not only a new era of gay and lesbian
activism but also more challenging and more productive endeavors for disciples of the newly emerging academic discipline of gay
and lesbian and queer studies.

Notes

Introduction

1. Bill Maher came to understand this only too well. On an October 2001 edition of his television show, "Politically Incorrect," Maher suggested that the U.S. use of military force toward Afghanistan was cowardly. In an attempt to silence all dissent toward the Bush administration's war efforts, many of Maher's sponsors and network affiliates threatened and carried out a withdrawal of support from his show.

2. Michel Foucault, *The History of Sexuality*, vol. 1, *An Introduction*, trans. Robert Hurley (New York: Pantheon Books, 1978), p. 11.

Chapter 1

1. See, for example, http://webpages.charter.nct/mckinlcyhousc for a booking into one of my favorite bed-and-breakfasts.

2. See, for example, *Bay Windows, The Advocate,* and the *Gay Yellow Pages.*

3. See, for example, "Alpha Flight," *Marvel Comics* 1, no. 106 (March 1992).

4. Dennis Altman, *The Homosexualization of America* (Boston: Beacon Press, 1982); Jeffrey Escoffier, "Sexual Revolution and the Politics of Gay Identity," *Socialist Review* 15, nos. 4–5 (1982–1983): 119–133; Steven Epstein, "Gay Politics, Ethnic Identity: The Limits of Social Constructionism," *Socialist Review* 93–94 (1987): 9–56.

5. The *New York Times*/CBS news poll, February 9–11, 1993. The poll's results were based on telephone interviews with 1,154 adults nationwide. The original wording for this question is somewhat awkward: "Do you think being homosexual is something people choose to be, or do you think it is something they cannot change?"

6. A 2001 Roper Center at the University of Connecticut poll sponsored by *Time* and CNN interviewed one thousand adults nationwide between January 10 and 11, 2001. The question was "Do you think that someone who is homosexual can change their sexual orientation if they choose to do so, or don't you think so?"

7. Martin Rein, *Social Science and Public Policy* (New York: Penguin Books, 1976), p. 13. Although Martin Rein is one of the few policy analysts who has shown true concern about the way that values affect the public policy process, he admits, "I do not reject the positivist tradition" (p. 14). In his "value critical" approach to policy studies, he takes values as the subject of analysis; values shape the policy process.

8. Aaron Wildavsky, *Speaking Truth to Power: The Art and Craft of Policy Analysis* (Boston: Little, Brown, 1979), p. 35.

9. Kathy Ferguson, *The Man Question: Visions of Subjectivity in Feminist Theory* (Berkeley and Los Angeles: University of California Press, 1993), p. 7.

10. Quoted in Philip Gleason, "Identifying Identity: A Semantic History," *Journal of American History* 69, no. 4 (1983): 910–931.

11. Quoted in ibid., p. 916.

12. Louis Althusser, "Ideology and Ideological State Apparatuses: Notes Toward an Investigation," in *Lenin and Philosophy and Other Essays*, trans. Ben Brewster (London: New Left Books, 1971), p. 79.

13. Tzvetan Todorov, *The Conquest of America: The Question of the Other* (New York: Harper Torchbooks, 1987), p. 249.

14. Epstein, "Gay Politics, Ethnic Identity," p. 11.

15. Diana Fuss, *Essentially Speaking: Feminism, Nature and Difference* (New York: Routledge, 1989), p. 1.

16. John Boswell makes this claim in his review of David F. Greenberg's *The Construction of Homosexuality* (see "Gay History," *Atlantic Monthly* [February 1989]: 74–78).

17. See Epstein, "Gay Politics, Ethnic Identity," and Boswell, "Gay History." In *Essentially Speaking*, Fuss argues that this has been accomplished, in part, through the encouragement of "more careful attention to historical specificities where perhaps we have hitherto been quick to universalize" (p. 1).

18. Vivienne C. Cass, "Homosexual Identity: A Concept in Need of Definition," in *Origins of Sexuality and Homosexuality*, ed. John DeCecco and Michael Shively (New York: Haworth Press, 1984), p. 105. The bibliographies that Cass examined include W. Parker, *Homosexuality: Selected Abstracts and Bibliography* (San Francisco: Society for Individual Rights, 1971), and M. S. Weinberg and A. Bell, *Homosexuality: An Annotated Bibliography* (New York: Harper and Row, 1972).

19. Jonathan Katz, *Gay American History* (New York: Cromwell, 1976), pp. 406–420.

20. Quoted in ibid., p. 412. For an extended discussion about the activities of the Mattachine Society, see also Toby Marrotta, *The Politics of Homosexuality* (Boston: Houghton Mifflin, 1981), pp. 8–21; John D'Emilio, *Sexual Politics, Sexual Communities: The Making of a Homosexual Minority in the United States, 1940–1970* (Chicago: University of Chicago Press, 1983), pp. 57–91; and Escoffier, "Sexual Revolution and the Politics of Gay Identity."

21. Escoffier, "Sexual Revolution and the Politics of Gay Identity," p. 128.

22. Ibid., p. 127.

23. Alfred C. Kinsey, Wardell B. Pomeroy, and Clyde E. Martin, *Sexual Behavior in the Human Male* (Philadelphia: Saunders, 1948); Staff of the Institute for Sex Research, Indiana University, Alfred C. Kinsey et al., *Sexual Behavior in the Human Female* (Philadelphia: Saunders, 1953); Donald Webster Corey, *The Homosexual in America* (New York: Greenberg, 1951).

24. D'Emilio, *Sexual Politics, Sexual Communities,* pp. 57–91; also quoted in part in Escoffier, "Sexual Revolution and the Politics of Gay Identity," pp. 127–128.

25. For more information about the gay and lesbian rights movement in the fifties and sixties, see D'Emilio, *Sexual Politics, Sexual Communities,* and Marrotta, *The Politics of Homosexuality.*

26. John Boswell, Wayne Dynes, and Edward Stein each make the argument that the social constructivists have really examined only one simplistic view of essentialism—one that serves to posit constructivism as clearly superior. (See Edward Stein, "Conclusion: The Essentials of Constructionism and the Construction of Essentialism," pp. 325–353; Wayne Dynes, "Wrestling with the Social Boa Constrictor," pp. 209–238; and John Boswell "Concepts, Experiences and Sexuality," pp. 133–174, all in *Forms of Desire: Sexual Orientation and the Social Constructivist Controversy,* ed. Edward Stein [New York: Garland Publishing, 1990]). Stein takes the most extreme position, although Dynes and Boswell would agree with his assessment that "essentialism is really only a construction of the social constructivists" (p. 327). John Boswell, "Revolutions, Universals, and Sexual Categories," *Salmagundi* 58–59 (Fall 1982–Winter 1983): 89–113, and Boswell, "Gay History," 74–78, both further the critique of constructivism.

27. For a complete account of the philosophic history of essentialism, see David Degrood, *Philosophies of Essence: An Examination of the Categories of Essence* (Amsterdam: B. R. Gruner Publishing, 1976); Rich-

ard Rorty, *Philosophy and the Mirror of Nature* (Princeton: Princeton University Press, 1979); Charlotte Witt, "Aristotelian Essentialist Revisited," *Journal of the History of Philosophy* 27 (1989): 285–299; and D. Wyatt Aiken, "Essence and Existence, Transcendentalism and Phenomenalism: Aristotle's Answer to the Questions of Ontology," *Review of Metaphysics* 45 (1991): 29–56.

28. Jean Jacques Rousseau, "A Discourse on Political Economy," in *The Social Contract and Discourses*, trans. G.D.H. Cole (London: J. M. Dent and Sons, 1973), p. 118.

29. See note 26 for a list of the current critics of constructivism who argue that constructivist views of essentialism are simplistic and serve only the role of straw man to the more elaborately developed constructivist critiques.

30. Examples of the various and diverse types of tenets that are sometimes attributed to social constructivism include Epstein's claim that, in addition to Mary McIntosh and Michel Foucault, the lineage includes the symbolic interactionists—for example, John Gagnon and William Simon—and labeling theorists Mary McIntosh (once again) and Kenneth Plummer. (See John Gagnon and William Simon, *Sexual Conduct* [Chicago: Aldine, 1973], and Kenneth Plummer, *Sexual Stigma* [London: Routledge and Keegan Paul, 1975].) Jeffrey Escoffier cites the importance of Herbert Marcuse, *Eros and Civilization* (Boston: Beacon Press, 1955); Norman O. Brown, *Life Against Death* (Middletown: Wesleyan University Press, 1959); and Paul Goodman, *Growing Up Absurd* (New York: Random House, 1966). Wayne Dynes adds others, such as Peter Berger and Tom Luckmann, *The Social Construction of Reality: A Treatise in the Sociology of Knowledge* (New York: Anchor Books, 1966), which he claims reflects the ideas of such continental thinkers as Karl Mannheim, Alfred Schutz, and Sigmund Freud. What all of these authors have in common, however, is their belief that Mary McIntosh and Michel Foucault are the major influences on the origins of the social constructivist position as it has developed in the study of sexuality.

31. Mary McIntosh, "The Homosexual Role," *Social Problems* 16 (1968): 182–192.

32. Michel Foucault, *The History of Sexuality*, vol. 1, *An Introduction*, trans. Robert Hurley (New York: Pantheon Books, 1978), p. 43.

33. Thomas Kuhn, *The Structure of Scientific Revolutions* (Chicago: University of Chicago Press, 1962).

34. Foucault, *The History of Sexuality*, p. 43.

35. Stein, *Forms of Desire*, p. 140 (emphasis mine).

36. Epstein argues that deterministic explanations for sexuality are central to the way that many gay men and lesbians perceive their own

experience and identity. He calls these deterministic explanations "folk essentialism," as they are widely understood and accepted as "truth" in the gay subculture.

37. Epstein, "Gay Politics, Ethnic Identity," p. 12.

38. Dynes, "Wrestling with the Social Boa Constrictor," p. 213.

39. Fuss, *Essentially Speaking,* p. xi.

40. Foucault, *The History of Sexuality,* p. 11.

41. Ibid., p. 128.

42. For interesting insights into the gay contribution to mainstream fashion, see Jeff Yarborough, "Vanity Fairies: How Gay Is the Condé Nast Empire? The Editors of *Vogue, GQ, Vanity Fair, Details* and *HG* Tell All," *The Advocate* March 10, 1992, pp. 30–37.

Chapter 2

Acknowledgment: I am indebted to Jonathan Katz, whose work first brought to my attention many of the U.S. medical journal articles discussed in this chapter (see note 48).

1. Aaron Wildavsky, *Speaking Truth to Power: The Art and Craft of Policy Analysis* (Boston: Little, Brown, 1979), p. 35.

2. Jeffrey Weeks, *Coming Out: Homosexual Politics in Britain from the Nineteenth Century to the Present* (London: Quartet Books, 1977), p. 5.

3. The relevant text reads as follows: "Anyone who in conformity with nature, proposes to re-establish the law as it was before Laios, declaring that it was right not to join with men and boys in sexual intercourse as with females, adducing as evidence the nature of animals and pointing out that [among them] male does not touch male for sexual purposes, since that is not natural, he could, I think make a very strong case" (Plato, *Laws,* 836c–e, trans. Thomas L. Pangle [Chicago: University of Chicago Press, 1988], p. 166).

4. John Boswell, *Christianity, Social Tolerance and Homosexuality: Gay People in Western Europe from the Beginning of the Christian Era to the Fourteenth Century* (Chicago: University of Chicago Press, 1980), pp. 15–20.

5. Ibid., p. 13. Realistic conceptions of nature, on the other hand, are related to the physical world and observations of it. Realistic definitions deploy "nature" in three ways: (1) as the "essence" or character of something; or, more broadly, (2) as the collection of properties and principles that apply with the force of law in the observable universe; or (3) as that which does or could occur without human intervention. In these "realistic" understandings of nature, "unnatural" means something uncharacteristic, something outside the boundaries of the observable universe, something characteristic only of human beings, or something simply ar-

tificial. For a complete discussion of both "realistic" and "idealized" conceptions of nature, see ibid., pp. 18–41. It is also interesting to note how much Boswell's arguments about "ideal nature" mirror those made by constructivists when they address sexual identity.

6. Ibid., p. 13.

7. See note 2.

8. Boswell, *Christianity, Social Tolerance and Homosexuality*, p. 12. For examples of references to homosexual behavior among animals in the wild and in captivity, see Bruce Bagemihl, *Biological Exuberance: Animal Homosexuality and Natural Diversity* (New York: St. Martin's Press, 1999); Wainwright Churchill, *Homosexual Behavior Among Males: A Cross-cultural and Cross-species Investigation* (New York: Hawthorn Books, 1967); John Kirsch and James Rodman, "The Natural History of Homosexuality," *Yale Scientific Magazine* 51, no. 3 (1977): 7–13; and George Hunt and Molly Hunt, "Female-Female Pairing in Western Gulls *(Laurus Occidentalis)* in Southern California," *Science* 196 (1977): 81–83.

9. Boswell, *Christianity, Social Tolerance and Homosexuality*, pp. 12–13.

10. Ibid., pp. 14–15.

11. Ibid.

12. Thomas Aquinas, *Summa Theologiae*, ed. Timothy McDermott (Westminster, Md.: Christian Classics, 1984), 1a, 2ae, quae. 91, art. 1.

13. Weeks, *Coming Out*, p. 4.

14. Quoted in ibid., p. 245.

15. See, for example, Cardinal Joseph Ratzinger's October 31, 1986, letter to the Catholic bishops: "To choose someone of the same sex for one's sexual activity is to annul the rich symbolism and meaning, not to mention the goals of the creator's sexual design."

16. It is clear that after the twelfth century, punishment, even to the point of death, became more frequent for those accused of sodomy. During the Inquisition, sodomy became one of the crimes that indicated the presence of the (d)evil and was therefore worthy of greater church concern and regulation.

17. Plato, *Collected Dialogues of Plato*, ed. Edith Hamilton and Huntington Cairns (Princeton: Princeton University Press, 1961), p. 1402 (emphasis mine).

18. Boswell, *Christianity, Social Tolerance and Homosexuality*, p. 12.

19. Boswell's *Christianity, Social Tolerance and Homosexuality* is recognized as the authoritative source on the history of the Catholic Church's attitude toward homosexuality during the first twelve centuries. This debate is far from settled, however. Theologian James P. Hanigan writes, "There would appear to be a quite clear condemnation of homosexual behavior in both the old and new testaments, the normative source . . .

of Christian ethics," and philosopher Michael Ruse has responded to the works of Bailey (see note 21) and Boswell by claiming that "however much reinterpretation you do, the Biblical prohibitions really are explicit." See James P. Hanigan, *Homosexuality: The Test Case for Christian Sexual Ethics* (New York: Paulist Press, 1988), p. 35, and Michael Ruse, *Homosexuality: A Philosophical Inquiry* (Oxford, England: Basil Blackwell, 1988), p. 182. The texts that both Hanigan and Ruse cite are the following: from Hebrew Scriptures, the Sodom and Gomorrah story (Gen. 19:1–29) and the texts from the Holiness Code (Lev. 18:22 and 20:13); and, from the New Testament, Rom. 1:26–27, I Cor. 6:9–10, and 1 Tim. 1:9–10.

20. Boswell explains that the heart of this debate is about translation and that two of the three New Testament texts (I Cor. 6:9–10 and I Tim. 1:9–10) have been interpreted as referring to homosexual acts only since the beginning of the twentieth century.

The third of the New Testament texts (Rom. 1:26–27) does not explicitly problematize homosexual acts, or any sexual acts per se; rather, it speaks of them in the context of the general infidelity of the Gentiles. Boswell notes, "There was a time, Paul implies, when monotheism was offered to or known by the Romans and they rejected it. The reference to homosexuality is simply a mundane analogy to this theological sin; it is patently not the crux of the argument" (*Christianity, Social Tolerance and Homosexuality*, pp. 108–109). For a complete discussion of New Testament texts, see Boswell, *Christianity, Social Tolerance and Homosexuality*, pp. 91–118. For a more traditional, if less sophisticated, discussion of these texts, see Hanigan, *Homosexuality*, pp. 35–58.

21. Derrick Bailey, *Homosexuality and the Western Christian Tradition* (London: Longmans, Green, 1955).

22. Boswell, *Christianity, Social Tolerance and Homosexuality*, p. 180.

23. Michael Goodich, *The Unmentionable Vice: Homosexuality in the Later Medieval Period* (London: American Bibliographical Center/Clio Press, 1979), p. 85.

24. Quoted in Weeks, *Coming Out*, p. 23.

25. *Revised Statutes*, 1881, paragraph 2005, quoted in Ronald Hammoway, "Preventive Medicine and the Criminalization of Sexual Immorality in Nineteenth Century America," in *Assessing the Criminal: Restitution, Retribution and the Legal Process*, ed. Randy E. Barnett and John Hagel III (Cambridge, Mass.: Ballinger, 1977), p. 142, and David Greenberg, *The Construction of Homosexuality* (Chicago: University of Chicago Press, 1988), p. 401. A 1913 court decision held that this statute could be interpreted as prohibiting fellatio. See *Glover v. State of Indiana*, 179 Ind. 459 (1919), and 101 S.E. 629 (1913).

26. In several works, Foucault has traced the connection between the development of medical discourse and its deployment: *The Birth of the Clinic* (New York: Vintage Books, 1973); *Madness and Civilization* (New York: Vintage Books, 1973); and *The History of Sexuality*, vol. 1, *An Introduction*, trans. Robert Hurley (New York: Pantheon Books, 1978). David Greenberg travels a similar historical road, reaching similar conclusions in *The Construction of Homosexuality*, pp. 398–399.

27. George Chauncey, "From Sexual Inversion to Homosexuality: Medicine and the Changing Conceptualization of Female Deviance," *Salmagundi* 58–59 (Fall 1982–Winter 1983): 133.

28. Kristin Luker, *Abortion and the Politics of Motherhood* (Berkeley and Los Angeles: University of California Press, 1984); Greenberg, *The Construction of Homosexuality*.

29. Robert A. Nye, *Crime, Madness and Politics in Modern France: The Medical Concept of National Decline* (Princeton, N.J.: Princeton University Press, 1984), p. 44.

30. Greenberg, *The Construction of Homosexuality*, p. 402.

31. In the middle years of the nineteenth century, the appeal of "utopian" communal experiments reached its peak in the United States. Shaker communities, started in the eighteenth century, prospered well into the nineteenth century. Robert Owen's New Harmony, Josiah Warren's Hopedale, John Humphrey Noyes's Oneida, and George Ripley's Brook Farm were in existence between 1825 and 1887. Noyes's community even boasted its own eugenics program, called stirpiculture.

32. Michel Foucault, "Body/Power," in *Power/Knowledge*, ed. Colin Gordon (New York: Pantheon Books, 1980), p. 62.

33. Ruse, *Homosexuality*, p. 203.

34. Quoted from an interview in Lawrence Mass, *Homosexuality as Behavior and Identity* (New York: Harrington Park Press, 1990), p. 167.

35. Shane Phelan, *Identity Politics: Lesbian Feminism and the Limits of Community* (Philadelphia: Temple University Press, 1989), p. 26.

36. Magnus Hirschfield claimed that, as an "expert" witness for the defense who had testified on many occasions that homosexuality is congenital, he had saved numerous individuals from a total of some six hundred years of confinement (*Sex in Human Relationships* [London: John Lane, 1935], p. xviii). David Greenberg and Phyllis Grosskurth have claimed that the efforts of Caesar Lombroso (discussed later in this chapter) to influence Italian public opinion may have prompted the repeal of the criminalization of consensual homosexual relations between adults in Italy in 1889 (Phyllis Grosskurth, *John Addington Symonds* (London: Longmans, Green, 1964), p. 283; Greenberg, *The Construction of Homosexuality*, p. 409; and Weeks, *Coming Out*, p. 27). However, legally sanc-

tioned homophobia seems to be on the rise again. As recently as July 1992, Nicaragua recriminalized sodomy.

37. This shift to a focus on "homosexual people" instead of acts and behaviors occurred even before the term "homosexual" had entered the medical lexicon.

38. Richard von Krafft-Ebing, *Psychopathia Sexualis: A Medico-forensic Study* (1886, reprint, New York: G .P. Putnam's Sons, 1965), pp. 357–358.

39. Vern Bullough, *Homosexuality: A History* (New York: Garland STPM Press, 1979).

40. Weeks, *Coming Out*, p. 127. Jeffrey Weeks's account of Benkert varies somewhat from Vern Bullough's, though both credit Benkert with the coining of the word "homosexuality."

41. Ulrichs published under the pseudonym Numa Numantius. His work is discussed in Greenberg, *The Construction of Homosexuality*, and Weeks, *Coming Out*.

42. Magnus Hirschfield, *Berlins Drittes Geschelet* (Berlin: H. Seeman Nachfolger, 1904), and idem, *Die Homosexualitat des Mannes und des Weibes* (Berlin: Louis Marcus, 1914). Both Benkert's and Hirschfield's works are discussed in much of the literature (see, for example, Greenberg, *The Construction of Homosexuality;* Jonathan Katz, *Gay American History: Lesbians and Gay Men in the U.S.A.: A Documentary* [New York: Harper and Row, 1976]; Bullough, *Homosexuality;* and Weeks, *Coming Out*).

43. For Hirschfield's own estimate of his success, see note 35.

44. Havelock Ellis, *Sexual Inversion* (London: Wilson and MacMillan, 1897; reprint, New York: Arno Press, 1975). Both environmental and degeneracy theories of homosexuality are discussed later.

45. Havelock Ellis, "Sexual Inversion with an Analysis of Thirty-three New Cases" *Medico-legal Journal* 13 (December 1895): 259. This paper was originally read before the Medico-legal Congress, September 1895.

46. Havelock Ellis, "Sexual Inversion in Women," *Alienist and Neurologist* 16, no. 2 (March 1895): 141–158.

47. Edward Carpenter, *The Intermediate Sex: A Study of Some Transitional Types of Men* (London: Mitchell Kennerly, 1908); idem, *Intermediate Types Among Primitive Folk* (London: George Allen, 1914).

48. Karl Freidrich Otto Westphal, "Die Kontrare Sexualempfindung: Symptom eines neuropathologischen (psychopathischen) Zustandes," *Archiv fur Psychiatrie und Nervenkrankheiten* 2 (1869): 73–108. A number of medical practitioners writing in U.S. journals translated sections of Westphal's article: G. Alder Blumer, "A Case of Perverted Instinct," *American Journal of Insanity* 39 (1882): 22–35, and J. C. Shaw and G. N. Ferris, "Perverted Sexual Instinct," *Journal of Nervous and Mental Diseases*, 10, no. 2

(1883): 185–204. Excerpts from both of these articles are published in Jonathan Ned Katz, *Gay/Lesbian Almanac: A New Documentary* (New York: Harper and Row, 1983), pp. 183, 189–191.

49. Paolo Mantegazza, *Sexual Relations of Mankind* (New York: Falstaff Press, 1932), p. 217.

50. James G. Kiernan, "Sexual Perversion and the White-Chapel Murders," *Medical Standard* 4, no. 3 (November 1888): 172; Robert W. Shufeldt, "Biography of a Passive Pederast," *American Journal of Urology and Sexology* 13, no. 10 (October 1917): 455.

51. Summaries of the work of Paul Moreau, Veniamin Tarnovsky, and Karl Westphal, and the Moreau quotation can be found in Weeks, *Coming Out*, pp. 27–28.

52. Paul Moreau, *On Aberrations of the Genesic Sense* (Paris: Asselin, 1882), p. 46. The book was reviewed by B. Salemi Pace in *Alienist and Neurologist* 5, no. 3 (1884): 367–385.

53. Frank Lydston, "Clinical Lecture: Sexual Perversion, Satyriasis and Nymphomania," *Medical and Surgical Reporter* 61, nos. 10–11 (1889): 253–284.

54. James Kiernan, "Androphobia," *Urologic and Cutaneous Review* 20, no. 2 (1916): 103–108. Earlier, Marc-Andre Rafflovich had also argued that "exaggerated modesty" in the presence of adult males was a sign of homosexuality in young boys (Marc-Andre Rafflovich, "Uranism, Congenital Sexual Inversion: Observations and Recommendations," trans. C. Judson Herrick, *Journal of Comparative Neurology* 5 [1895]: 61). And George Shrady contended that young homosexual boys often manifest "an inclination to adopt the manners and practices of girls or women" (George Shrady, "Perverted Sexual Instinct," *Medical Record* 26 [July 1884]: 70).

55. William Howard, "The Sexual Pervert in Life Insurance," *Medical Examiner* 16 (July 1906): 206–207.

56. Edward J. Kempf, "Social and Sexual Behavior of Infra-human Primates with Some Comparable Facts in Human Behavior," *Psychoanalytic Review* 4, no. 2 (1917): 129.

57. Kiernan, "Sexual Perversion and the White-Chapel Murders," p. 172. See also Kiernan, "Sexual Perversion" *Medical Standard* 4, no. 4 (1888): 483–484.

58. G. W. Henry, "Psychogenic and Constitutional Factors in Homosexuality," *Psychiatric Quarterly* 8 (1934): 245.

59. Lydston, "Clinical Lecture," p. 262.

60. Kiernan, "Androphobia," p. 105.

61. Shrady, "Perverted Sexual Instinct," p. 71.

62. Douglas McMurtie, "Lesbian Assemblies," *American Journal of Urology* 10, no. 9 (1914): 433.

63. Rafflovich, "Uranism, Congenital Sexual Inversion," p. 61.

64. Clarence Oberndorf, "Diverse Forms of Homosexuality," *Urologic and Cutaneous Review* 33, no. 8 (1929): 521.

65. W. C. Rivers, "A New Homosexual Trait(?)," *Alienist and Neurologist* 41, no. 1 (1920): 23.

66. Weeks, *Coming Out*, p. 24. Foucault makes a similar argument in *The History of Sexuality*, vol. 1. David Greenberg discusses a number of reasons that the category of childhood was redefined during the late nineteenth century: "As the commercial and industrial revolutions increased the educational requirements for many jobs, middle class parents began to keep their children in the French Lycees and English public schools longer. First in the United States, then in other countries, the democratic ethos led petit bourgeois and some working-class parents to seek expanded, publicly funded educational opportunities for their children. New paternalistic labor legislation barred children from working in many occupations and forced them into school. Economic dependency kept them at home longer. The decline of apprenticeships and family farms . . . left juveniles more excluded from adult life than ever before." Greenberg concludes that "these developments reduced opportunities for sexual connections across generational lines," which in turn led to the desexualization of children (*The Construction of Homosexuality*, p. 399).

67. Greenberg, *The Construction of Homosexuality*, p. 399.

68. Alfred Adler, "The Homosexual Problem," *Alienist and Neurologist* 38, no. 3 (August 1917): 274.

69. Shrady, "Perverted Sexual Instinct," p. 71.

70. William Howard, *Confidential Chats with Males* (New York: Edward J. Clode, 1911), p. 102.

71. Rafflovich, "Uranism, Congenital Sexual Inversion" (reprinted in part, with editorial commentary, in *Katz, Gay/Lesbian Almanac*, p. 266).

72. E. H. Smith, "Masturbation in the Female," *Pacific Medical Journal* 96, no. 1 (1903): 77.

73. Lilburn Merrill, "A Summary of Findings in a Study of Sexualism Among One Hundred Delinquent Boys," *Journal of Delinquency* 3 (1918): 258 (reprinted in *American Journal of Urology and Sexology* 15 [1919]: 254).

74. Ibid.

75. John D'Emmilio, "Capitalism and Gay Identity," in *Powers of Desire*, ed. Ann Snitow, Christine Stansell, and Sharon Thompson (New York: Monthly Review Press, 1983), p. 105.

76. Horace Frink, *Morbid Fears and Compulsions: Their Psychoanalytic Treatment* (New York: Dodd, Meade, 1918), p. 136. Earlier, James Weir had argued that "every woman who has been at all prominent in advancing the cause of equal rights in its entirety has either given evidence

of masculo-feminity (Viraginity), or shown, conclusively, that she was the victim of psycho-sexual aberrancy" ("The Effect of Female Suffrage on Posterity," *American Naturalist* 24, no. 345 [1895]: 819).

77. Shrady, "Perverted Sexual Instinct," p. 70.

78. The psychological and psychiatric explanations for homosexuality are as entertaining to read as are the "scientific" theories of physicians who sought congenital, environmental, and physiological causes (these are discussed in greater detail later). It is important to remember that arguments that linked homosexual desire and madness circulated contemporaneously with these "medical" theories. Medical theorists often sought out the causes of this madness in the environment or in the cells or genes of the individual rather than in his or her psyche.

79. Sigmund Freud, "Three Essays on the Theory of Sexuality (1905)," in *Standard Edition*, vol. 7 (London: Hogarth Press, 1958), p. 133.

80. Sigmund Freud, "Letter to an American Mother," *American Journal of Psychiatry* 107 (1951): 786–787.

81. Wilhelm Stekel, "Masked Homosexuality," trans. S. A. Tannenbaum, *American Medicine* 9, no. 8 (August 1914): 533.

82. Constance Long, "A Psychoanalytic Study of the Basic Character," *Proceedings of the International Conference of Women Physicians, 1919*, vol. 4, *Moral Codes and Personality* (New York: Woman's Press, 1920), p. 77.

83. Charles Socarides, *The Overt Homosexual* (New York: Gruene and Stratton, 1968), p. 5.

84. Ibid., p. 11.

85. Otto Fenichel, *The Psychoanalytic Theory of Neurosis* (New York: W. W. Norton, 1945), pp. 340–343.

86. Anna Freud, "Homosexuality," *Bulletins of the American Psychoanalytic Association* 7 (1951): 117–118. Charles Socarides also includes "narcissistic inferiority" in his long list of causes of homosexuality (*The Overt Homosexual*, p. 5).

87. G. L. Bibring, "On an Oral Component in Masculine Inversion," *International Z. Psychoanalysis* 25 (1940): 128. The same argument is found in H. Nunberg, "Homosexuality, Magic and Aggression," *International Journal of Psychoanalysis* 19 (1938): 1–16.

88. M. Sherman and T. Sherman, "The Factor of Parental Attachment in Homosexuality," *Psychoanalytic Review* 13, no. 3 (1926): 32–37; Carl Jung, *Psychology of the Unconscious* (New York: Moffett, Yard, 1916); and Socarides, *The Overt Homosexual*, p. 14.

89. George Henry, "Psychogenic Factors in Overt Homosexuality," *American Journal of Psychiatry* 93, no. 4 (1937): 889–908.

90. The American Psychological Association declassified homosexuality as a mental disorder in 1974 on a mail vote of 5,854 to 3,810. How-

ever, the 1980 *International Classification of Disease* (Department of Health and Human Services, Centers for Disease Control and Prevention—National Center for Health Statistics DHHS Publication PHS00-1260, 9th ed.) still lists homosexuality as a disease.

91. Socarides, *The Overt Homosexual,* p. 8.

92. Charles Socarides, "How America Went Gay," *American,* November 18, 1995.

93. The active way in which psychiatrists and psychologists supplanted their physician colleagues as the experts of homosexuality is evidenced in Chapter 3, which describes how they sought an institutionalized role with the military by claiming that they could best "detect" homosexuals for separation.

94. The MMPI and its subset of "queer" questions are treated with a bit too much respect by Philip Ruse in *Homosexuality* (New York: Basil Blackwell, 1988), pp. 216–218. (Responding "true" to the first two questions and "false" to the second two is supposed to be indicative of a homosexual personality. How did you do?)

95. Sodomy laws are still on the books in thirty-four U.S. states. They are not, however, widely enforced. When they have been, the U.S. Supreme Court has ruled that states have the right to forbid acts of sodomy, as there exists no constitutional right to privacy that extends to the protection of "homosexual acts." See, for example, the U.S. Supreme Court's opinion in *Bowers v. Hardwick,* 478 U.S. 186 (1986).

96. See Bullough, *Homosexuality;* Weeks, *Coming Out;* and Jeffrey Weeks, *Sexuality and Its Discontents: Meanings, Myths, and Modern Sexualities* (London: Routledge, 1985).

97. Thomas Szasz, *The Manufacture of Madness* (London: Routledge and Keegan Paul, 1971), p. 172.

98. Ibid., p. 173.

99. William Hammond, *Sexual Impotence in the Male and Female* (New York: Bermingham, 1883; reprint, New York: Arno Press, 1974), p. 68.

100. James Kiernan, "Sexual Perversion," *Detroit Lancet* 7, no. 11 (May 1884): 184.

101. Graeme M. Hammond, "The Bicycle in the Treatment of Nervous Diseases," *Journal of Nervous and Mental Diseases* 17, no. 1 (1892): 38.

102. Francis Anthony, "The Question of Responsibility in Cases of Sexual Perversion," *Boston Medical and Surgical Journal* 139, no. 12, September 22, 1898, p. 291. C. H. Hughes also called for the incarceration of homosexuals ("Erotopathia—Morbid Eroticism," *Alienist and Neurologist* 14 no. 4 [1893]: 531–578). And Italian criminologist Caesar Lombroso, who is often included among those who were sympathetic to homosexuals, was one of the first to call for this treatment (see Weeks, *Coming Out,* p. 27).

103. Arlo Karlen, *Sexuality and Homosexuality* (New York: W. W. Norton, 1971), p. 325. See also idem, "The Homosexual Heresy," *Chaucer Review* 6 (1971): pp. 44–63.

104. Karlen, *Sexuality and Homosexuality.*

105. Weeks, *Coming Out,* p. 31.

106. Emil Oberhoffer, "The Influence of Castration on the Libido," *American Journal of Urology and Sexology* 12 (1916): 58–60.

107. Hughes, "Erotopathia," p. 537.

108. Hirschfield, *Sex in Human Relationships.*

109. Richard von Krafft-Ebing, "Perversion of the Sexual Instinct," trans. H. M. Jewett, *Alienist and Neurologist* 9, no. 4 (1888): 565–581; Havelock Ellis, *The Criminal* (London: W. Scott, 1890).

110. Weeks, *Coming Out,* p. 27. Lombroso's argument that homosexuals, like criminals, were throwbacks to an earlier stage of civilization and therefore should be treated in asylums rather than imprisoned can hardly be seen as a ringing endorsement of homosexuals, however.

111. Johann Ludwig Casper, *Vierteljahrsschrift fur geriichtliche und offentliche Medizin,* vol. 1 (Berlin: August Hirschwald, 1852), and Ambrose Tardieu, *Étude medico-legale sur les attentats aux moeurs* (Paris: J. B. Bailleiere, 1857), are discussed in Karlen, *Sexuality and Homosexuality,* pp. 183–184, and in Greenberg, *The Construction of Homosexuality,* pp. 397–433.

112. Karlen, *Sexuality and Homosexuality,* p. 185.

113. Allen McLane Hamilton and Lawrence Godkin, *A System of Legal Medicine,* 2 vols. (New York: E. B. Treat, 1894).

114. Shrady, "Perverted Sexual Instinct," p. 71.

115. Douglas McMurtie, "Notes on Homosexuality," *Vermont Medical Monthly* 19 (1913): 69.

116. Hughes, "Erotopathia," p. 563.

117. Adler, "The Homosexual Problem," p. 273.

118. F. E. Daniels, "Should Insane Criminals or Sexual Perverts Be Permitted to Procreate?" originally published in the December 1893 *Medico-legal Journal* and reprinted as "Castration of Sexual Perverts," *Texas Mecial Journal* 27, no. 10 (1893): 372.

119. Ibid., p. 375.

120. Ibid., p. 381.

121. Edward J. Kempf, "Social and Sexual Behavior of Infra-human Primates with Some Comparable Facts in Human Behavior," *Psychoanalytic Review* 4, no. 2 (1917): 141.

122. Merrill, "A Study of Sexualism Among One Hundred Delinquent Boys." Using his position as a diagnostician with the Juvenile Court of Seattle, Washington, to conduct studies of the sexual behavior

of young boys, Merrill again combined State power with the scientific investigatory power of modern medical science.

123. R. C. Lewontin, Steven Rose, and Leon J. Kamin, *Not in Our Genes: Biology, Ideology and Human Nature* (New York: Pantheon Books, 1984), p. 8.

124. Greenberg, *The Construction of Homosexuality*, p. 402.

125. Ibid., p. 414.

126. Hughes, "Erotopathia," p. 533.

127. William J. Robinson, "My Views on Homosexuality," *American Journal of Urology* 10 (1914): 551.

128. Harold Moyer, "Is Sexual Perversion Insanity?" *Alienist and Neurologist* 28, no. 2 (1907): 197.

129. Irving C. Rosse, "Sexual Hypochondriasis and Perversion of the Genesic Instinct," *Journal of Nervous and Mental Disease* 17, no. 11 (1892): 798.

130. James G. Kiernan, "Psychical Treatment of Congenital Sexual Inversion," *Review of Insanity and Nervous Disease* 4, no. 4 (1894): 294.

131. Douglas McMurtie, "Some Observations on the Psychology of Sexual Inversion in Women," *Lancet Clinic* 108, no. 18 (1912): 489.

132. Krafft-Ebing, "Perversion of the Sexual Instinct," p. 302. An anonymous U.S. reviewer of Krafft-Ebing's *Psychopathia Sexualis* (see *Alienist and Neurologist* 14, no. 3 [1893]: 526–527) softly reproached him for not defending Dr. G.'s position. He noted that Krafft-Ebing's own claim that homosexuality was an inborn mental condition should have led him to call for the decriminalization of homosexuality.

Chapter 3

1. For a more complete discussion, see Raphael Sealey, *Women and Law in Classical Greece* (Chapel Hill: University of North Carolina Press, 1990). I pursue the related question of women and their exclusion from combat only as it pertains to lesbians. Suffice it to say that gender differences seem to present threats to troop morale and discipline similar to those of sexual differences. The combined effects seem almost too much for the armed forces to bear, as witnessed by the fact that significantly higher percentages of lesbians than gay men are separated from military duty because of homosexuality.

2. In fact, twenty-three of the fifty U.S. states still have some form of sodomy law on the books today.

3. 10 USCS, sec. 925, August 10, 1956, ch. 1041, sec. 1, 70A Stat. 74.

4. See Chapters 1 and 2. See also John Boswell, *Christianity, Social Tolerance and Homosexuality: Gay People in Western Europe from the Beginning*

of the Christian Era to the Fourteenth Century (Chicago: University of Chicago Press, 1980), pp. 11–14.

5. *Grant v. United States,* 162 Ct. Cl. 601 (1963). The fact that few heterosexuals have been discharged for violation of Article 125 opens the question of whether the past homosexual encounters present in the court record of *Grant v. United States* have had more to do with the court's willingness to uphold the discharge than the court was willing to admit. The fact that this case represents one of only two contested discharges for heterosexual sodomy lends strength to this interpretation. The other case, *United States v. Doherty,* also supports this interpretation.

6. *Grant v. United States* at 603.

7. *United States v. Phillips,* 3 USCMA 137 (1953) at 137.

8. U.S. Senate Armed Services Committee, "Hearings on Homosexuals in the Military," May 7, 1993, p. 144. Another exchange only minutes later also deserves noting:

> *Kerry:* Today you have gays working in the workplace. You have them right here in the Senate. It is against the law. Has Senator Thurmond, or have the Capitol Police arrested anybody because we have people up here that we know practice sodomy? No. Do we do it out in the workplace every day? No.
>
> *Thurmond:* Do you want them arrested for that?
>
> *Kerry:* Do you, Sir? I mean my question is are we going to apply . . .
>
> *Thurmond:* If they are practicing sodomy and it's against the law why shouldn't it [*sic*] be arrested?

9. *Maryland v. McGowen,* 81 S. Ct. 1101 (1969).

10. *Hatheway v. Secretary of the Army,* 641 F. 2d 1376 (1981) at 1383–1384. It should again be noted that Article 125 deals with both heterosexual and homosexual acts of sodomy, but the court speaks only to the "legitimate justifications" for preventing homosexual conduct.

11. Eric Schmitt, "Forum on Military's Gay Ban Starts, and Stays, Shrill," *New York Times,* March 25, 1993, p. A11.

12. Daniel Brown, a driver at the headquarters of the Lejeune Service Support Schools, made this comment to B. Drummond Ayres Jr. (see "Marine Corps: Even the Thought Is Off-Limits," *New York Times,* January 28, 1993, p. A16).

13. Brian Grenard made this comment to Larry Rohter (see "Open Hostility to Homosexuals Outside Navy Base," *New York Times,* January 31, 1993, p. 20).

14. Albert Abrams, "Homosexuality—a Military Menace," *Medical Review of Reviews* 24 (1918): 528–529.

15. *United States v. Adkins*, 5 USCMA 492 (1955) at 499.

16. Army Regulation No. 40-105 (1921).

17. Ibid.

18. See William C. Menninger, *Psychiatry in a Troubled War: Yesterday's War and Today's Challenge* (New York: Macmillan, 1948), p. 228.

19. Jane Gross, "Gay Sailor's Colleagues Unsettled and Unheard," *New York Times*, April 5, 1993, p. A5.

20. Gustaff D. Tillman, "Detecting Schizoid and Pre-schizophrenic Personalities," *Bulletin of the Menninger Clinic 5*, no. 5 (September 1941): 167–170, quoted in Alan Berube, *Coming Out Under Fire* (New York: Free Press, 1990), p. 20.

21. Berube, *Coming Out Under Fire*, p. 20.

22. Jane Gross, "Navy Is Urged to Root Out Lesbians Despite Abilities," *New York Times*, November 2, 1990, p. A11.

23. Berube, *Coming Out Under Fire*, p. 10.

24. There is little doubt not only that psychiatrists saw the military as their ticket to legitimation but also that their active lobbying of the military for greater participation in the selective service process was fired by a desire to achieve that legitimacy. In a quite frank and amazingly unself-reflective manner, William Menninger, the father of U.S. psychiatry, makes just this explanation (see *Psychiatry in a Troubled War*).

25. Harry Stack Sullivan, "Psychiatry and the National Defense," *Psychiatry 4* (May 1941): 201–217, cited in Alan Berube, *Coming Out Under Fire*, p. 10.

26. "The William Alanson White Psychiatric Foundation Bulletin: A Minimum Psychiatric Inspection of Registrants," October 27, 1940, published in *Psychiatry 3* (November 1940): 625–627.

27. Patrick S. Madigan, "Military Psychiatry," *Psychiatry 4* (May 1941): 228–229. In January 1941, the navy issued its own directive, which created regulations for the separation and exclusion of the "neuropsychiatrically unfit." It declared unfit those men "whose sexual behavior is such that it would endanger or disturb the morale of the military unit" (Forrest Harrison, "Psychiatry in the Navy," *War Medicine 3* [February 1943]: 122).

28. Abrams, "Homosexuality," p. 382.

29. Arthur Weider et al., "The Cornell Selectee Index: A Method for Quick Testing of Selectees for the Armed Forces," *Journal of the American Medical Association 124*, January 22, 1944, pp. 224–228. Berube also discusses this form (see *Coming Out Under Fire*, p. 20).

30. *Crawford v. Davis*, 249 F. Supp. 943 (1966) at 944.

31. Ibid., p. 946.

32. *Murray v. United States*, 154 Ct. Cl. 185 (1961) at 187.

33. *Clackum v. United States,* 296 F. 2d 226 (1960) at 230. This case also reveals that the service member's psychiatric evaluation, which was the only "evidence" ever considered after an anonymous tip regarding her homosexuality was sent to investigators, lasted all of twenty minutes.

34. *Nelson v. Miller,* 373 F. 2d 474 (1967) at 475.

35. *Falk v. Secretary of the Army,* 870 F. 2d 941 (1989) at 943.

36. Berube, *Coming Out Under Fire,* p. 146.

37. Ibid., p. 147.

38. *Rich v. Secretary of the Army,* 516 F. Supp 621 (1981) at 625.

39. Department of Defense Directive 1332.14, January 28, 1982, p. 2.

40. *United States v. Viches,* 17 MJ 851 (1984). "Chicken hawk" is slang for an older man who finds younger men (chickens) attractive.

41. *United States v. Marcey,* 9 USCMA 137 (1958).

42. Gross, "Navy Is Urged to Root Out Lesbians Despite Abilities," p. A11.

43. One radar instructor who elected not to fly with Keith Meinhold explained that Meinhold's presence in the cockpit would distract him from his responsibilities: "I'd rather have my whole thinking on the safety of the flight and not on what he just said and why did he say it." One of Meinhold's supervisors explained that some of the service members who had opted out of flying with Meinhold were unwilling to risk the incidental contact that would be inevitable in a small aircraft or flight simulator: "They didn't want to touch him, like he had cooties" (quoted in Gross, "Gay Sailor's Colleagues Unsettled and Unheard," p. A18).

Jason Alexander, a twenty-year-old airman, declared, "We're all crammed together in the showers, and I don't want to worry that some gay guy is staring at me." Another airman asked a *New York Times* reporter, "Now how am I going to feel if I walk into a dormitory and see pictures on the wall from *Playgirl* magazine?" Still another commented, "I couldn't sleep at night. I'd be worried that some homosexual is going to sneak over and make a pass at me" (quoted in Dirk Johnson, "Air Force: Are Homosexuals the New Enemy?" *New York Times,* January 28, 1993, p. A16).

44. Dan Coats, "Clinton's Big Mistake," *New York Times,* January 30, 1993, p. A21 (emphasis mine).

45. *Augenblick v. United States,* 509 F. 2d 1157 (1975) at 1160.

46. Quoted in Eric Schmitt, "Calm Analysis Dominates Panel Hearing on Gay Ban," *New York Times,* April 1, 1993, p. A1.

47. *Beller v. Middendorf,* 632 F. 2d 788 (1980).

48. "Court Reinstates Lesbian's Lawsuit Against Army," *New York Times,* August 20, 1991, p. A22.

49. *United States v. Scoby,* 5 MJ 160 (1978) at 161.

50. *United States v. Brown,* 5 MJ 501 (1979) at 503.

51. Office of the Attorney, "Regarding Defensibility of the New Policy on Homosexual Conduct in the Military," July 19, 1993 (for the full text of this memo, see the Queer Resources Directory on-line: http://vector.intercon.com/pub/QRD/qrd/military/janet.reno.memo.on.New.ban).

52. *Gay Veterans v. Secretary of Defense,* 668 F. Supp. 11 (1987) at 11.

53. U.S. Senate Armed Services Committee Hearings on Homosexuals in the Military, May 7, 1993.

54. See Michael Wines, "This Time Nunn Tests a Democrat," *New York Times,* January 30, 1993, p. A1. Some have charged that the hearings were not objective. One navy admiral commented, "Nunn's already made up his mind," to which Nunn replied, "We've had as fair a hearing as I know how to put forth." Undercutting his own claim, Nunn added, "Is everyone in this town supposed to have an opinion but me?" (quoted in Jill Smolowe, "Hearts and Minefields," *Time,* May 24, 1993, pp. 41–42).

55. Quoted in Wines, "This Time Nunn Tests a Democrat," p. A14.

56. *United States v. Miller,* 3 MJ 292 (1977) at 294. In this case, the victim was constructed as both dishonest and promiscuous. The court seemed to suggest that consent is not an issue. A homosexual, it would appear, loses the right to say no to unwanted sexual advances.

57. *Rich v. Secretary of the Army,* 516 F. Supp. 621 (1981). See also *Rich v. Secretary of the Army,* 753 F. 2d 1220 (1984).

58. Tamar Lewin, "Gay Cadet Is Asked to Repay R.O.T.C. Scholarship," *New York Times,* March 4, 1990, p. A7.

59. Shane Phelan, *Getting Specific: Postmodern Lesbian Politics* (Minneapolis: University of Minnesota Press, 1994), p. 62.

60. *United States v. Kindler,* 14 USCMA 394 (1964) at 395. In both this case and the 1990 example of James Holobaugh, the armed services did not accept the word of the accused, as if homosexuality affected a person's veracity. The armed services, it is clear, will not entertain the possibility that sexual identity can develop later for some people than for others.

61. *Clackum v. United States.*

62. *United States v. Phillips* at 137.

63. *United States v. Marcey* at 141.

64. Ibid., p. 142.

65. *United States v. Adkins* at 493. Navy fireman Adkins won the right to a new hearing; however, he did so based on the testimony of a naval investigator concerning the likelihood that Adkins's childhood sleeping arrangement (three or four children in a single bed) must necessarily have made him a homosexual.

66. Quoted in Schmitt, "Calm Analysis," p. A1.

67. Equal protection law requires that, when such distinctions between groups of people are made, these distinctions be "rational" and legitimate. When distinctions made by government actions are "suspect" or "quasi-suspect," when the government employs as the basis for differentiation certain characteristics that bear no apparent relationship to the subject in question, the courts must apply a more rigorous standard of scrutiny in reviewing the government's actions. The onus is on the government to demonstrate a compelling State interest if the group in question is determined to be a "suspect class." If the group is determined to be a "quasi-suspect" class, the government must show that its justification for discriminating is substantially related to a legitimate State interest. In all equal protection cases, whatever status the group involved is determined to have, the government must demonstrate a legitimate and rational basis for its policy. In their book about *Steffan v. Cheney*, Ken Sherrill and Marc Wolinsky have noted that in the determination of whether a group constitutes a suspect or quasi-suspect class, the courts have focused on five questions:

1. Has the group suffered a history of purposeful discrimination?
2. Is the group defined by a trait that frequently bears no relation to ability to perform or contribute to society?
3. Is the trait defining the class "immutable" or, in other words, is the trait a product of an accident of birth?
4. Has the group been saddled with unique disabilities because of prejudice or absurd stereotypes?
5. Does the group burdened by discrimination lack the political power to obtain redress through the political process?

Marc Wolinsky and Kenneth Sherrill, eds. *Gays and the Military: Joseph Steffan Versus the United States Military* (Princeton, N.J.: Princeton University Press, 1993), p. xvi.

68. Craig Stoltz, "Gays in the Military," *USA Weekend*, August 7–9, 1992, pp. 4–5.

69. Quoted in ibid., p. 4 (emphasis mine).

70. *Rich v. Secretary of the Army* at 623.

71. Even one's choice of reading material can be regarded as symptom and threat by signaling sexual orientation to others. During the U.S. Senate Armed Services Committee hearings, Senator Carl Levin asked General Norman Schwarzkopf if reading a magazine that catered to homosexuals constituted homosexual activity. The general answered no but then added that if a soldier were to read the magazine "in the barracks on a continuous basis to the point where it cause[ed] all around [him or her] to be concerned about [his or her] sexual orientation and it

started to cause polarization within [the] outfit," then the offending service member should be removed. Quoted in Eric Schmitt, "Compromise on Military Gay Ban Gaining Support Among Senators," *New York Times*, May 12, 1993, p. A1.

Chapter 4

1. Billy Bragg, "Tender Comrade," Workers Playtime, Electra Communications, 1988. Lyrics used with permission of Billy Bragg and published by BMG Music Publishing.

2. See, for example, Alan Berube, *Coming Out Under Fire: The History of Gay Men and Women in World War Two* (New York: Free Press, 1990); Randy Shilts, *Conduct Unbecoming: Gays and Lesbians in the U.S. Military* (New York, St. Martin's Press, 1993); and Tom Brokaw, *The Greatest Generation* (New York: Random House, 1998).

3. 10 USCS, sec. 925, August 10, 1956, ch. 1041, sec. 1, 70A Stat.74.

4. *United States v. Doherty*, 4 USCMA 287 (1954) at 290.

5. Ibid.

6. Secretary of the Navy Instruction 1620.1, July 19, 1953.

7. *Nelson v. Miller*, 373 F. 2d 474 (1967) at 475. The form was prescribed by 32 C.F.R. 730.15(h) in 1961 and again in 1964.

8. Army Regulations AR 635-89, April 15, 1955; Air Force Regulations AFR 35-66; and Secretary of the Navy Instructions 1900.9, and 1620.1 all distinguish between three classes of homosexuality, all of which are grounds for separation from the military.

9. *Rich v. Secretary of the Army*, 516 F. Supp. 621 (1981) at 622.

10. Ibid., p. 223.

11. Department of Defense Directive 1332.14, "Enlisted Administrative Separations," January 28, 1982, p. 1.

12. Ibid., p. 2.

13. Ibid., p. 2.

14. See, for example, *United States v. Phillips*, 3 USCMA 137 (1953); *Augenblick v. United States*, 509 F. 2d 1157 (1975); *United States v. Miller*, 3 MJ 292 (1977); *United States v. Scoby*, 5 MJ 160 (1978); *Beller v. Middendorf*, 633 F. 2d 788 (1890); *Hatheway v. Secretary of the Army*, 641 F. 2d 1376 (1981); and *Gay Veterans v. Secretary of Defense*, 668 F. Supp. 11 (1987).

15. *Pruitt v. Cheney*, 943 F. 2d 989 (1991) at 991.

16. Ibid., pp. 146–150.

17. *Clackum v. United States*, 296 F. 2d 226 (1961) at 227.

18. See, for example, the courts' decisions in *Clackum v. United States*, 148 Ct. Cl. 404 (1960); *Harmon v. Bruckner* 355 U.S. 579 (1958); *Murray v. United States*, 154 Ct. Cl. 185 (1961); *Middleton v. United States*, 179 Ct. Cl. 36 (1965); *Conn v. United States*, 180 Ct. Cl. 120 (1966); and *Glidden v.*

United States, 185 Ct. Cl. 515 (1968). See also Colin J. Williams and Martin S. Weinberg, *Homosexuals and the Military: A Study of Less Than Honorable Discharges* (New York: Harper and Row, 1971).

19. *Glidden v. United States,* at 516.

20. *Murray v. United States,* 154 Ct. Cl. 188 (1961) at 189. The air force's categorization of women in the service as "female airmen" and the navy's categorization of women as "female seamen" are reflective of the general attitude of the armed services about the accommodation of difference.

21. Department of Defense enlistment/reenlistment forms all contain the following questions:

  a. Are you a homosexual or bisexual? ("Homosexual" is defined as: sexual desire or behavior directed at person(s) of one's own sex. "Bisexual" is defined as: a person sexually responsive to both sexes.)
  b. Do you intend to engage in homosexual acts (sexual relations with another person of the same sex)?

22. Rick Harding, "Commanders Quietly Ignore Antigay Rule to Build Gulf Forces," *The Advocate,* February 26, 1991, p. 20.

23. Ibid.

24. Randy Shilts, "What's Fair in Love and War," *Newsweek,* February 1, 1993, p. 58.

25. Discharge statistics for the period from 1966 to 1970 were unavailable. The numbers for 1960 to 1961 represent discharges issued by the army, navy, and marines (Subcommittee on Constitutional Rights of the Senate Judiciary Committee, 87th Congress, 2nd Session, 1962, p. 913). The numbers for 1962 to 1963 include the air force discharges for that period (Subcommittee on Constitutional Rights of the Senate Judiciary Committee, 89th Congress, 2nd Session, 1966, pp. 697, 1001, 1004). The army discharges for the six years from 1960 to 1965 were available only as a total; I have figured an average of 818 per year. See Williams and Weinberg, *Homosexuals and the Military,* pp. 47–48. See also the 1966 Subcommittee on Constitutional Rights for the Senate Judiciary Committee hearings, pp. 697, 919, 1001, 1004. The numbers for the period from 1970 to 1982 are from the Department of Defense (see Eric Schmitt, "Pentagon Aides to Study Option of Segregation for Gay Soldiers," *New York Times,* January 31, 1993, p. A1, and U.S. General Accounting Office, "Defense Force Management: DOD's Policy on Homosexuality," GAO/NSIAD-92-98, June 12, 1992).

26. "National News," *The Advocate,* April 23, 1991, p. 38.

27. Rick Harding, "Commanders Quietly Ignore Antigay Rule," p. 20. According to the article, Miriam Ben-Shalom, founder of the politi-

cal and support group Gay, Lesbian, and Bisexual Veterans of America, reported hearing from at least ten gay and lesbian reservists that they were scheduled for Gulf War duty after telling their commanding officers about their sexual orientation.

28. Ibid.

29. Ibid.

30. "In Debate Over Military Gay Ban, Attention Is Turning to Lesbians," *New York Times*, May 4, 1993, p. A23.

31. Quoted in John Gallagher, "GAO: Military Spent $500 Million Discharging Gays," *The Advocate*, July 30, 1992, p. 21.

32. Quoted in "Attention Is Turning to Lesbians," p. A23.

33. Francis Wilkerson, "The Gay Cadet," *Village Voice*, March 13, 1990, p. 25.

34. Richard Rouilard, "Editor's Comments," *The Advocate*, August 27, 1991, pp. 6–7; Scott Shuger, "American Inquisition: The Military vs. Itself," *New Republic*, December 7, 1992, pp. 23–29.

35. "News in Brief," *The Advocate*, July 30, 1991, p. 28.

36. Shuger, "American Inquisition," p. 26.

37. Quoted in Eric Schmitt, "Military's Gay Subculture Off Limits but Flourishing," *New York Times*, December 1, 1992, p. A1.

38. Quoted in ibid.

39. "Military Maneuvers," *The Advocate*, August 13, 1991, p. 2.

40. Quoted in Seth Mydans, "Navy Is Ordered to Return Job to a Gay Sailor," *New York Times*, November 11, 1992, p. A14.

41. Georges Clemenceau, *Discours de Guerre* (Paris: University of Paris, 1969).

42. "Transcript: Radio Interview of President Clinton by CBS News," distributed by Office of International Information Programs, U.S. Department of State, December 11, 1999.

43. Servicemember's Legal Defense Network (SLDN), Sixth Annual Report on "Don't Ask, Don't Tell, Don't Pursue, Don't Harass."

44. "Cohen Orders Probe of Harassment of Gay Troops," Reuters wire release, December 14, 1999.

45. Linda D. Kozaryn and Jim Garamone, "Cohen Adds 'Don't Harass' to Homosexual Policy, Says It Can Work." American Forces Press Service, December 29, 1999.

46. SLDN, Sixth Annual Report on "Don't Ask, Don't Tell, Don't Pursue, Don't Harass," p. 4.

47. Ibid, p. 5.

48. SLDN, Seventh Annual Report on "Don't Ask, Don't Tell, Don't Pursue, Don't Harass."

49. Ibid, p. iii.

50. SLDN, Sixth Annual Report on "Don't Ask, Don't Tell, Don't Pursue, Don't Harass," p. 6.

51. Eric Schmitt, "Joint Chiefs Hear Clinton Vow Anew to Ease Gay Policy," *New York Times*, January 26, 1993, p. A1.

52. Ibid. Schmitt reports, "A spokeswoman for [General Powell] said that by 6 P.M. today his office had received 681 calls to keep the ban and only 21 to lift it" (p. A1).

53. On two separate occasions, military personnel who answered the phones in General Powell's office attempted to explain to me why my opinion that the ban should be lifted was ill informed and, indeed, dangerous both to the defense of the country, as it would undermine preparedness for war, and to those gay men and lesbians who might openly serve. Similar reports were widespread on Queernet, a computer-generated distribution/e-mail list that acts as a clearinghouse for information about the activities, protests, and demonstrations of the gay activist group Queer Nation. The lobbying campaign by General Powell's office seemed too widespread to be merely coincidental.

54. Eric Schmitt, "R.O.T.C. Uses Oath on Homosexuality," *New York Times*, November 19, 1992, p. A10.

55. Quoted in Eric Schmitt, "Joint Chiefs Fighting Clinton Plan to Allow Homosexuals in Military," *New York Times*, January 23, 1993, p. 1.

56. See Peter Applebome, "Army: Ranks Are Split, as in Society," *New York Times*, January 28, 1993; B. Drummond Ayres Jr., "Marine Corps: Even the Thought Is Off Limits," *New York Times*, January 28, 1993, p. A16; Dirk Johnson, "Air Force: Are Homosexuals the New Enemy?" *New York Times*, January 28, 1993, p. A16; and Eric Schmitt, "Forum on Gay Ban Starts and Stays Shrill," *New York Times*, March 25, 1993, p. A13.

57. *Pruitt v. Cheney*, at 989.

58. Ibid., p. 990. This standard is much more permissive than the standard that courts use for racial discrimination. See "Court Reinstates Lesbian's Lawsuits Against Army," *New York Times*, August 20, 1991, p. A22, and John Gallagher, "U.S. Appeals Panel, Psychological Group Chip Away at Gay Ban, *The Advocate*, September 24, 1991, p. 16.

59. *Meinhold v. Secretary of Defense*, 808 F. Supp. 1455 (1993) at 1459. See also Thomas Friedman, "Judge Rules Military's Ban on Homosexuals Is Void," *New York Times*, January 29, 1993, p. A12.

60. Defense Personnel Security Research and Education Center, "Nonconforming Sexual Orientations and Military Suitability," prepared by Theodore R. Sarbin, Ph.D., and Kenneth E. Karols, M.D. Ph.D., December 1988, p. 35.

61. Quoted in Craig Stoltz, "Gays in the Military," *USA Weekend*, August 7–9, 1992, pp. 4–5. See also Ronald Sullivan, "The Military Balked at Truman's Order, Too," *New York Times*, January 31, 1993, section 1, p. 21.

62. Stoltz, "Gays in the Military," pp. 4–5. See the discussion in Chapter 3.

63. Quoted in ibid.

Chapter 5

1. David Cohen, "Notes on a Grecian Yearn: Pederasty in Thebes and Sparta," *New York Times*, March 31, 1993, p. A23.

2. Michel Foucault, *The History of Sexuality*, vol. 1, *An Introduction*, trans. Robert Hurley (New York: Pantheon Books, 1978); Mark Blasius, *Gay and Lesbian Politics: Sexuality and the Emergence of a New Ethic* (Philadelphia: Temple University Press, 1994).

3. Department of Defense Directive 1332.14, "Enlisted Administrative Separations," January 28, 1982, p. 2.

4. Ibid.

5. In every one of the dozens of radio call-in programs on which I was an invited guest in 1992 and 1993, the issue of sharing showers with gay men emerged as listeners' single biggest objection to allowing gays to serve in the military.

6. U.S. Navy, *Report of the Board Appointed to Prepare and Submit Recommendations to the Secretary of the Navy for the Revision of Policies, Procedures and Directives Dealing with Homosexuality*, prepared by Chairman S. H. Crittenden (Washington, D.C.: Government Printing Office, 1957).

7. E. L. Gibson, *Get Off My Ship* (New York: Avon, 1978), contains the history of the suppression and subsequent release of the Crittenden Report.

8. Department of Defense Directive 1332.14.

9. Timothy Egan, "Dismissed from Army as Lesbian, Colonel Will Fight Homosexual Ban," *New York Times*, May 31, 1992, p. 18.

10. Quoted in Jeffrey Schmalz, "Difficult First Step: Promises and Reality Clash as Clinton Is Moving to End Military's Gay Ban," *New York Times*, November 15, 1992, p. 22.

11. Defense Personnel Security Research and Education Center (PERSEREC), "Nonconforming Sexual Orientations and Military Suitability," prepared by Theodore R. Sarbin, Ph.D., and Kenneth E. Karols, M.D. Ph.D., December 1988, p. 33.

12. The PERSEREC report and the Pentagon memos, with an introduction to the politics that surrounded the report's release by Gerry Studds, are published in Kate Dyer, ed., *Gays in Uniform: The Pentagon's Secret Report* (Boston: Alyson Publications, 1990).

13. PERSEREC, "Preservice Adjustment of Homosexual and Heterosexual Military Accessions: Implications for Security Clearance Suitability," prepared by Michael A. McDaniel, January 1989, p. 19.

14. National Defense Research Institute (Rand Corporation), "Sexual Orientation and U.S. Military Personnel Policy: Options and Assessments," MR-323-OSD, 1993.

15. Quoted in John Gallagher, "Terrible Timing," *The Advocate*, October 5, 1993, p. 28.

16. PERSEREC, "Preservice Adjustment of Homosexual and Heterosexual Accessions," p. 21.

17. Quoted in Jane Gross, "Navy Is Urged to Root Out Lesbians Despite Abilities," *New York Times*, November 2, 1990, p. A11.

18. U.S. General Accounting Office, "Defense Force Management: DOD's Policy on Homosexuality: A Report to Congressional Requesters," GAO/NSIAD-92-98, June 12, 1992, p. 13.

19. Ibid. p. 14.

20. For example, Miriam Ben-Shalom, president of Gay, Lesbian, and Bisexual Veterans of America, makes this claim. See John Gallagher, "GAO: Military Spent $500 Million Discharging Gays," *The Advocate*, July 30, 1992, pp. 19–20.

21. Quoted in Eric Schmitt, "Joint Chiefs Fighting Clinton Plan to Allow Homosexuals in Military," *New York Times*, January 23, 1993, p. 1.

22. Eric Schmitt, "Joint Chiefs Hear Clinton Vow Anew to Ease Gay Policy," *New York Times*, January 26, 1993, p. A1; Schmitt, "Joint Chiefs Fighting Clinton Plan," p. 1; Eric Schmitt, "Pentagon Chief Warns Clinton on Gay Policy," *New York Times*, January 25, 1993, p. A1.

23. Schmitt, "Joint Chiefs Fighting Clinton Plan," p. 1.

24. Quoted in Chris Bull, "Judge Gasch Cites AIDS While Upholding Enlistment Ban," *The Advocate*, January 14, 1992, p. 19.

25. *Steffan v. Cheney*, 780 F. Supp. 1 (1991) at 2. Paula Ettelbrick, then legal director of the gay public interest law firm that represented Steffan (Lambda Legal Defense and Education Fund) was not surprised by Judge Gasch's decision. "We have known exactly what kind of judge we were dealing with ever since the hearings—when he repeatedly called our client a 'homo,'" she said. When Gasch's prejudicial language became the basis of a motion to remove him from the case, he refused to step aside (quoted in Greg Scott, "A Good Liberal Gone Sour," *The Advocate*, January 14, 1992, p. 55).

26. A similar relationship exists in the military's claim about unit cohesion.

Chapter 6

1. "Ego and Error on the Gay Issue," *New York Times*, January 29, 1993, p. A26.

2. Anthony Lewis, "The Issue Is Bigotry," *New York Times,* January 29, 1993, p. A23.

3. Peter Applebome, "Gay Issue Mobilizes Conservatives Against Clinton," *New York Times,* February 1, 1993, p. A14.

4. Professor John Green, at the University of Akron, quoted in ibid.

5. Ibid.

6. USC, section 654, November 30, 1993, p. 3.

7. Ibid., p. 3. See also Les Aspin, "Memorandum for the Secretary of the Army, Secretary of the Navy, Secretary of the Air Force, Chairman, Joint Chiefs of Staff Regarding Policy on Homosexual Conduct in the Armed Forces," July 19, 1993.

8. C. Dixon Osborne and Michelle Benecke (co-executive directors of the Servicemember's Legal Defense Network [SLDN], "Conduct Unbecoming: The Second Annual Report on 'Don't Ask, Don't Tell, Don't Pursue' Violations: March 1, 1995–February 27, 1996." The SLDN documented over seventy-seven violations of the Don't Ask provision in 1996 alone.

9. Quoted in Neff Hudson, "Is 'Don't Ask, Don't Tell' Working? Depends on Who You Ask," *Army Times,* June 13, 1994, p. 14.

10. John Gallagher, "Some Things Never Change," *The Advocate,* May 17, 1994, p. 46.

11. Osborne and Benecke, "Conduct Unbecoming." The report explains, "The cost figures for 1991–1995 are based on the ratio of discharges in year X divided by the costs in year X set equal to the ratio of discharges in years 1980–1990 divided by the costs in years 1980–1990. *The cost figures have not been adjusted for inflation"* (p. 32).

12. SLDN, Sixth Annual Report on "Don't Ask, Don't Tell, Don't Pursue, Don't Harass," p. 29.

13. Ibid., pp. 1–20.

14. Quoted in ibid., pp. 48–49.

15. SLDN, Seventh Annual Report on "Don't Ask, Don't Tell, Don't Pursue, Don't Harass," p. 2.

16. "Cohen Orders Probe of Harassment of Gay Troops," Reuters wire release, December 14, 1999. See also SLDN, Seventh Annual Report on "Don't Ask, Don't Tell, Don't Pursue, Don't Harass."

17. *Thomasson v. Perry,* 80 F. 3d 915 (4th Cir.) (en banc), cert. denied, 519 U.S. 948 (1996); *Selland v. Perry,* 905 F. Supp. 260 (D. Md. 1995), aff'd, 100 F. 3d 950 (4th Cir. 1996), cert. denied, 520 U.S. 1210 (1997); *Richenberg v. Perry,* 97 F. 3d 256 (8th Cir. 1996), cert. denied, 118 S. Ct. 45 (1997); *Able v. United States,* 88 F. 3d 1280 (2d Cir. 1996) (sustaining act against First Amendment and equal protection challenge, provided its underlying prohibition of homosexual acts is valid); after remand, *Able v. United*

States, 153 F. 3d 628 (2d Cir. 1998) (sustaining act's prohibition of homosexual acts); *Philips v. Perry,* 106 F. 3d 1420 (9th Cir. 1997) (sustaining act's prohibition of homosexual acts); *Thorne v. Department of Defense,* 139 F. 3d 893 (4th Cir. 1997), cert. denied, No. 98-91, October 19, 1998.

18. Sarah Schulman, *My American History: Lesbian and Gay Life During the Reagan/Bush Years* (New York: Routledge, 1994), p. 13.

19. Quoted in Jeff Yarbrough, "The Life and Times of Randy Shilts," *The Advocate,* June 15, 1993, p. 36.

20. Tim McFeeley, letter to Human Rights Campaign Fund members, June 25, 1992.

21. Quoted in John Gallagher, "Half a Loaf," *The Advocate,* May 4, 1993, p. 25.

22. Barney Frank, letter to Campaign for Military Justice, May 20, 1993.

23. Quoted in Chris Bull, "No Frankness," *The Advocate,* June 29, 1993, p. 27.

24. Ibid., p. 29.

25. Ken Sherrill has argued that thrusting upon the lesbian and gay community the complete responsibility for breaking this iron triangle not only represents the Clinton administration's greatest sin but also doomed the proposed changes to failure: "A new President, with much undistributed patronage at his disposal and with a reservoir of good will, might have had a chance against the complex. To assign the responsibility was to throw us to the lions" (personal communication, November 4, 1995). I believe that Sherrill is largely right. But as a president without a mandate, without even the support of a majority of voters, and with a history of serious campaign issues surrounding his own military service, Clinton never had a reservoir of good will—especially with those in the military industrial complex he hoped to influence—that was very substantial.

26. Barbara Smith, "Where's the Revolution?" *The Nation,* July 5, 1993, p. 14.

Chapter 7

1. Jean Bethke Elshtain, "Homosexual Politics: The Paradox of Gay Liberation," *Salmagundi* 58–59 (Fall 1982–Winter 1983): 252.

2. Jean Bethke Elshtain, "Battered Reason," *New Republic,* October 5, 1992, p. 25.

3. Dennis Altman, *Coming Out in the Seventies* (Boston: Alyson Publications, 1981); Stuart Byron, "The Closet Syndrome," in Jay and Young, *Out of the Closets,* pp. 58–65; Edward William Delph, *The Silent Homo-*

sexual Community: Public Homosexual Encounters (Beverly Hills, Calif.: Age Publications, 1978); Richard Goldstein, "Sex on Parole," *Village Voice*, August 20–26, 1980, pp. 20–23; John Murphy, *Homosexual Liberation* (New York: Praeger, 1971); Carl Whitman, "A Gay Manifesto," in *Out of the Closets: Voices of Gay Liberation*, ed. Karla Jay and Allen Young (New York: Douglas Books, 1972), pp. 330–341; Allen Young, "Out of the Closets, into the Streets," in Jay and Young, *Out of the Closets*, pp. 6–30.

4. Young, "Out of the Closets," p. 9.

5. Whitman, "A Gay Manifesto," p. 331.

6. Radicalesbians, "Woman-Identified Woman," in Jay and Young, *Out of the Closets*, p. 172.

7. Martha Shelly, "Gay Is Good," in Jay and Young, *Out of the Closets*, pp. 31–34.

8. Whitman, "A Gay Manifesto," p. 331.

9. Young, "Out of the Closets," p. 29.

10. Ibid, p. 17.

11. Ibid.

12. Radicalesbians, "Woman-Identified Woman," p. 172.

13. Byron, "The Closet Syndrome," p. 59 (emphasis in original).

14. Young, "Out of the Closets," p. 8.

15. Radicalesbians, "Woman-Identified Woman," p. 172.

16. Shelly, "Gay Is Good," p. 34.

17. Whitman, "A Gay Manifesto," p. 341.

18. Elshtain, "Homosexual Politics," p. 255.

19. Ibid., p. 276.

20. Ibid., p. 253.

21. Ibid.

22. See, for example, Jean Bethke Elshtain, *Public Man, Private Woman: Women in Social and Political Thought* (Princeton: Princeton University Press, 1981), especially pp. 87, 104, 202–203, 226, 256–284, 344.

23. Elshtain, "Homosexual Politics," p. 252.

24. Jay, "Introduction," in Jay and Young, *Out of the Closets*, p. lxi.

25. Young, "Out of the Closets," p. 30.

26. Ibid., p. 28.

27. Elshtain, "Homosexual Politics," p. 254.

28. Ibid., pp. 253–254. In *Public Man, Private Woman*, Elshtain argues that this same imperative is at work among "feminist analysts who urge that 'the personal is political' totally and *simpliciter*" (p. 104).

29. Elshtain, *Public Man, Private Woman*, p. 104.

30. Elshtain, "Homosexual Politics," p. 267 (emphasis in original).

31. Ibid., p. 254.

32. This Jacobin terror surfaces again in Elshtain's "Stories and Political Life," *PS* 28, no. 2 (June 1995).

33. Elshtain, "Homosexual Politics," p. 262.

34. Ibid., p. 253.

35. Elshtain's anxiety about a more fluid understanding of gender is manifested again in "Against Androgyny," *Telos* (Spring 1981).

36. Elshtain, "Homosexual Politics," p. 275.

37. Shelley, "Gay Is Good," p. 32.

38. Elshtain, "Homosexual Politics," p. 275.

39. *Bowers v. Hardwick,* 478 U.S. 186 (1986).

40. Elshtain, "Homosexual Politics," p, 254.

41. Ibid., p. 256 (emphasis mine).

42. Justice Harry Blackmun's dissent makes it clear that *Bowers* was, indeed, about more than the majority had indicated: "This case is no more about 'a fundamental right to engage in homosexual sodomy' . . . than a [leading obscenity case] was about a fundamental right to watch obscene movies. This case is about the most comprehensive of rights and the right most valued by civilized men, namely, 'the right to be let alone'" (*Bowers v. Hardwick,* p. 199).

43. Michelangelo Signorile, *Queer in America: Sex, the Media, and the Closets of Power* (New York: Random House, 1993).

44. See, for example, Jean Bethke Elshtain, "The Family in Trouble," *National Forum* 75, no. 1 (Winter 1995); idem, "The Ties That Bind," *Chronicles: A Magazine of American Culture* 13, no. 10, October 1, 1989; and idem, "Feminism and Politics," *Partisan Review,* 57, no. 2 (Spring 1990).

45. A 1989 federal study indicated that 30 percent of the youths who commit suicide each year are gay and lesbian—double or triple the rate for straight youths. See U.S. Department of Health and Human Services, "Report of the Secretary's Task Force on Youth Teen Suicide," 1989.

46. Catherine MacKinnon, *Feminism Unmodified* (Cambridge, Mass.: Harvard University Press, 1987), chap. 8. For an extension of this argument that includes lesbian and gay rights, see Kendall Thomas, "Beyond the Privacy Principle," *Columbia Law Review* (October 1992). For a rebuttal of this position, see Morris Kaplan, "Intimacy and Equality: The Question of Lesbian and Gay Marriage," *Philosophical Forum* 25, no. 4 (Summer 1994).

47. Michel Foucault, *The History of Sexuality,* vol. 1, *An Introduction,* trans. Robert Hurley (New York: Pantheon Books, 1978).

48. Elshtain, "Homosexual Politics," p. 280.

49. Judith Butler, "Imitation and Gender Subordination," in *The Lesbian and Gay Studies Reader,* ed. Henry Abelove, Michelle Barale, and David Halperin (New York: Routledge, 1993), p. 314.

50. Elshtain, "Homosexual Politics," p. 254.

51. Daniel Ortiz, "Creating Controversy: Essentialism and Constructivism and the Politics of Gay Identity," *Virginia Law Review* 79, no. 1833 (1993), p. 163.

52. Michel Foucault, *Herculine Barbin: On the Recently Discovered Diaries of a Nineteenth Century French Hermaphrodite* (New York: Pantheon Books, 1980); Ann Fausto-Sterling, *Myths of Gender: Biological Theories About Women and Men* (New York: Basic Books, 1985); and Cheshire Calhoun, "Denaturalizing and Desexualizing Lesbian and Gay Identity," *Virginia Law Review* 79, no. 1859 (1993).

53. Adrienne Rich argues that, rather than a "natural outcome," heterosexuality is an institution that depends on a great amount of power, energy, and violence in order to be maintained. See her "Compulsory Heterosexuality and Lesbian Existence," *Signs* 5, no. 4 (1980): 631–660.

54. Stephen Epstein, "Gay Politics, Ethnic Identity: The Limits of Social Constructionism," *Socialist Review* 93–94 (1987): 12.

55. Department of Defense Directive 1332.14, January 28, 1982.

56. *Romer v. Evans*, 517 U.S. 620 (1996).

57. Ibid, p. 632.

58. Ibid, p. 632.

59. Ibid, p. 633.

60. In a June 16, 1992, editorial, *The Advocate* called NEA Acting Chair Anne-Imelda Radice "a new doormat homosexual who could give [the Bush] administration's self hating blacks and male identified women a serious run for their money" (p. 47). Vivian Shapiro, the former chair of the HRCF, called Radice "a lesbian from hell" (quoted in ibid, p. 47).

61. Warren Leary, "U.S. Agency Shreds List of Gay Workers and Plans Inquiry," *New York Times*, May 19, 1992, p. A17.

62. Quoted in Kevin Sack, "Judge's Ouster Sought After Antigay Remark," *New York Times*, February 20, 2002, p. A2.

63. Ortiz, "Creating Controversy"; Thomas, "Beyond the Privacy Principle"; Kaplan, "Intimacy and Equality"; Calhoun, "Denaturalizing and Desexualizing Lesbian and Gay Identity."

64. The Defense of Marriage Act was introduced in the U.S. House of Representatives as H.R. 3396 on May 7, 1996. An identical bill was introduced in the Senate as S. 1740 on May 8, 1996.

65. Elshtain, "Homosexual Politics," p. 254.

66. *Baehr v. Lewin*, 853 P. 2d 44 (1993).

67. *Loving v. Virginia*, 388 U.S. 1 (1967).

68. Kaplan, "Intimacy and Equality," p. 337.

69. Ibid, p. 336.

70. Ibid, p. 353.

71. Jean Bethke Elshtain, "Against Gay Marriage," *Commonweal* 118, no. 20, November 22, 1991, p. 147.

72. Ibid, p. 147.

73. John Boswell, "Concepts, Experience and Sexuality," *Forms of Desire: Sexual Orientation and the Social Constructionist Controversy*, ed. Edward Stein (New York: Garland Publishing, 1990), p. 147.

74. Foucault, *Herculine Barbin*, p. ix.

75. Elshtain, "Homosexual Politics," pp. 259–260. Elshtain quotes Altman, *Coming Out in the Seventies*, p. 36.

76. Tzvetan Todorov, *The Conquest of America: The Question of the Other* (New York: Harper Torchbooks, 1987), p. 249.

Conclusion

1. Quoted in Timothy Egan, "Dismissed from Army as Lesbian, Colonel Will Fight Homosexual Ban," *New York Times*, May 31, 1992, p. 18.

2. Hannah Arendt, *The Origins of Totalitarianism* (New York: Harcourt Brace Jovanovich, 1973), p. 87.

3. Ibid., p. 80.

4. Joe Dolce, "G(r)AY Matter," *The Advocate*, June 1, 1993, p. 38.

5. Lawrence Mass, *"Homosexual* as Acts or Persons: A Conversation with John De Cecco," in *Homosexuality as Behavior and Identity* (New York: Harrington Park Press, 1990), p. 167.

6. See Felicity Barringer, "Sex Survey of American Men Finds 1% Are Gay," *New York Times*, April 15, 1993, p. A1.

7. Andrew Sullivan, *Virtually Normal: An Argument About Homosexuality* (New York: Random House, 1995).

8. Michel Foucault, "Right of Death and Power over Life," *The History of Sexuality*, vol. 1, *An Introduction*, trans. Robert Hurley (New York: Pantheon Books, 1978), pp. 135–159.

9. Interestingly, under this scenario, the present position of religious right-to-life groups and liberal pro-choice organizations could be reversed, with liberals arguing against persecution of unborn gays and conservatives allied with the right to correct these sexual abnormalities.

10. Diana Fuss, *Essentially Speaking: Feminism, Nature and Difference* (New York: Routledge, 1989), p. xi.

11. Judith Butler, *Gender Trouble: Feminism and the Subversion of Identity* (New York: Routledge, 1990), p. 136.

12. Ibid.

13. Adrienne Rich, "Compulsory Heterosexuality and Lesbian Existence," *Signs* (Summer 1980), p. 637.

Index

223